THE POLYTHINK SYNDROME

THE POLYTHINK
SYNDROME

*U.S. Foreign Policy Decisions on 9/11,
Afghanistan, Iraq, Iran, Syria, and ISIS*

Alex Mintz and Carly Wayne

Stanford University Press
Stanford, California

Stanford University Press
Stanford, California

Printed in the United States of America on acid-free, archival-quality paper

Library of Congress Cataloging-in-Publication Data

Mintz, Alex, 1953- author.
  The polythink syndrome : U.S. foreign policy decisions on 9/11, Afghanistan, Iraq, Iran, Syria, and ISIS / Alex Mintz and Carly Wayne.
    pages cm
  Includes bibliographical references and index.
  ISBN 978-0-8047-9515-9 (cloth : alk. paper) -- ISBN 978-0-8047-9676-7 (pbk. : alk. paper) -- ISBN 978-0-8047-9677-4 (electronic)
  1. United States--Foreign relations--2001-2009--Decision making--Case studies.
  2. United States--Foreign relations--2009---Decision making--Case studies. 3. National security--United States--Decision making--Case studies. 4. Group decision making--United States--Case studies. I. Wayne, Carly, author. II. Title.
  JZ1480.M564 2015
  327.73056--dc23
                            2015030662

Typeset by Bruce Lundquist in 10/14 Minion

Table of Contents

Preface

How do presidents and their advisors make war and peace decisions on military intervention, escalation, de-escalation, and termination of conflicts? Why do they often make sub-optimal decisions? Why do important policy goals, plans, and aspirations frequently result in inaction? The leading concept of group dynamics, Groupthink, offers one explanation—cohesive policy-making groups, such as advisors to the President, often make sub-optimal decisions due to their desire for uniformity over dissent, while ignoring important limitations of chosen policies, overestimating the odds for success and failing to consider other relevant policy options or possibilities. But presidential advisory groups are often fragmented and divisive. We thus introduce Polythink, a group decision-making dynamic whereby different members in a decision-making unit espouse a *plurality* of opinions and offer divergent policy prescriptions, which can result in intragroup conflict, a disjointed decision-making process, and decision paralysis and inaction as each group member pushes for his or her preferred policy direction.

In *The Polythink Syndrome*, we analyze U.S. national security and foreign policy decisions such as the pre-9/11 national security choices, the decisions to enter into and withdraw from Afghanistan and Iraq, the crisis over the Iranian nuclear program (analyzed from both the American and the Israeli perspectives), the summer 2012 UN Security Council debate on the civil war in Syria, decisions in the 2013–14 Israeli–Palestinian peace negotiations, and the 2014 U.S. decision to attack ISIS. We illuminate the prevalence of Polythink, a phenomenon no less problematic or common than Groupthink, demonstrating how otherwise smart, experienced decision makers can engage in flawed decision-making processes that deeply affect the security and welfare of a country. We also discuss how Polythink characterizes many corporate and business decisions and day-to-day decisions and can thus have important implications for group-based decision-making processes outside of the political realm, such as in marketing, R&D, and financial decisions.

Furthermore, we explain how leaders and other decision makers (for example, in business) can transform Destructive Polythink into Productive Polythink, illuminating the potential ways in which this group dynamic may be effectively directed toward sound decisions. By shining a light on Polythink's symptoms and consequences, and on the factors that lead to Polythink, we seek to offer actionable policy prescriptions for elite decision makers to offset the negative attributes of this phenomenon and engage in more optimal policy-making processes.

Acknowledgments

We thank Mrs. Miri Furst-Homa and Dr. Ehud Eiran for comments and valuable input on various sections of this book. We have also benefited from comments given to Alex Mintz in seminars and presentations at the Davis Institute of the Hebrew University of Jerusalem, the 2012 International Society of Political Psychology Meeting in Chicago, the 2012 Columbia-Lauder Dialogue Group at IDC Herzliya, and the 2014 Science for Peace Conference in Milan, Italy.

1 The Polythink Syndrome

Pearl Harbor and September 11

On September 11, 2001, the United States of America was attacked by al-Qaeda terrorists who flew three American jetliners into the World Trade Center towers in New York City and the Pentagon in Washington, D.C. The terrorists even aimed a fourth plane at the U.S. Capitol building or the White House before resistance from the plane's passengers forced them to change course. The plane crashed in Shanksville, Pennsylvania, killing all on board. More than 3,000 people were killed in these devastating events, including 2,606 in the World Trade Center, 246 victims on the four airline flights, and 125 in the Pentagon. The overwhelming majority of these casualties were civilians. Fifty-five military personnel were killed in the assault on Washington. These attacks were carefully planned and executed by Osama bin Laden and his covert fundamentalist Islamic terrorist group, al-Qaeda.

Since the 9/11 attacks, the U.S., and the world, have never been the same. Following the attacks, the U.S. entered the costly War on Terror, launching two wars in Afghanistan and Iraq. Today, ongoing unrest in Iraq, Syria, and Afghanistan, the ISIS threat, and other terrorist attacks around the globe continue, with offensive operations by the U.S. in Iraq, Syria, and other countries in the region occurring as well.

Thus, as most academics, politicians, and pundits agree, the War on Terror continues to have profound implications for American citizens and others around the globe in an array of arenas—affecting the economy; individual freedoms and civil liberties; the security of airline transportation; the personal safety of civilians in the U.S., the Middle East, and other parts of the world; and even the conduct of modern warfare itself. However, American foreign policy decisions during these turbulent years have often been criticized as sub-optimal or even damaging to America's interests and security. The central goal of this book is to address this troubling paradox—how do smart, experienced decision makers make faulty policy decisions or experience decision paralysis and inaction in the face of critical foreign policy crises?

Polythink

At first glance, many analysts and laymen alike draw parallels between September 11 and the last devastating attack on American soil that similarly transformed the world. On December 7, 1941, "a date which will live in infamy,"[1] U.S. forces in Pearl Harbor, Hawaii, were stunned in a deadly surprise attack by Japanese forces, leaving 2,402 Americans dead and another 1,282 wounded. Altogether, the Japanese sank or severely damaged eighteen ships, including eight battleships, three light cruisers, and three destroyers. On the airfields, the Japanese destroyed 161 American planes and seriously damaged 102 (World War II History Info 2010). As with September 11, 2001, this attack was arguably the main catalyst for the U.S. entry into a global war of epic proportions that truly changed the face of the world as we know it today.

But how is it that such a powerful and sophisticated nation as the U.S. allowed both of these deadly attacks to happen in the first place? More generally, how is it that presidents and their policy-making teams—including foreign policy and national security experts—made policy decisions that led to such negative outcomes? Were similar factors at play in both instances? Or was it, as we will demonstrate in this book, the result of two very different, but similarly destructive, types of sub-optimal group decision-making processes at the elite level? Were these foreign and national security decisions and policies that allowed a seemingly militarily inferior enemy to inflict such damage on the American homeland a result of the distinct group dynamics among the military, intelligence, and diplomatic arms of the U.S. government? Namely, were these attacks the result of the phenomenon of *Groupthink* or of the dynamic we call *Polythink*?

As we will demonstrate, the group dynamic of a decision-making unit is indeed a vital variable that should be examined in order to understand how policies are ultimately formulated and executed (or *fail* to be executed at all).

Indeed, "foreign-policy making is not simply a matter of a rationalist calculus, which merely requires realist inputs about power and interests to determine choices and outcomes . . . Instead we must think of the decision process as a fundamentally human one . . . To understand how a state arrives at a decision, we must carefully examine the human processes behind that decision" (Schafer and Crichlow 2010, 8).

In *The Polythink Syndrome*, we focus on the *Polythink* group dynamic, a phenomenon that can cause otherwise rational decision makers to engage in flawed decision-making processes that deeply affect the security and welfare of a country. Polythink is a group dynamic whereby different members in a decision-making unit espouse a plurality of opinions and offer divergent policy prescriptions, and even dissent, which can result in intragroup conflict and a fragmented, disjointed decision-making process. Members of a Polythink decision-making unit, by virtue of their disparate worldviews, institutional and political affiliations, and decision-making styles, typically have deep disagreements over the same decision problem. Consequently, members of Polythink-type groups will often be unable to appreciate or accept the perspectives of other group members, and thus will fail to benefit from the consideration of various viewpoints.

This book will analyze eleven key national security and foreign policy decisions: (1) the national security policy designed prior to the terrorist attacks of 9/11; (2) the decision to enter into Afghanistan; (3) the decision to withdraw from Afghanistan; (4) the Iraq War entry decision; (5) the decision on the Surge in Iraq; (6) the decision to withdraw from Iraq; (7) and (8) the crisis over the Iranian nuclear program (analyzed from both the American and the Israeli perspectives); (9) the 2012 UN Security Council decision on the Syrian Civil War; (10) the 2013–14 Kerry peace negotiations between the Israelis and Palestinians; and (11) the 2014 decision by the U.S. to engage in targeted strikes against the emergent ISIS threat. Through our analysis of these decisions, we conclude that many of these national security and foreign policy decisions of the U.S. indeed exhibited key symptoms of the Polythink syndrome.

Polythink vs. Groupthink

The surprise attack on the Pearl Harbor base on the island of Oahu, Hawaii, has been characterized by scholars as a prototypical example of a policy "fiasco" that was triggered by the Groupthink decision-making syndrome (Janis 1982a). Groupthink is "a mode of thinking that people engage in when they are deeply involved in a cohesive in-group, when the members' strivings for unanimity override their motivation to realistically appraise alternative courses of action" (Janis 1982a, 9). At the national level, this means that cohesive policy-making groups, such as the advisors to the President, often make sub-optimal decisions as a result of their conscious or subconscious desire for consensus over dissent, which leads to ignoring important limitations of chosen policies, overestimating the odds for success, and failing to consider other relevant policy options or possibilities. The implications of this phenomenon for national security decision making are clear. In a Groupthink scenario, the overarching tendency to strive for consensus and unanimity rather than carefully reviewing a set of diverse policy options and the risks and benefits that accompany each leads to sub-optimal decision-making processes that in turn result in the many policy "fiascoes" with which we are all too familiar, such as the attack on Pearl Harbor (Janis 1982b).

And in fact, since the introduction of Groupthink in the 1970s, much emphasis has been placed in national security and foreign policy decision-making circles on the procedures, processes, methods, and techniques that can be utilized to prevent Groupthink from occurring, such as a leader remaining impartial rather than stating a particular view; dividing the group into subgroups to hammer out differences; bringing in outside experts to challenge policymakers' views; and assigning specific members of the group to play the role of "devil's advocate" (George 1972). However, Janis and others have also recognized that many of these policy prescriptions could have detrimental effects if they are poorly managed. These strategies could lead to prolonged debates that could be costly when a crisis requires immediate action, or they might damage good relations between group members. Thus, oftentimes the prescriptions provided by theorists and practitioners for addressing Groupthink leave decision makers at risk of swinging too far in the other direction and contributing to the advent of a very different, but no less detrimental phenomenon that we term *Polythink*.

While at first glance the Pearl Harbor and September 11 attacks appear to be similar due to their deadly nature, the U.S.'s astonishment and unpreparedness, and the attacks' resulting massive impact on the global political stage, the reasons the U.S. failed to prevent these attacks were actually quite distinct. Though there was a striking similarity of inaction in the face of increasingly alarming intelligence reports before both attacks, the *causes* of this inaction were starkly different. While the failure to prevent the attack on Pearl Harbor occurred in part because of the overarching effects of Groupthink, and the resulting overconfidence of diplomatic and military officials in existing defense preparations, we show in this book that the failure to prevent 9/11, like many U.S. decisions in the War on Terror, was a result of Polythink among and within key governmental decision-making branches.

Indeed, the authors of *The 9/11 Commission Report* (2004), tasked with exploring the national security failures that preceded the attack, summarize their findings as follows:

> We learned of fault lines within our government—between foreign and domestic intelligence, and between and within agencies . . . We learned of the pervasive problems of managing and sharing information across a large and unwieldy government that had been built in a different era to confront different dangers . . . The massive departments and agencies [of the federal government] . . . must work together in new ways, so that all the instruments of national power can be combined. (xvi)

These symptoms are all hallmarks of the Polythink dynamic that we will explore in depth throughout this book (see Chapter 3 for the case study on Polythink prior to 9/11 and Chapters 4–7 for case studies of post-9/11 decisions on Afghanistan, Iraq, Iran, Syria, the Israeli-Palestinian peace negotiations, and ISIS).

Polythink is a general phenomenon; that is to say, it is a horizontal concept that can be applied to myriad realms. Indeed, Polythink is relevant to any group (not just decision units), including multiple groups within a decision unit. It has far-reaching implications for decision makers in the arenas of foreign policy, domestic policy, business, national security, and any other small-group decisions in individuals' daily lives, from group projects in school to decisions about what to do on a Saturday night with friends. In this book, we show how Polythink is applied to the realms of national security and foreign policymaking, areas in which Polythink's detrimental consequences can be particularly problematic and destructive. We also show how leaders can move from Destructive Polythink to Constructive Polythink (a dynamic we term "Productive Polythink") and benefit from diverse points of view among group members.

The Groupthink-Polythink Continuum

Polythink is essentially the opposite of Groupthink on a *continuum* of decision making from "completely cohesive" (Groupthink) to "completely fragmented" (Polythink). While Polythink is defined as a plurality of opinions, views, and perceptions among group members, Groupthink tends toward overwhelming conformity and unanimity. The divergence of opinions present in Polythink groups will often lead to myriad interpretations of reality, and policy prescriptions, making it difficult to formulate cohesive policies. Polythink can thus be seen as a mode of thinking that results from a highly *disjointed* group rather than a highly cohesive one. For example, some of the symptoms of Polythink are intragroup conflict and the existence of contradictory interests among group members (Mintz, Mishal, and Morag 2005), which may lead to a situation where it becomes virtually impossible for group members to reach a common interpretation of reality and common policy goals.

In the context of decision-unit dynamics, it is important to distinguish Polythink from the concept of "multiple advocacy," in which decision makers "harness diversity of views and interests in the interest of rational policy making" (George 1972, 751). Rather, the multiple advocacy model can actually be construed as a type of structured Polythink process, in which the leader strategically capitalizes on the already existing Polythink dynamic to carefully lead and bring the divergent opinions of group members into a single, cohesive policy direction. Thus, whereas multiple advocacy is a type of Polythink, it is important to note that most forms, structures, and variants of Polythink are *not* multiple advocacy (see Chapter 2 for a detailed discussion of concepts related to the Polythink syndrome).

Both Polythink and Groupthink should also be considered as "pure" types. In real-world decision-making situations, there is rarely a case of pure or extreme Polythink or Groupthink. It is therefore more useful to think of these two concepts as extremes on a continuum in which "good" decision-making processes typically lie toward the middle and defective decision-making processes fall closer to one of two extremes—the group conformity of Groupthink or the group disunity of Polythink. The case of September 11 provides an illustration of this continuum. While both the Clinton and the Bush Administrations exhibited a mainly Polythink dynamic in their approach to national security and counter-terrorism policy in the pre-9/11 years, there was also a Groupthink-like nearly unanimous sentiment that an attack on the American homeland was impossible.

The Con-Div Dynamic

On the Groupthink-Polythink continuum, there is also a range in the middle in which neither Groupthink nor Polythink dominates. We call this area *Con-Div*, the range in which the *convergence* and *divergence* of group members' viewpoints are more or less balanced and in equilibrium. In this situation, group members do not all share the same viewpoint and opinions, although they do

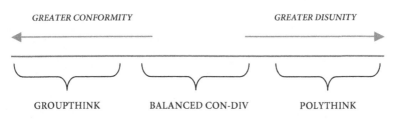

FIGURE 1.1 Continuum of Group Decision-Making Dynamics

share the general vision of the organization. In this scenario, the group is most likely to benefit from thorough yet productive decision-making processes that consider a multitude of options but ultimately reach some sort of consensus or agreement and execute well-formulated policies and actions. This is very different from either Groupthink or Polythink, which are both characterized by more extreme cohesion or dissent, respectively. Con-Div's balanced nature should benefit group leaders as they can assess diverse inputs that are nonetheless reviewed in the context of overall consensus about vision and key goals.

Symptoms and Consequences of Polythink

A number of important symptoms are unique to Polythink due to the wide-ranging chorus of viewpoints and policy prescriptions that members of the group espouse. The presence of these symptoms in decisions taken by a decision-making unit can be utilized to diagnose whether the group indeed suffers from a Polythink syndrome as compared to Con-Div or Groupthink:

1. Greater likelihood of group conflict and turf battles

2. Greater likelihood of leaks

3. Greater likelihood of confusion and lack of communication

4. Greater likelihood of framing and counter-framing

5. Limited review of policy options (similar to Groupthink)

6. No room for reappraisal of previously rejected policy options (similar to Groupthink)

7. Adoption of positions with the lowest common denominator

8. Decision paralysis

These critical symptoms and consequences of Polythink will be explored further and elaborated upon in Chapter 2.

Causes of Polythink

The reasons for Polythink at the national level boil down to a few key factors. First, the pluralism of views by different units and sub-units often means that diverse sets of decision makers must work together to develop cohesive, beneficial policies for the nation while at the same time effectively representing their various constituencies, political parties, governmental branches, and institutions. Second, individuals in decision-making groups bring with them vastly different types of decision-making styles, experiences, and roles within the group. These diverse perspectives hinder the ability of individual group members to see eye to eye on important issues. Finally, the vast scale and number of different agencies and decision-making units at the federal level often lead to a lack of communication flow that severely impedes the timely, uniform information processing necessary in order to make informed decisions at the national level.

Thus, Polythink can be thought of as a contingent phenomenon—dependent on a variety of issues such as government structure, leader decision-making style, advisory group makeup, and more. In the following chapters we will review several key explanations for the Polythink syndrome and apply Polythink symptoms and explanations to a series of case studies. The key explanations of Polythink are (Mintz, Mishal, and Morag 2005):

- Institutional "turf war" battles
- Political considerations
- Normative differences
- Expert-novice divides
- Leader-followers realtionship

These factors can drastically affect the judgment of key decision makers, leading to conflicting viewpoints, policy prescriptions, and interpretations of the situation or threat at hand—often leaving decision-making groups hopelessly paralyzed or relegated to taking only non-controversial "lowest-common-denominator" stances that are not in the best interests of the country as a whole.

One of the key insights of this book is that U.S. decisions to enter wars in the post-9/11 period have been characterized more often by a Groupthink dynamic, whereas U.S. decisions to exit wars more closely resembled the Polythink dynamic. Another important insight is that U.S. decisions at the strategic level have more often been characterized by Groupthink, whereas U.S. decisions at the tactical level post-9/11 have exhibited more of a Polythink dynamic.[2]

Organization of the Book

Following this introductory chapter, which provided an overview of the Poly-think syndrome, we will, in Chapter 2, further elaborate on the Polythink dynamic and its symptoms, causes, and implications for national security and foreign policy decision making. Then, to better understand how Polythink affects war and peace decisions, we will examine several key case studies, from the miscalculations that led to 9/11, to the subsequent national security decisions made in the decade following the attack—the decision to invade Afghanistan, and the decision to terminate that war; the 2003 decision to attack Iraq, the 2007 Surge in Iraq, and the 2009 decision to withdraw from Iraq; and decisions regarding Iran's nuclear program—the 2009 Iran Policy Review by the U.S. and the 2012 Israeli decision not to attack Iran's nuclear facilities. We will also look at the 2012 UN decision on Syria, the 2013–2014 Kerry peace negotiations between the Israelis and Palestinians, and the 2014 U.S. decision to attack ISIS. These case studies serve to illustrate the Polythink process and demonstrate its impact on the type and quality of policy decisions. They represent significant American foreign policy decisions in the Middle East since the 9/11 attacks, an area of tremendous strategic interest and policy importance for the U.S. and the world. Analyzing such key foreign policy decisions will enable us to better understand, predict, and obviate the detrimental symptoms of Polythink that can contribute to defective decision making.

Our book utilizes a diverse array of primary and secondary sources, primarily memoirs of former administration officials and advisors, published interviews, government reports, and scholarly analysis, while using news reports as illustrative examples.[3] Because Polythink and Groupthink are two extremes on a continuum of group decision making, this approach is sufficient to distinguish between these two dynamics.

In Chapter 3, we analyze September 11 as a case study of Polythink. We will further support our claim that while Pearl Harbor can be classified as a case of Groupthink, September 11 is much more typical of Polythink. Chapter 4 will move to post-9/11 decisions, showing how Groupthink contributed to the decisions to invade Afghanistan and how Polythink has plagued the decision-making process in the years since, as decision makers have struggled to chart a strategic military exit from this war.

Chapter 5 will demonstrate a similar dynamic in Iraq—Groupthink in and Polythink out, a dynamic that is often repeated in the context of war initiation and termination. Using a variety of sources, we will show how the overarching desire for conformity and clarity in the wake of the September 11 attacks led to a decision to invade Afghanistan (and later Iraq) without the necessary preparations for American involvement *after* a military victory over the government's forces. In contrast, in the decade since these wars began, we find that the U.S. administration's decision-making processes on how to end wars have typically been wracked by the symptoms of Polythink. These symptoms include serious disagreements, dissent, intragroup conflict, confusion, and more. It is important to note, however, that these case studies are located at various points on the continuum of group decision making. The 2007 Surge decision, as we will demonstrate, is much more indicative of a Con-Div decision-making process, in which the decision-making unit exhibited both convergence and divergence of policy views, making for a more balanced decision process.

Chapter 6 will turn to the important foreign policy dilemmas surrounding Iran's nuclear weapons program, analyzing the ways in which top governmental national security teams in both the U.S. and Israel responded to this challenge. We will also briefly explore the international components of Polythink on this critical issue, reviewing the divergent states' perspectives that have contributed to the somewhat listless response of the UN Security Council.

Chapter 7 will look at recent challenges in the international arena, particularly the United Nations' paralysis regarding the conflict in Syria, Secretary Kerry's diplomatic push for Israeli-Palestinian peace negotiations in 2013–14, and the 2014 U.S. decision to launch air strikes against ISIS in Iraq and Syria.

We will conclude by exploring the ways in which a decision maker can successfully manage Polythink, turning this particular group dynamic into a positive and productive strategy to maximize information search and result in more optimal decisions. We will look at specific strategies and tools for what we call Productive Polythink, such as a decision-unit architecture, which a leader can utilize to restrain the more negative side effects of Polythink, while simultaneously benefiting from Polythink's strengths. We will also address key implications and externalities of the Polythink phenomenon, and prescriptions for avoiding and/or overcoming this dynamic, curtailing the types of foreign policy fiascoes that often continue to plague democratic governments and institutions around the world.

2 Symptoms, Causes, and Consequences of Polythink

The Concept

What factors can cause experienced and knowledgeable leaders to make critical errors in judgment and decision making on vital issues of national security and foreign policy? Why are so many governmental and non-governmental goals not achieved nor advanced through policy decisions? Polythink is one key explanation. Polythink is a plurality of opinions and views that leads to disagreement among group members. Polythink is thus essentially the opposite of Groupthink on a continuum of decision making. In the following pages, we develop the Polythink concept, identify Polythink's symptoms and consequences, and introduce key explanations and predictors of Polythink. We also show how analysts can assess whether Polythink or Groupthink exists in a group. Finally, we compare the Polythink dynamic with the Groupthink dynamic and with Con-Div—the middle range between these two extremes.

The word "Polythink" is derived from the word "poly," meaning "many" ways of perceiving the same decision problem, goals, or solutions (Mintz, Mishal, and Morag 2005). Polythink is essentially the presence of disagreement and dissent within the group making the decision. It can be contrasted with the homogeneous, uniform, monolithic viewpoint of groups characterized by Groupthink. The sheer level of dissension in a Polythink group may create a situation in which it becomes virtually impossible for group members to reach a common interpretation of reality and common policy goals. As a result, Polythink can often lead to sub-optimal or even bad decisions. Polythink can also lead to paralysis and inaction. In other words, big plans and programs may be paralyzed because of disagreements within the decision-making unit.

Polythink characterizes many decision units and contributes to shaping the review of policy options and policy decisions. It is thus likely that a decision unit handicapped by Polythink will reach a very different decision than a group plagued by Groupthink.[1]

Symptoms of Polythink

There are a number of important symptoms of Polythink, some of which (confusion, leaks, and framing) can be counterintuitive:

1. *Greater likelihood of intragroup conflict.* Since group members hold different, sometimes even opposing views of the situation and of potential solutions, there is greater likelihood for group conflict and personal disagreements in Polythink. This dynamic contrasts with that of Groupthink, in which group members share more common views. Group conflict may impede not only short-term decisions but also long-term planning and policy implementation.

2. *Greater likelihood of leaks.* Since group members do not hold uniform views of the situation under Polythink, they are more likely to leak information in order to undermine positions that they oppose.

3. *Greater likelihood of confusion and lack of communication.* Polythink may increase confusion through willful lack of communication between advisors, mixed messages sent from different members of the decision-making unit, and inadvertent failures to effectively communicate between and within a diverse decision-making structure. This is likely to confuse the decision maker and obscure the optimal course of action.

4. *Greater likelihood of framing effects.* Polythink may cause some group members to advance biased or selective information in order to effectively make their point and "rise above the crowd" of other group members and advisors. Some members may use this selective information to frame offers, proposals, counterproposals, and even disagreements in different ways: some may give it a positive spin, while others may give it a negative spin. The likelihood of members of the group framing a decision problem in opposite directions is greater under Polythink than when there is a group consensus, as in Groupthink.[2]

5. *Adoption of positions with lowest common denominator.* Polythink may create decision situations in which the lowest common denominator becomes the dominant product of the group. Since group members express different or opposing views of the situation and of potential solutions, there is less likelihood that the group will speak in one voice under Polythink. This is also the case because, to reach a policy decision that will be palatable to the majority of the group, each member of the group needs to make some concessions in his or her organizational and political agenda.

6. *Decision paralysis.* The decision paralysis triggered by the Polythink dynamic often means either a complete failure to act to prevent potential crises or the adoption of sub-optimal, satisficing policies that are often shortsighted and in fact inhibit the kind of long-term planning that is required in war and peace decisions. The many divergent viewpoints within the decision-making unit make it incredibly difficult to reach consensus and clarity. Consequently, leaders may freeze up, since they are unclear whether their choice is correct and unsure whether it will be acceptable to the rest of their decision-making unit. Thus, decision paralysis is a primary characteristic of Polythink.

    Some of the symptoms of Polythink are similar to those of Groupthink. This is the case not because members of the group are thinking alike or sharing the same views but "because the group is *failing* to carry out any significant collective thinking" (Mintz, Mishal, and Morag 2005, 8). As is the case with Groupthink, Polythink is likely to lead to:

7. *Limited review of policy options.* Paradoxically, Polythink can lead to a limited review of policy options even though each advisor has distinct policy preferences. The lack of consensus and the presence of dissent in the group prevent the discussion and review of a large number of options. Thus, decision makers will often quickly exclude some of the options from consideration in order to construct a more manageable set of items for more thorough consideration (Mintz 2004).

8. *No room for reappraisal of previously rejected policy options.* A Polythink group is also less likely to revise its policies if and when other policy options are brought back up for further discussion, as any updating of policies may result in the time-consuming rehashing of previous disagreements among group members.

As does Groupthink, Polythink is likely to lead, in many situations, to *defective*, sub-optimal decisions; however, the mechanism for these flawed decision-making processes is the group's disunity and diversity rather than the group's unity and conformity.

Explaining Polythink

In Chapter 1, we introduced several explanations of Polythink. We now elaborate on each.

The Institutional, "Turf Wars" Explanation

The well-known phrase "where you stand depends on where you sit," coined by Rufus Miles Jr. in 1949 (see also 1978) and popularized by Graham Allison (1971), adeptly summarizes the type of "institutional thinking" that can contribute to Polythink. According to this explanation, the goal of members of the group is to represent their own bureaucracy/organization.[3] Thus, presidential advisors, members of the military, intelligence officials, and Cabinet members all interpret and advance plans and proposals from their own perspectives (e.g., political, coalitionary, institutional, etc.).[4] This well-known tendency to negotiate among various institutional positions is evident in Kissinger's famed observation, "The conclusions of both the Joint Chiefs of Staff and the National Security Council reflect the attainable consensus among sovereign departments rather than a sense of direction" (Kissinger 1969, 227).

Institutional rivalries can also contribute to Polythink. Due to intragroup and intergroup institutional competition (for resources, attention, time, credit, promotion), turf battles can arise that hamper information sharing across intelligence and security agencies, such as the CIA, the FBI, and the NSA, thus triggering confusion and miscommunication, key symptoms of Polythink. Moreover, multiple gatekeepers at various organizations may emerge, holding information at control points (Sullivan 2007) and keeping the information close to their chest (for a variety of organizational and bureaucratic reasons) instead of sharing it.

The Political Explanation

Robert Putnam (1988) coined the term "two-level games" to describe a typical negotiation setting where negotiators "play" at both the international level and the domestic level, taking into account international considerations as well as domestic political considerations (such as political audience costs; see Schultz

2003). Audiences play an important part in shaping the behavior of negotiators (Rubin and Brown 1975). In parliamentary democracies, for example, where governments typically consist of representatives from different parties with different platforms, agendas, constituencies, and interests, a two-level game can contribute to Polythink, as each member of the group represents not only the national interest but also his party's and constituencies' interests. Each member/delegate has to view his move in light of the coalition formation process with different potential partners. Lack of strong group cohesion, for example, because group members come from different political parties or represent different political constituencies, can increase the likelihood of Polythink. In contrast, authoritarian systems are less likely to suffer from Polythink because of the top-down control and fear advisors have of giving dissenting opinions.

The Normative Explanation

Members of the group can be hawkish or dovish, conservative or liberal. Stephen Walker and associates (1999) analyzed presidential "operational codes" and belief systems, and pointed to the importance of normative differences in beliefs among leaders in predicting decisions and action. These operational codes and normative perspectives also apply to presidential advisors. Members of groups represent not only the national interest but also their own personal values and worldviews. Moreover, they have different personal backgrounds inside and outside of government, while growing up, and throughout their careers. The relative lack of formal "rules of the game" in presidential advisory groups can exacerbate these differences and contribute to what we call "normative thinking," in which the goal of members of the decision-making unit is to represent their own worldview and normative belief system (Taber 1992).

The Expert–Novice Explanation

Fiske, Kinder, and Larter (1983, 393) found that novices "employ knowledge-based strategies that differ from those of experts." They process information and recall information in different ways than experts do. Specifically, whereas experts often focus on disconfirming evidence and information, novices typically focus on confirming information and strategies (Fiske, Kinder, and Larter 1983). Naturally, this can have a drastic effect on Polythink. In national security and foreign policy decision-making units, the expert-novice divide generally exists between security experts, diplomatic experts, and political experts, who, given the tendency to specialize, are most likely novices in the others' field of expertise (i.e., a career diplomat will likely not have a strong military background and a military leader will likely not have been trained as a diplomat). This divide can thus be particularly pronounced when military leaders weigh in on diplomatic solutions and when diplomatic advisors seek to address military concerns.

The Leader–Followers Explanation

Studies have shown that leaders place significant constraints on their advisors' freedom of action (Hermann 2001). The frequent reluctance of leaders to share goals, objectives, or strategies with group members, whether due to fear of leaks or the desire to maintain impartiality and prevent Groupthink, may also contribute to Polythink. For example, though a "hands-off" management style may give subordinates a wide degree of autonomy, it may also contribute to Polythink by inflating each group member's perceived independence and influence.

· · ·

In sum, the above discussion would seem to suggest that bureaucracies, constituencies, parties, worldviews, group leaders, and expertise place significant constraints on the freedom of action of leaders of the decision-making unit, and the "psychological presence" of these audiences acts to curtail the cognitive processes and "information search" of each member. Each team member evaluates collective considerations that are competing with interest-based considerations (institutional, domestic-political, and personal) (Mintz, Mishal, and Morag 2005).

The five explanations of Polythink listed above are not mutually exclusive. Some natural overlap exists; for example, the political positions of members of the coalition and their personal worldviews are related constructs that often interact.

The Groupthink-Polythink Continuum

As discussed in Chapter 1, Groupthink-Polythink is a continuum ranging from a highly cohesive, monolithic group dynamic at one end (Groupthink)[5] to a highly disjointed, pluralistic group dynamic (Polythink) at the other. Not surprisingly, other group configurations are also possible on this continuum. For example, some groups do not exhibit characteristics or symptoms of either Groupthink or Polythink. Members of such groups do not share exactly the same views and opinions, nor do they have completely pluralistic views. Some groups fall closer to the Groupthink position on the continuum, while others are closer to the Polythink position.

In a group dynamic that we call Con-Div, for example, group members are more balanced in the distribution of their opinions and so there is some *convergence* and some *divergence* of opinions. A major consequence of Con-Div is that group members will likely provide the decision maker with pros and cons of a variety of potential courses of action. This is because the different members are likely to advocate more than one set of policy options toward the same goal. Therefore, the decision maker can benefit from a balanced view of the situation and courses of action.

Subgroups in the Polythink Syndrome

Group decision-making entities, such as advisory boards, delegations, and committees, often consist of subgroups. One interesting feature of a Polythink environment is that although the group opinion is typically heterogeneous, it may encompass subgroups that exhibit Groupthink or Con-Div characteristics. For example, in coalition governments, one can identify parties that exhibit strong tendencies of Groupthink, yet, in the general makeup of the government, are part of a Polythink regime (in which each party has a different view on many domestic and foreign issues, while representing its constituencies). Thus, subgroups can subscribe to a Groupthink, Polythink or a Con-Div orientation and yet be part of a larger decision body that exhibits Polythink. Similarly, commercial firms and companies are often susceptible to Groupthink within their R&D, sales, and marketing units, but overall a company may actually exhibit Polythink symptoms because these subgroups frequently do not share the same vision of the company, its priorities, or strategic plan. Also conceivable are situations in which groups of different character (Polythink or Groupthink) interact with one another, as is often the case in negotiations, arbitration, or mediation. For example, there may be interactions of subgroups that may take the form of:

- Groupthink vs. Polythink

- Groupthink vs. Groupthink

- Polythink vs. Polythink

Such interactions are likewise possible with Con-Div groups. Key differences in the chances for successful outcomes depend probabilistically on the characteristics of these groups and their interactions. It is expected, for example, that in a Polythink-Polythink interaction, the groups will have difficulty updating or revising their initial offers in negotiations. This is due to intragroup conflict, leaks, confusion, framing, counter-framing, and other symptoms of Polythink. In contrast, Groupthink-Groupthink interactions are likely to result in sub-optimal decisions due to group pressure, poor information search, or lack of consideration of non-obvious risks.[6]

Can Polythink Be Beneficial?
The Productive Polythink Dynamic

As we have seen, Destructive Polythink often leads to decision paralysis and poor decisions. However, under what conditions might Polythink result in good decisions? In other words, how can Polythink be beneficial? Political leaders, business executives, managers, and other group leaders can benefit from Polythink if they can positively leverage the plurality of opinions presented to them in a group setting en route to forming a decision. For example, if a leader can take the diverse feedback of group members and channel it into one comprehensive viewpoint, articulated in one unified voice, it may actually prove beneficial to have diverse input in the decision.

In some cases diverse opinions and viewpoints can be reconciled and result in a positive policy outcome. The decision on the Surge of U.S. forces in Iraq (analyzed in Chapter 5 of this book) is a prime example of this approach. The Administration consulted with multiple groups and experts to make a relatively "good," Con-Div decision in terms of evaluating multiple, even conflicting views and reconciling them to formulate a cohesive policy. Likewise, President Obama's decision to draw down the number of troops in Iraq involved some serious disagreements, despite being supported by nearly 75 percent of the U.S. electorate (Jones 2011), who considered it better than the status quo outcome—at least at the time the decision was taken (though this view is increasingly being challenged by some as ISIS has emerged as a major threat in Iraq and Syria). Stated differently, divergent opinions do not always lead to a bad decision. Managed, Productive Polythink can even be beneficial to the decision maker, as it could reduce the group's biases. In Chapter 8, we will review potential strategies by which leaders can leverage Polythink to produce better decision-making outcomes.

Polythink and Biases in Group Decision Making

Surprisingly, and counterintuitively, Polythink can actually *reduce* biases of information processing, judgment, and choice in group settings. Cognitive biases are defined as "predictable errors in the ways that individuals interpret information and make decisions" (Kahneman and Renshon 2009, 79). Scholars of decision making under risk have detected several common biases that Polythink may help prevent (Forman and Selly 1996; Jervis 1976; Mintz and DeRouen 2010). This is not the case with Groupthink, which typically raises the likelihood that a group may exhibit such cognitive and information-processing biases. Interestingly, many of these cognitive biases are more "hawkish" in that decision makers are "not only more likely to see threats as more dire than an objective observer would perceive, but also [are more] likely to act in a way that will produce unnecessary conflict" (Kahneman and Renshon 2009, 79). Some of the more well-known biases include:

1. *Shooting from the hip.* This bias involves making spur-of-the-moment, unplanned decisions. Since group members in a Polythink dynamic express a plurality of opinions, including dissenting views, it is less likely that the group as a whole will be able to make a shoot-from-the-hip decision. Group members who have opposing views are simply more likely than in a Groupthink setting to introduce such views and challenge the prevailing one, making it hard, all things being equal, for the group leader to make less-calculated, impulsive decisions.

2. *Locking in.* This bias focuses exclusively on a preferred policy option while ignoring critical information that contradicts this option. This bias is much more likely to occur in a Groupthink setting than in a Polythink dynamic, because in Polythink, the existing plurality of opinions and views reduces the probability of all group members sharing and advocating the same policy option. With Polythink, there is a probability of dissent among group members, including the introduction of an alternative course of action or even a set of competing alternatives.

3. *Engaging in wishful thinking.* Though some views within a Polythink group may represent wishful thinking, others are unlikely to exhibit such bias. Consequently, compared with Groupthink, there is less likelihood for wishful thinking when people express (and are thus exposed to) multiple views than when they share the same (potentially misguided) view.

4. *Ignoring critical information.* In a Polythink dynamic, group members are less likely to ignore critical information than in a Groupthink dynamic. This is because the diverse group is more likely to point out obstacles and challenges to the preferred course of action. However, because members of the group suffer from the Polythink syndrome, their collective view may be

more radical than the view of each one of them, a phenomenon known in the psychological literature as "risky shift" (or group polarization effect). This may lead to the radicalization of the group's recommendation.

5. *Exhibiting poliheuristic bias.* This bias refers to the practice of making decisions only after the elimination of options that are particularly negative on a singular non-compensatory dimension, usually political (Mintz 2004). In other words, decisions can be considered on a number of dimensions (military, political, diplomatic, etc.), but if a given policy results in a negative score on one very important dimension (e.g., it is bad for the leader politically), it may not be selected, even if its overall score is highest. The poliheuristic bias is less likely to occur in a Polythink dynamic because conflicting political and institutional agendas and interests often neutralize one another. In other words, group members have diverse opinions in a Polythink setting, so while some members may be susceptible to a poliheuristic bias, the group as a whole may actually be less so.

6. *Focusing on short-term benefits rather than on long-term costs.* In a Polythink environment, it is more likely that some members will focus on short-term gains whereas others will focus on long-term costs. This can be more beneficial to a decision maker than the homogeneity of Groupthink because leaders will gain a broader picture of costs and benefits.

7. *Reducing the preference over preference heuristic.* Closely related to the "locking in" bias is the "preference over preference" bias of group members. This bias is when one overarching course of action is preferred (e.g., military action), but the preference ordering of the sub-options is not pre-determined (e.g., ground forces or missile attacks). This bias is more likely to occur in a Groupthink process with a directive leader than in a Polythink process. This is because divergent opinions represent a plurality of preferences. In contrast, in Groupthink overarching preferences often govern the decision and the ultimate choice.

8. *Minimizing overconfidence.* The Polythink group as a whole may be less susceptible to the overconfidence bias or "positive illusions" (Kahneman and Renshon 2009), as various members of the group who exhibit opposing views may cancel/neutralize one another in overconfidence and underconfidence. In fact, the plurality of viewpoints may hinder overconfidence, since a counterargument can be advanced for many of the views presented.

Predicting Polythink

If one can predict a Polythink dynamic in a group, it might be possible to miti-gate some of the associated negative symptoms and outcomes associated with this group dynamic. Below, we enumerate some specific factors that can either exacerbate or mitigate Polythink, many of which are tied to the causes of Poly-think discussed above.

1. *Type of advisory system.* The decision-making literature typically identifies three main forms of advisory groups: competitive, collegial, and formal (Burke 2005; Johnson 1974; Mitchell 2005). Each system has the potential to mitigate or exacerbate Polythink and other group decision-making pro-cesses in different ways (Hermann and Hermann 1989). For example, a col-legial style will be more likely to lead to Groupthink as a result of the close relationship fostered between the leader and his advisors. The competitive system, on the other hand, may be more predictive of Polythink, since dis-senting views of various group members are freely expressed, perhaps even leading to group conflict. The formal advisory system provides a more structured format that guides group decision-making processes. Thus, the particular leader–followers' relationship and expert-novice makeup of the group are in many ways a consequence of the type of advisory system a leader chooses.

2. *Situational conditions.* Variables such as the relative openness of the group to new information (rather than monolithic worldviews) and conflicting bureaucratic, institutional, and political agendas and interests of group members are likely to increase the probability of Polythink.

3. *Leadership style.* Leadership style affects the way advisory systems are struc-tured (Hermann and Preston 1994). Margaret Hermann and colleagues (2001) produced a typology of leadership style featuring four categories: crusader, opportunistic, strategic, and pragmatic. We claim that this typol-ogy can help predict Polythink and especially whether Polythink will be Productive or Destructive. The crusader leader challenges political con-straints and is closed to new information (Hermann 2001). The opportu-nistic leader, in contrast, "is mindful of political constraints and pursues information" (Mintz and DeRouen 2010, 117). Leaders with this leadership style will also not risk alienating politically important actors. The strate-gic leader "challenges constraints but is open to information" (Mintz and DeRouen 2010, 117). This leader is politically bold "but circumspect when

it comes to acting out these ambitious aspirations" (117). Finally, the pragmatic leader respects political constraints but is closed to information.

Which type of leadership style can best predict Productive Polythink? It is clear that a prerequisite for Productive Polythink is openness of the leader to information from group members, even if the information they provide contradicts that which the leader seeks. Consequently, the pragmatic leader and the opportunistic one are more likely to benefit from Polythink, whereas the crusader and the strategic leader may either ignore divisions within their advisory system or even forbid such divisions.

4. *Conflicting interests.* Opposing, or even conflicting institutional interests and agendas can be exacerbated by different types of governmental systems. For example, whether a system is authoritarian, presidential, or parliamentary can affect the political interests of group members and shape the group dynamic in collaborative or adversarial ways.

Therefore, like Groupthink, Polythink can be viewed as "a contingent phenomenon" rather than as a "general property" of all decision-making groups ('t Hart, Stern, and Sundelius 1997, in reference to Groupthink). Clearly, Polythink is dependent on the political views and interests of group members, bureaucratic and institutional considerations, gatekeepers, management style, and type of leadership. These factors can provoke divergence or convergence of views.

In Polythink, each group member typically takes into account "a bewildering array of considerations. Furthermore, as groups and coalitions become more brittle and issues more controversial, Polythink becomes more relevant" (Mintz, Mishal, and Morag 2005). The existence of multiple power bases, multiple gatekeepers, diverse institutional interests and competing bureaucratic agendas within a group may serve as an "advance warning" for unsuccessful outcomes in decision making and negotiations (Mintz, Mishal, and Morag 2005).

The predictive utility of the Polythink model is important as a practical tool for policymakers and other group leaders. Indeed, if a group leader can predict such a dynamic a-priori when building a decision unit, she or he can mitigate the negative symptoms of Polythink and transform Destructive Polythink into Productive Polythink (see Chapter 8).

Applications of Polythink

Polythink is applicable to group dynamics at the federal, state, and local levels. It can exist in any group: in the National Security Council, in the UN Security

Council, in a security cabinet, in a governmental coalition, or in congressional committees. It is much less likely, of course, to exist in non-democratic settings, and in other hierarchical systems, although intragroup rivalries are documented across many authoritarian political systems (Kinne 2005). As a generic concept, Polythink applies to any small-group dynamics in government, business, industry, military, or politics. This encompasses many advisory systems, boards of directors, management teams, R&D teams, marketing and sales teams, school boards, and other groups.

Polythink within a decision-making unit may significantly hinder collective success at the federal, state, local, committee, and company levels. Executives and managers may make poor decisions if they are paralyzed by the multiple views presented to them, instead of taking advantage of the plurality of viewpoints. Furthermore, numerous companies that are characterized by a hierarchical structure with a strong leader/executive (chairman/president/CEO) are more prone to exhibit signs of Groupthink, whereas many start-ups encourage and reward pluralism of ideas (but see Apple and Google, which also exhibit such pluralistic structures). In contrast, shared mental models such as those in Groupthink increase speed and flexibility in decision making by emphasizing the most salient dimensions and solutions, although often the wrong ones (Cannon-Bowers, Salas, and Converse 1993).

According to Greenhalgh (1986), conflict resolution involves moving from a "zero-sum game" situation to a "win-win" situation. It would appear that it is thus predicated on the existence of shared mental models within and between delegations to negotiations, which can then be refashioned during the course of the conflict resolution process. The lack of shared mental models would then seem to suggest a diminished likelihood of achieving conflict resolution (Greenhalgh 1986).

Polythink characterizes group dynamics not only in the domestic, political, and economic arenas, but also at the international level. States' national interests often differ. States also see things differently. Essentially, *where you stand on international issues often depends on where you sit politically or economically.* For example, citizens in countries with very high percentages of Muslim voters naturally have different opinions on the Israeli-Palestinian issue than those in countries such as the U.S., Canada, or Australia. Linkage politics—the impact of domestic politics on foreign policy—often explains foreign policy decisions and behavior (James and Rioux 1998; Rosenau 1969). Economic calculations also influence decisions of states and non-state actors in the international system, as do geopolitical and geostrategic goals.

Measuring Polythink

Polythink can be operationalized and measured. In addition to examining the number and severity of the above symptoms present in a decision-making process (as we do in this book), one can also determine empirically whether Polythink or Groupthink exists in a group by examining the number of overlapping choice sets of alternatives and dimension sets of group members (Mintz, Mishal, and Morag 2005). Such an analysis can reveal the extent of overlap in individuals' "decision matrices." A decision matrix consists of a set of decision alternatives (for example, Do Nothing, Apply Sanctions, Negotiate, Attack) and a set of decision dimensions or criteria (such as political considerations, diplomatic considerations, military considerations, economic considerations) (Mintz 1993). By comparing whether the alternative sets and dimension sets (a) are completely identical, (b) are partially similar, or (c) have little overlap in the choice sets and the dimension sets, one can determine whether a Polythink, a Con-Div, or a Groupthink dynamic characterizes the group. Conceptually and empirically, it is thus possible to think about decision-making groups in several different ways, each of which has important ramifications for the operationalization and measurement of Polythink.

1. *Content of the choice set and the dimension set.* This refers to whether the group members' alternatives (e.g., choices) and dimensions (e.g., different aspects of each choice) are similar or different and the extent of such variations.

2. *Binary (bi-categorical) mode of decision making versus multi-categorical mode.* In foreign policy, for example, state decision makers evaluate alternatives such as use force or do not use force; sponsor terrorism or oppose terrorism; or, in a multi-categorical mode: attack, do not attack, negotiate, apply sanctions. One measure of Polythink is the number of alternatives in the choice set of *each* decision maker (Mintz, Mishal, and Morag, 2005).

3. *Multidimensional versus unidimensional reasoning.* A choice can be multidimensional, meaning it is based on several criteria/dimensions such as the military balance, political audience costs, or deterrence; or it can be unidimensional, such as a decision based solely on whether the decision will help

the leader politically. Consequently, another measure of Polythink is the number of dimensions/criteria in each member's matrix.

4. *Size of the decision matrix* (Maoz 1990). Some decision makers conceptualize a decision problem in a relatively narrow way, while others may take a more comprehensive view (e.g., by using a multi-categorical choice set and a multidimensional dimension set). The size of the decision matrix equals the number of alternatives multiplied by the number of dimensions. When the size and content of the decision matrices and the ultimate choice vary between group members, it is evidence for the prevalence of Polythink.

Refuting Polythink

It is important to consider, as well, how the Polythink thesis can be refuted. In order for the Polythink syndrome to exist in a given group, several symptoms, such as leaks, competing framing efforts, and intragroup conflict should also be present. Polythink is not *only* multiple viewpoints among group members, which might be normal for any group; in Polythink, disagreement and dissent are important components as well.

Indeed, one way to distinguish Polythink from Groupthink and the Con-Div dynamic is by showing that the group has *disagreements* among its members. This was clearly the case in the Israeli 2012 decision not to attack Iran, as described in Chapter 6. The three subgroups that influenced this important decision were (a) the top political echelon in Israel (the Israeli Prime Minister and the Defense Minister), (b) former and then present top members of the Israeli military establishment, and (c) U.S. Administration officials. Serious disagreements among these subgroups characterized the 2012 debate on Iran before the U.S. November election.

However, it is possible to refute Polythink by showing that the group dynamic fits better with the Con-Div or Groupthink symptoms. The overarching prerequisite of Polythink is the plurality of opinions and disagreement among group members. Moreover, for Polythink to exist, the majority of symptoms (although not all) need to be present. The symptoms of Polythink thus offer a systematic and testable set of hypotheses. For example, groups characterized by Polythink will likely exhibit more intragroup conflict, leaks, and confusion than Groupthink or Con-Div groups.[7] In subsequent chapters, we will illustrate the Polythink symptoms and their consequences using several case studies of U.S. foreign and national security policy.

Symptoms of Con-Div

Con-Div has its unique symptoms as well. Its key characteristics are:

1. *Clearer policy direction than in Polythink, with little or no confusion over direction.* Since group members in Con-Div share the same goals and have no major disagreements over general policy, there will be less confusion than in Polythink on action items, but probably more than in Groupthink, where the group has consensus on its specific recommendations.

2. *Fewer group information processing biases than in Groupthink.* Con-Div is likely to lead to fewer group cognitive biases, such as "shooting from the hip," "plunging in," or even the "preference over preference bias" (Mintz and DeRouen 2010), as there is some diversity in the group (though less than in Polythink). For example, as group members in Con-Div can have different opinions on specific policy recommendations, the group is less likely to "plunge in" and make a (wrong) decision.

3. *Less likelihood of ignoring critical information than in Groupthink.* Due to the plurality of opinions in the Con-Div group (although not quite as pronounced as in Polythink), critical information that may affect the decision is less likely to be ignored than in Groupthink.

4. *Operating in one voice.* As group members share the same goals and vision for the organization, the group is likely to speak with one voice, especially if its leader sets a clear direction. Of course, rivalries among group members may still naturally exist and lead to some off-message comments.

5. *Too much harmony that may hinder real debate.* Because group members in Con-Div share the same goals (though they may have different opinions with regard to specific policy directions), a leader's dominant view may trigger an excess of harmony that will in turn lead to less debate over policy. In other words, the harmony associated with Con-Div (though less than in Groupthink) may lead to recommendations that are not challenged enough by group members especially if the views of the leader are perceived as too dominant or strong. Although in Con-Div there can be a debate where various opinions are presented, the ultimate decision will typically be made by the leader of the group, and group members will follow. In other words, the lack of dissent in Con-Div, though often constructive to the group's deliberations, may not provide a sufficient challenge to the leader's view. Importantly, some debate can be helpful for the decision unit, as it can illuminate logical errors in thinking or factual misjudgments.

6. *Less likelihood of decision paralysis.* Con-Div is less likely to result in decision paralysis than Polythink, especially if the group has a strong leader who sets a clear vision for the organization that motivates group members and other followers.[8] However, deliberations may be prolonged en route to a decision if this dynamic exists in a group.

7. *Greater likelihood of "good" decisions compared with decisions under Groupthink or Polythink.* In Con-Div, plurality of opinions, viewpoints, and even debate are often channeled into more informed and good decisions, as group members share the same goals and vision. Thus, a plurality of opinions can provide useful input for leaders' decisions, without the dissent and paralysis that Polythink groups often experience. Moreover, unlike Groupthink, in Con-Div, a plurality of opinions serves to challenge mind guards and prevent the narrowing of vision associated with cohesive groups. Con-Div may result in more-balanced and superior advice to the group leader.

   Under Con-Div, group members who share the same general goals and objectives may be able to rise above smaller disagreements, if there are any. This may also lead to better decisions and more optimal outcomes.

   However, Con-div is not necessarily a prerequisite for optimal decisions, although this group dynamic is generally superior to Groupthink and Polythink because it facilitates more balanced recommendations for action. Often, Con-Div requires a leader with a clear vision and strong presence to bridge policy differences in pursuit of the goals of the organization.

   Thus, working in a Con-Div environment does not *necessarily* guarantee a a good outcome. There have been cases of government cabinets and executives working in harmony, sharing the same vision, the same key goals, and agendas, while debating policy alternatives, yet producing bad decisions.[9]

Causes of Con-Div

What may trigger Con-Div? The midrange on the Groupthink-Polythink continuum can evolve from several factors:

1. Poor or defective decision outcomes in a previous important case or in a series of events or incidents may induce the group leader to reshape and reconstruct the group as Con-Div, hoping that this structure will result in better decisions.

2. A leader who sets a clear vision with regard to the priorities and goals of the organization, yet allows open discussion of the dilemmas facing the group, can reduce the likelihood of Groupthink and Polythink and lead to the more balanced Con-Div dynamic.

3. Leaders and group members often learn from experience how to deal with the Groupthink or Polythink syndromes and how to structure their decision unit to foster a Con-Div dynamic and shape group membership to avoid extremes. The Con-Div process is not set in stone; it can change as the decision unit continually evolves, learns from past experience, and tries to improve its decision-making ability.

4. Electoral defeat or the fear of such defeat often prompts a reshuffling of the elite group decision-making structure that can reshape the decision-unit dynamic. For example, following the 2014 midterm elections, President Obama and Secretary of Defense Chuck Hagel parted ways, as Obama was seeking a leader who would not bow to military demands as easily and would be more vocal and present during strategy meetings (Starr 2014b).

5. Commissions of inquiry into a fiasco often lead to a shake-up and a more diverse yet professionally balanced group of advisory group members.

6. Some politically and organizationally astute leaders deliberately and strategically build advisory groups in a more balanced way in order to achieve optimal results in a less-challenging environment than Polythink yet in a more diverse setting than Groupthink.

Groupthink and Polythink: Similarities and Differences

What are the similarities and differences between Groupthink and Polythink? How does the Con-Div process relate to these group dynamics? How can group dynamics lead to better decisions? As was pointed out above, both Groupthink and Polythink represent extremes on a continuum that runs from an ultra-cohesive group to an ultra-diverse group. Because process is relate to outcome (Schafer and Crichlow 2010), both Groupthink and Polythink often lead (unless managed carefully and creatively) to defective decisions. However, there are also significant differences between Polythink and Groupthink. In Polythink, the key reason that group dynamics lead to defective decisions is the lack of any consensus in a group, and, often, the presence of open dissent. In Groupthink, on the other hand, it is too much consensus with no dissent at all that leads to sub-optimal decisions.[10]

The distinction between Groupthink and Polythink with regard to each group dynamic's symptoms is substantial, as Polythink is characterized by group conflict, leaks, framing and counter-framing by group members, whereas the Groupthink dynamic leads to overarching consensus and the funneling of ideas and policy options to essentially one viewpoint.

Often, the focus on preventing a Groupthink dynamic via multiple advocacy, a competitive advisory system, or some other mechanisms can inadvertently lead to Polythink. This is because efforts to make groups more pluralistic or less cohesive can obviously result in disagreements and fragmentation of the decision unit. Various strategies are recommended in this book for the prevention and preemption of Polythink by leaders. Among them are the divide and conquer strategy; the leveraging of group divisions and pluralism of opinion for brainstorming; and the use of sophisticated analytic techniques and decision support systems to present and assess a range of alternatives (see Chapter 8). There is a strong need for decision-unit architecture in order to create a Con-Div dynamic that can result in a more balanced group dynamic and lead to more optimal decision-making processes and outcomes (Jones 2001).

Table 2.1 provides a direct comparison of Polythink with Groupthink. Interestingly, some of the prevention tactics of Groupthink advocated by Janis (1982a) may lead to Polythink.

Comparing Groupthink and Polythink to Con-Div

In Con-Div groups, there will be greater likelihood of reviewing more policy options than in Groupthink (and Polythink), but for different reasons. In Groupthink, other policy options are not introduced because the views of the group are monolithic and/or because social pressure of the group discourages members from advocating other perspectives. In Polythink, options may also, paradoxically, be limited, as the decision maker attempts to tamp down divisive conflict or paralyzing debate by limiting the policy choice set. In Con-Div, however, the social pressure for conformity (caused by Groupthink) or the leader's restriction of the choice set (caused by Polythink) will be greatly diminished, and so group members will be freer to express and debate different policy options.

Con-Div is, by definition, less homogeneous than Groupthink but less heterogeneous than Polythink. Thus, in Con-Div the group is less likely to possess the Groupthink symptoms described by Janis (1982a). Namely, Con-Div groups are less likely to engage in an incomplete survey of alternatives and objectives,

TABLE 2.1 Comparing Groupthink and Polythink

	Groupthink	Polythink
Symptoms	Closed-mindedness Overestimations of the group's power and morality Rationalization to discount warnings Stereotyped views Pressure toward uniformity such as self-censorship, the illusion of unanimity, pressure on dissenters through self-appointed mind-guards (Janis 1982)	Intragroup disagreements; dissent Intragroup conflict Lack of communication and confusion Leaks Framing and counter-framing Selective review of information Multiple gatekeepers Limited review of alternatives Failure to reappraise previously rejected alternatives
Causes	A high degree of group cohesiveness A high level of insulation of the policy-making group from outside criticism and input No tradition of impartial leadership A lack of norms requiring methodical decision-making procedures Relative homogeneity of group members' social backgrounds and ideologies High stress from external threats Low self-esteem among decision makers. (Janis 1982)	Institutional agendas and turf wars Political and coalitionary considerations Normative differences in worldviews Expert vs. novice decision-making styles Leader/followers/advisors relationship
Consequences	An incomplete survey of alternatives An incomplete survey of objectives Failure to examine risks emanating from the preferred choice Failure to reappraise initially rejected alternatives Poor information search Selective bias in processing information at hand Failure to work out contingency plans (Janis 1982)	Lowest-common-denominator decision making Decision paralysis Lack of long-term planning

	Groupthink	Polythink
Prevention	The leader should assign the role of critical evaluator to each member, encouraging the group to give high priority to airing objections and doubts.	Decision unit architecture
		Group brainstorming
		Use of a divide-and-conquer tactic
	The leader should be impartial rather than stating a particular view	Subdivision of the decision problem into smaller, more manageable problems
	An administrative practice of setting up several independent policy groups should be utilized	Use of decision support systems and other analytic techniques
	Subgroups could be formed to hammer out differences	
	Group members should discuss deliberations with trusted outside associates	
	Outside experts should be brought in to challenge views	
	At every meeting, one member should be assigned the role of devil's advocate	
	A significant amount of time should be devoted to surveying all warning signals from the opposing side and constructing alternative scenarios of the rival's intentions	
	After reaching a preliminary consensus, the group should hold a second-chance meeting to rethink the decision	
	(Janis 1982)	

and are less likely to use poor information search or to engage in selective bias in information processing. Such groups will be more likely to review competing alternatives, survey a more complete set of objectives, examine risks and rewards, reappraise previously rejected alternatives, and prepare a contingency plan. This is because group members who converge on the same goals in Con-Div are nevertheless not necessarily in complete agreement over a preferred alternative.

Likewise, in accordance with the symptoms of Polythink, we expect to find in Con-Div group conflict, turf interests, leaks, framing and counter-framing efforts by group members, but much less pronounced than in Polythink, as the group is characterized by convergence of key group goals, agendas, and direction. In Con-Div, some group members are still likely to introduce competing frames and use leaks; however, there is enough convergence that these competing frames are more likely to be reconcilable and fit into an overarching policy framework. This results in less confusion and less intragroup conflict.

The Con-Div dynamic thus has the potential to strike a balance between Groupthink and Polythink, encouraging reappraisal of rejected options, without the paralysis of indecision and endless debate. Furthermore, the group leader will typically reach a decision after listening to input from various group members.[11]

Alternatives to Polythink

Previous work on group decision-making processes, including presidential advisory systems, has identified several related but distinct concepts relevant to the Polythink dynamic. Below, we outline various strategies and structures of group decision making that may directly affect the prevalence of Polythink in group decision-making processes.

Multiple Advocacy

With the multiple advocacy model, Alexander George introduced his own method for preventing the advent of Groupthink in decision-making processes of complex organizations such as the Executive Branch of the U.S. government (George 1972). This model, rather than "discouraging or neutralizing internal disagreements over policy," would "harness diversity of views and interests in the interest of rational policy making" (George 1972, 751). George relies on a centralized management model in order to avoid devolving into a nonstructured and unbalanced debate that could potentially paralyze the decision-making process. However, oftentimes this structured style of management is faulty or nonexistent—when the decision-making group does not agree with the leader, when the leader himself is confused or conflicted, when there are too many competing voices, and more. This multiple advocacy model can be construed as a type of structured, "ideal" Polythink process, with productive consequences, provided that the group leader adequately structures and brings together the divergent opinions of group members into a single, cohesive policy direction.

Whereas multiple advocacy is a type of Polythink, it is important to note that most forms, structures, and variants of Polythink are not multiple advocacy. Polythink is a by-product of group dynamics that often triggers destructive consequences, rather than a strategic policy, such as multiple advocacy, that is directed and designed by a leader for the purpose of making informed foreign policy decisions.

Distributed Decision Making (DDM)

Distributed decision making can be defined as "the design and coordination of connected decisions" (Schneeweiss 2003, 3). In other words, it is a model featuring a set of related decisions that are distributed across a set of organizational decision makers. Distributed decision making constitutes, therefore, a concept that is related to but distinct from Polythink. The concept originated in the literature on social movements (Brown and Hosking 1986; Klandermans 1988), whose distributed, weblike leadership structure did not fit into typical centralized models of leadership. Not all decisions are made by a single decision maker. The decisions are related in that the consequences of one may affect another and hence must be coordinated in some manner. The decision makers are related by means of their organizational roles, which give them full or partial authority and responsibility for certain areas of the decision domain (Sage 1991). However, this DDM can also have a highly hierarchical relationship between various decision makers in some cases.

Thus, it is clear that distributed decision making is somewhat related to Polythink in that it involves a variety of decision makers, each with expertise and responsibility for decisions within his or her own field of expertise. However, ultimately each decision is intertwined with and somewhat dependent on other decisions. This interrelated web of decisions by various key decision makers is in fact a factor that can contribute to Polythink. If this process is not properly managed at the top, it can easily devolve into chaos or paralysis as each decision maker inserts his or her own opinions, values, and worldview into each of the interrelated decisions. Indeed, often in national security policy, it is possible to witness the way in which distributed decision making exacerbates Polythink.

The State Department will make decisions, for example, on foreign aid and diplomacy; the Department of Defense will work to strengthen national defense and homeland security; the CIA will focus on intelligence; the army will seek to maintain military gains in the field. However, in the end, each of these decisions affects the others and must be coordinated up the hierarchical ladder to the President, who is meant to ensure the cohesion of the overall foreign policy picture, counteracting the military-industrial bureaucracy's distributed nature.

The Competitive Advisory System

The competitive advisory system is another strategy that has often been put forth as a method of counteracting Groupthink (Johnson 1974). Rather than seek cohesion among advisors, as in the collegial system, presidents who subscribe to the competitive advisory system will encourage advisors to vigorously debate and argue their relative perspectives among themselves. The President in the meantime will keep his own views on the issue hidden or neutral until late in the decision-making process. The President is thus effectively playing "the neutral or honest broker" role himself (Burke 2005). FDR is a prime example of this strategy (George 1980; Pfiffner 2005).

In contrast to the competitive advisory system, Polythink is more of a reflection of the group *dynamic.* Leaders do not seek or engineer it. It is a description of reality. Similar to the idea of multiple advocacy, the competitive advisory strategy can be effective in combating Groupthink, but it can also easily descend into Destructive Polythink if the process is not effectively managed by the leader.

·   ·   ·

In the following chapters, we will use the diagnostic criteria listed in this chapter (symptoms) to identify the dynamic that characterized presidential administrations as they made key foreign policy and national security decisions. Specifically, we will examine the set of policy decisions made surrounding the 9/11 terrorist attacks and the subsequent War on Terror. An analysis of key U.S. decisions with regard to Afghanistan, Iraq, Iran, Syria, the Israeli-Palestinian Conflict, and ISIS provides a broad spectrum of post-9/11 national security and foreign policy decisions in a crucial regional and policy area—the Middle East and the War on Terror—and helps us understand the effect of group composition and dynamics on the actual decision. Determining the prevalence of Polythink, and its political consequences, in this context has important implications for policymakers and analysts.

3   The 9/11 Attacks

Polythink in National Security

It Can't Happen Here: 9/11 and Pearl Harbor

For much of its nearly three-hundred-year history as a nation, the U.S. has felt secure in its relative insulation and safety from the tumultuous events occurring oceans away in Europe, the Middle East, Africa, Latin America, Oceania, or Asia. Yet, on two clear mornings—Sunday, December 7, 1941, and Tuesday, September 11, 2001—this illusion of safety and security was strikingly challenged, as thousands of American citizens perished in carefully executed attacks carried out by foreign enemies on the American homeland. These attacks, in addition to fundamentally and permanently altering the international system, forced the U.S. government to look inward and address the errors in judgment that contributed to its stark failure to protect its citizens. How was it possible, given the amount of intelligence that warned of an impending attack, that the U.S. government was unable to predict and prevent these tragedies? Because of the massive impact of both attacks on the future course of global events, these attacks are often compared and equated. However, such a comparison is inherently problematic and fails to take into account the many differences between the decision-making processes of the federal government in each case.

Irving Janis convincingly argues in *Victims of Groupthink* (1982a) that the attack on Pearl Harbor in 1942 was caused in large part by the American military strivings for unanimity and consensus. This motivation appeared to supersede its motivation to realistically appraise alternative courses of action and its own potential vulnerabilities to enemy attack. Janis points to the widespread belief held by most senior military strategists, including Admiral Husband Kimmel, the Commander in Chief of the U.S. Pacific Fleet, and his advisors, that "it can't happen here." Janis emphasizes the nearly unanimous sense of extreme invulnerability among senior naval personnel that led to a completely "unwarranted feeling of immunity from attack" (described by Admiral Ernest Joseph King).[1] Guided by uninformed stereotypes about Japanese inferiority, American military planners failed to adequately prepare for a potential attack on the U.S. Pacific Fleet by the Japanese. This failure occurred despite the nearly miraculous cracking of the Japanese military code, named MAGIC, which indicated that the Japanese were preparing for a major military operation, although it did not specify exactly where. This source of ambiguity enabled American military personnel to engage in "wishful thinking," a hallmark of Groupthink (Janis 1982a), which resulted in the lack of preparation for an assault on the American Pacific Fleet.

This inaction in the face of increasingly alarming intelligence reports does resemble the similar decision paralysis prior to the September 11 attacks. However, the reasons behind the inaction in each case are starkly different. In other words, while the *outcome* was similar, the decision-making *process* was not. At Pearl Harbor, the military and political decision units were characterized by Groupthink. In the military, Admiral Kimmel's group of advisors was largely cohesive, and subordinates shared strong feelings of loyalty to their leader (Janis 1982a). This contributed to a practice of suppressing dissension and questioning of the admiral's military preparations for a potential attack, even though many at the lower echelons of the Navy were much more skeptical about Kimmel's optimistic perception of the U.S. invulnerability to such an attack. Moreover, the group developed shared rationalizations that were not subjected to critical evaluation: the idea that Japan was too scared at the idea of open war with the U.S. to risk an attack; that Pearl Harbor was too shallow to be vulnerable to torpedo bombs; and that the U.S. would certainly be able to detect and counteract any attempted attack well before any damage was inflicted (Janis 1982a). All of these rationalizations served to reinforce the idea of American invulnerability and contributed to the selective bias in the processing of intelligence reports from the Japanese (Janis 1982a).

Also, at Pearl Harbor, in contrast to 9/11, the many interlocking policy groups of the national security apparatus served only to reinforce the viewpoints and perspectives of each (rather than critique them, as we will show was the case with 9/11). For example, Janis mentions the viewpoints of the U.S. Army, of the

U.S. Naval Command in Washington, and President Roosevelt's circle of advisors as markedly similar: These entities understated the threat posed by the Japanese and failed to take into account alternative hypotheses that the Japanese might attack the U.S. first, before attacking British or Dutch targets in the Pacific. This phenomenon, of different policy-making groups reinforcing the Groupthink perspective of other policy-making groups, was caused and exacerbated by the fact that each group, in attempting to reassure the others, suppressed internal doubts, failing almost completely to discuss the issue of Hawaii. This ultimately strengthened the illusion of unanimity in the decision-making process that proved so disastrous on December 7, 1941.

The failure of the defense establishment to prevent the attacks of September 11, in contrast, was the result of a much different set of circumstances and problematic decision-making processes. Rather than striving for unanimity or conformity, the policymakers and defense officials charged with protecting the homeland from attack were divided, hampered by poor information-sharing processes, institutional disagreements, bureaucratic hurdles, and a general lack of a cohesive vision of what the threat of attack was and how to effectively address it. Thus, in the case of 9/11, the failure to anticipate and prevent the attacks was in part caused by Polythink, not Groupthink, at the highest levels of the federal government.

This chapter will provide an in-depth review of the events leading up to the 9/11 attacks, focusing on the decision-making processes of key diplomatic and security groups, including the CIA, the Presidential Cabinet and advisory team, the State Department, and more, to assess the key signs and symptoms of Polythink that were present in the decision-making processes of these groups and that ultimately contributed to the failure to prevent this staggering attack.

Polythink and Groupthink as "Pure" Types

It is important to note that throughout this book we treat both Groupthink and Polythink as "pure" types. In real-world decision-making situations, there is rarely a case of "pure" or extreme Polythink or Groupthink. For example, though Janis (1982a) clearly qualifies the attacks on Pearl Harbor as an example of Groupthink, several scholars have critiqued his categorization as too extreme, based on a small and restricted sample and perhaps failing to account for the non-Groupthink elements present in the decision-making process (Aldag and Fuller 1993; Baron 2005; Kramer 1998). Likewise with the September 11 attacks, though these attacks are much closer to Polythink on the group decision-making spectrum, there are, of course, elements that are not—for example, the widespread wishful thinking belief (though not unanimous) that the U.S. homeland could not or would not be attacked. It is therefore more useful to think of these two concepts as extremes, where defective decision-making processes lean closer to one of two poles—the group conformity of Groupthink (with Pearl Harbor as a key example) or the group disunity of Polythink (with September 11 as a key example).[2]

A Breakdown of 9/11—A Chronicle of Miscalculations

On September 11, 2001, a team of al-Qaeda terrorists launched a coordinated multi-pronged attack against the U.S., simultaneously hijacking four airplanes and crashing the fuel-laden planes into the symbolic centers of American economic and military might—the World Trade Center and the Pentagon. The hijackers failed only in their fourth target, the White House or the U.S. Capitol building, because of the heroic efforts of the plane's passengers, who crashed the plane in a field in Shanksville, Pennsylvania. This sophisticated, well-planned attack stunned the U.S. and the world. How could such a seemingly inferior enemy inflict such extensive damage to the U.S., the major military power in the world?

In analyzing the reasons behind this stunning national security breakdown, *The 9/11 Commission Report* (2004) pointed out several key faults in the decision-making process, all symptomatic of the Polythink syndrome: communication failures, lack of sharing of intelligence information, and the ill-preparedness of various security agencies in the U.S., each working separately, to prevent an attack on the homeland, both leading up to and on the day of the attack. In *The 9/11 Commission Report* (2004), the authors find that key fault lines between various government agencies contributed to information sharing problems and confusion that allowed the al-Qaeda terrorists to slip through the cracks.

In short, *The 9/11 Commission Report* pointed to huge failures in coordination and communication between key decision-making groups in the lead-up to the 9/11 attacks, problems that were symptomatic of the Polythink dynamic. This in turn led to a fundamental misunderstanding of the threats that America faced from Osama bin Laden and his al-Qaeda terrorist network, in both the Clinton and the Bush Administrations. Following the attacks, America began a War on Terror designed to eradicate al-Qaeda and organizations like it. But, in the words of Richard Clarke, former National Coordinator for Security, Infrastructure Protection, and Counter-terrorism (under both Clinton and Bush), "We would begin a long fight against al Qaeda, with no holds barred. But it was too late. They had proven the superpower was vulnerable, that they were smarter, they had killed thousands" (Clarke 2004, 17).

Symptoms of Polythink in 9/11

As discussed in Chapter 2, some of the symptoms of Polythink look similar to those of Groupthink and can also lead to defective, sub-optimal decisions: limited review of alternatives, objectives, and risks, and selective use of information. However, this is the case not because the group members are thinking alike or sharing the same views, but because the group is actually failing to engage in any significant collective thinking. Nevertheless, a number of symptoms are clearly unique to Polythink. For example, because of the failure to think collectively, Polythink often results in paralysis in the decision-making process. In addition, Polythink is characterized by a greater likelihood for group conflict and disunity (accompanied by a greater likelihood for leaks and turf interests), group confusion and miscommunication, and the adoption of positions with the lowest common denominator. The national security decisions preceding 9/11 were, unfortunately, characterized by *nearly all of these symptoms.* According to former counterterrorism "czar" Richard Clarke (2004), the story of 9/11 is "the story of how America was *unable to develop a consensus* that the threat was significant and was unable to do all that was necessary to deal with a new threat until that threat actually killed thousands of Americans" (preface, emphasis added).

Polythink Symptom #1:
Intragroup Conflict—Infighting and Turf Interests

Many symptoms of biased decision making plague decision-making processes on both ends of the Groupthink-Polythink decision-making continuum. Internal group conflict, on the other hand, characterizes only Polythink decisions. The reason is fairly obvious—the many competing viewpoints, interpretations of the situation at hand, and potential courses of action available are all hotly debated among group members, increasing the likelihood for destructive group conflict and chronic dissent—particularly if this process is not effectively managed by the leader. This divisive conflict in turn impedes optimal decision making by retarding the ability of group members to overcome personal animosity, concede refuted ideas, and successfully collaborate in developing optimal policies. In this way, group conflict is cyclical, both caused by and causing the Polythink syndrome.

In the case of 9/11, the destructiveness of this internal governmental conflict to the decision-making process was clear. Chronic disagreement between key branches of the advisory group often impeded successful cooperation on policy development. This bickering demonstrated that, indeed, "turf is a powerful thing in Washington" (Clarke 2004, 194), and, as documented by Richard Shultz, Director of the International Security Studies Program at the Fletcher School, it often triggered power struggles among the CIA, the FBI, and the military, as the "competing power centers . . . jockey[ed] for influence over counterterrorism policy" (Shultz 2004, 33). For example, there were "some in the intelligence community who jealously guarded 'their' channels" of communication and were reluctant to share this information with others (Clark 2004, 194). A fear of leaks was one factor that contributed to this, as will be discussed below, but much of this failure to cooperate stemmed from deep-seated turf battles and "ego" issues between governmental branches. This competition and failure to share information exacerbated the already dissenting viewpoints held by officials from different government organizations and triggered both conflict and confusion within the Administration—two key symptoms of Polythink.

A central example of this problem is the "endemic" tensions between the Department of Defense and the Department of State (Rice 2011, 15). Historically, the major divides existing between these two departments have inhibited maximum collaboration between the two central arms of the U.S. government's national security establishment. Rice (2011) attributes this general antipathy to the fact that

> Secretaries of State find the Pentagon all too willing to exert influence in foreign policy . . . With a budget nearly forty times that of the State Department, the Defense Department possesses an awe-inspiring logistical capacity, and State sometimes finds itself dependent on and resentful of the military's reach . . . It is State that must deliver, but everyone has views about how to get it done, and often those individuals [in the Office of the Secretary of Defense] are vocally critical of how State is doing its work. (15)

In the months leading up to the 9/11 attacks, the tension between Secretary of State Colin Powell and Secretary of Defense Donald Rumsfeld was palpable and encouraged the advent of Polythink in the Bush Administra-

tion's foreign and security policy. The two leaders advocated staunchly opposite perspectives and failed to cooperate and fully share information from
their respective departments. Rice (2011) describes their difficult relationship
as follows: "In the case of Colin Powell and Don Rumsfeld, [the problem]
went beyond such almost inescapable tensions . . . There was an equal measure of distrust . . . Don would send memos (snowflakes, we called them) that
implicitly—and sometimes explicitly—criticized what State or the NSC was
doing . . . This led to tensions with and frustrations for Colin" (16). This conflict was at times exacerbated by the personal leadership style of Secretary of
Defense Donald Rumsfeld (Rice 2011), and demonstrates the critical role that
leadership style can play in enhancing or limiting the advent of Polythink.
Colin Powell was a "cautious consensus builder," while Donald Rumsfeld was,
according to Rice (2011, 20), a "confrontational" leader who "rarely saw shades
of gray on an issue, while Colin almost always saw nuances." Rice's role at
the National Security Council (NSC) thus increasingly focused on "working
around the personal distrust between the two men, a task that became harder
as the problems became more difficult" (22).[3]

Moreover, Colin Powell and the State Department often found themselves
at odds with the President's office as well. In Rice's (2011) words: "There is a
tendency of Foreign Service officers to regard the President and his political advisors as a passing phenomenon without the deep expertise that they, the professionals, bring to diplomacy. . . . As [former Secretary of State Dean] Acheson
. . . put it in his memoir *Present at the Creation,* 'The attitude that presidents
and secretaries may come and go but the Department goes on forever has led
many presidents to distrust and dislike the Department of State'" (17).

One of the other major institutional conflicts to emerge out of the 9/11
attacks was about the "historical animosity" between the CIA and FBI (Tenet
2007, 192). The constant turf battles and distrust between these two central
intelligence branches of the U.S. government is often named as a key contributory factor to the failure to piece together disparate intelligence items and
prevent the 9/11 attacks. In June 2002, two competing news stories emerged in
the press. The first, released June 3, ran in *Time Magazine* with the headline
"How the FBI Blew the Case." It detailed how an FBI agent named Coleen
Rowley, in an e-mail message sent to FBI Director Bob Mueller and the Senate
Intelligence Committee, "unspools in furious detail how, in the weeks leading
up to the hijackings, officials at FBI headquarters systematically dismissed
and undermined requests from Rowley's Minneapolis field office for permis-

sion to obtain a warrant to wiretap and search the computer and belongings of Zacarias Moussaoui, the French-Moroccan operative arrested in Minnesota last August and facing trial this fall as the sole person charged with conspiring in the attacks" (Ratnesar and Weisskopf 2002). This report, coming on the heels of the explosive Phoenix Memo (Behar 2002), in which yet another FBI agent faulted the FBI for not heeding his request to track foreign nationals at U.S. flight schools for potential terrorist ties, was highly embarrassing to the FBI.

Needless to say, following this public, vitriolic attack on its capabilities as a security agency, the FBI struck back—casting blame on its historical rival, the CIA. Less than one week later, on June 9, an article titled "The Hijackers We Let Escape" appeared in *Newsweek*, stating: "The CIA tracked two suspected terrorists to a Qaeda summit in Malaysia in January 2000, then looked on as they re-entered America and began preparations for September 11" (Isikoff and Klaidman 2002). The article goes on to cite "confidential" FBI sources in recounting how, despite tracking both men to America, "the CIA did nothing with this information."

The full extent of the accuracy of these reports is debated by both George Tenet (former CIA Director) and Louis Freeh (former FBI Director) in their respective memoirs. However, these competing reports illustrate the critical communication errors between these two organizations in the years leading up to the 9/11 terrorist attacks. This intergroup conflict exacerbated the chronic level of Polythink that characterized the U.S. national security apparatus prior to 9/11. Thus, this ongoing conflict between America's two key intelligence apparatuses greatly contributed to the lack of the kind of cooperation and communication that would have been necessary in order to fully anticipate and prevent the September 11 attacks.

Polythink Symptom #2: Leaks and Fear of Leaks

Much of the reluctance on the part of each agency to share information could be attributed to an overwhelming concern over the possibility of security leaks—and perhaps rightfully so. There had been many times in the past when sensitive information regarding tactics and planned military missions had been leaked to the media, disrupting key operations and putting American lives at risk. This overwhelming concern about security leaks surrounding the issue of terrorism deeply affected the formation of security policy and military action. In the words of Condoleezza Rice (2011), "leaks are debilitating, sowing distrust among the officials who have to work together and coloring the President's options [yet] people do it to show that they are in the know or to advance a position" (22). This preoccupation with leaks, born of the simple fact that the policy-making group was so large and so diverse, at times caused fundamental miscommunications that exacerbated the problem of Polythink and hampered the federal government in its fight against the impending terrorist threat.

Polythink Symptom #3: Confusion and Lack of Communication

Another related bureaucratic failure before the 9/11 attacks was the oft-cited inability of various key agencies to communicate with one another. And in fact, analysts often bemoan the fact that "somewhere in CIA there was information that two known al Qaeda terrorists had come into the United States . . . Somewhere in FBI there was information that strange things had been going on at flight schools in the United States" (Clarke 2004, 236), yet no one was able to pull these threads of information together to form a complete picture of the impending threat, due to the inability and lack of will of various agencies to share what they knew. For example, the CIA sometimes failed to share information with key decision makers (Clarke 2004). Clarke (2004) recounts one experience hours after the attack:

> I stepped out and called [Dale] Watson [of the FBI]. [He said,] "We got the passenger manifests from the airlines. We recognize some names, Dick. They're al Qaeda." I was stunned, not that the attack was al Qaeda but that there were al Qaeda operatives on board aircraft using names that FBI knew were al Qaeda . . . "CIA forgot to tell us about them" . . . It became clear that CIA had taken months to tell FBI that the terrorists were in the country. When FBI did learn, they failed to find them. (24)

This confusion and lack of communication relate directly to the Polythink syndrome. The size and heterogeneity of the group of policymakers and advisors that constituted the federal security and defense apparatus naturally led to inter-agency competition and concerns regarding security leaks that heightened bureaucratic issues of access to information.[4]

The CIA was not alone in its communications breakdowns with other key governmental branches concerning the specifics about the 9/11 attacks. Louis Freeh (2005) admits in his book to the failures of the FBI in communicating critical intelligence to decision makers in the White House, bemoaning the fact that "[the FBI] let what could have been vital intelligence get trapped in the bureaucracy" (278). Clarke (2004) echoes this sentiment, claiming that "[the FBI] had specific information about individual terrorists from which one could have deduced what was about to happen . . . None of that information got to me or the White House" (236–237). And in fact, at the beginning of the Bush Administration, Clarke's position as the National Coordinator for Security, Infrastructure Protection, and Counter-terrorism—a position in many ways explicitly created as a response to the growing al-Qaeda threat— was *downgraded* from being part of the Cabinet-level Principals Committee to the Deputy Secretaries Committee. This meant that in many cases Clarke did not have access to classified documents, and thus his ability to gain a fuller picture of intelligence collected on al-Qaeda would have been inhibited (Clarke 2004). It also meant that his early warnings could not be conveyed directly to key decision makers and would instead go through a series of intermediary players and "gatekeepers." George Tenet's position as Director of Central Intelligence was also downgraded from Cabinet level during the Bush Administration (Tenet 2007, 136).

This lack of communication between key members of the interlocking decision groups led to another hallmark of Polythink—confusion. Particularly in the few months before the 9/11 attacks, confusion about the level (and target) of the impending threat was rampant. In the words of George Bush (2010), "The CIA had been worried about al Qaeda before 9/11, but their intelligence pointed to an attack overseas" (135). The FBI, meanwhile, received several signals about a threat to the homeland but was never able to piece the disparate pieces of information together. Louis Freeh (2005) bemoans this failure, and explains that "sifting through the millions of bits and bytes of intelligence gathered every day by the FBI, the CIA, the National Security Agency, and many other outposts was like drinking from a fire hydrant" (303). Indeed, the threat reporting in the summer of 2011 was "maddeningly nebulous" (Rice 2011, 66), contributing to an overall feeling of confusion and discord about where and when the next strike would be and what could be done to prevent it.

Thus, the institutional culture and large bureaucracy of the national security apparatus contributed to Polythink by causing communication lapses, unwillingness (or inability) to share information for fear of leaks or preoccupation with turf battles, and an overall sense of confusion and uncertainty. This hampered efforts to develop an effective and cohesive national policy to prevent and eliminate the growing terrorist threat.

Polythink Symptom #4:
Limited Review of Policy Alternatives, Objectives, Risks, and Contingencies
Often Polythink situations present many potential policy alternatives to consider, given the relatively large number of viewpoints and opinions among decision makers. Paradoxically, however, this can mean that each potential policy option receives only a limited review, due to the lack of consensus about which options will enter the choice set to begin with and the time constraints placed on elite decision makers. This frustration may lead decision makers to immediately discount certain options in order to reach a more manageable choice set with which to work. This was most certainly the case in the months and years leading up to the 9/11 attacks.

In general, policy options pursued by the Clinton and Bush Administrations as they related to the al-Qaeda threat were very limited. In fact, Richard Shultz (2004) contends that, though Clinton had promised to "find out who is responsible and hold them accountable" in response to the bombing of the USS *Cole*, not one of the aggressive offensive actions developed by the military or the CIA was ever executed (26). Thus, American policy toward al-Qaeda was limited to intelligence gathering and the fortification of foreign embassies. Other, more aggressive policies, such as support for the Northern Alliance in Afghanistan, preemptive military action and lethal covert operations to kidnap or kill bin Laden, received little traction. Why was there hesitancy to more thoroughly consider a broader range of more proactive approaches to the al-Qaeda threat?

It was not because policymakers and security experts were unanimous in their rejection of these alternative options. In fact, just the opposite was true. Many key members of Clinton's national security team supported such tactics. Most notable of these security stalwarts were Richard Clarke and George Tenet, both of whom rang early warning bells concerning the danger of bin Laden and al-Qaeda and advocated more aggressive, preemptive military operations against this threat. Yet these alternative options were almost always shelved as soon as they had been proposed. Tenet (2007) explains, "Instead of considering alternative approaches to the less-than-ideal cruise missile attacks, policy makers seemed to want to have things both ways: they wanted to hit bin Laden but without endangering U.S. troops or putting at significant risk our diplomatic relations" (123). In many ways, this failure to consider more-aggressive options was also a reflection of political constraints (Clarke 2004). Ironically, in the absence of a major attack against the homeland, the national security policies needed to prevent such an attack may not have been politically tenable.[5]

However, the reason for this limited review of potential policy alternatives is also rooted in the repercussions of the Polythink syndrome. Because military action is inherently risky (in blood, treasure, and reputation), and because individuals tend to be loss-averse (Kahneman and Tversky 1979), policymakers often hesitate to use military force unless there is a strong consensus on its strategic necessity and probability of success. In the Polythink atmosphere preceding 9/11, no such consensus existed. For example, General Hugh Shelton, the Chairman of the Joint Chiefs of Staff under President Clinton, was always incredibly cautious about launching an attack against bin Laden and al-Qaeda. He explains in his memoir, "I always tended to err on the side of conservativism when it came to target selection, intelligence verification, and minimization of collateral damage . . . You have to consider how it will look in the postmortem, because they will go back and dissect every target of every operation" (Shelton, Levinson, and McConnell 2010, 350). Thus, this chorus of opinions as to the necessity and feasibility of military options allowed the President and his advisory team (both under Clinton and under Bush) to quickly reject these options, focusing instead on a more limited range of less risky options that, in hindsight, were ineffectual in preventing the impending threat to the United States.

Polythink Symptom #5:
Failure to Reappraise Previously Rejected Alternatives

A related symptom of Polythink in group decision-making processes is the permanent removal of key options from the table. Because arriving at consensus is so arduous when such a number of conflicting perspectives and policy prescriptions is involved, group leaders are often loath to reopen discussion on a previously rejected alternative for fear of nearly endless debate on a potentially time-sensitive decision. Combined with the limited review of alternatives, this means that alternatives that were not given a full airing at the outset will most likely not return to the table to be reconsidered at a later date.

This phenomenon was evidenced by the refusal of key members of the Clinton and Bush Administrations to reconsider preemptive military force as an option in the fight against al-Qaeda, before the September 11 attacks. Despite increasingly alarming evidence as to the scope of the threat posed by al-Qaeda to the U.S., from the 1993 World Trade Center attack to the 1998 U.S. Embassy bombings in Kenya and Tanzania to the 2000 USS *Cole* assault, military options were almost immediately shelved because of concern about domestic public opinion, overly high-risk calculations, and ambiguity of incoming intelligence

(Schultz 2004). For example, "when support for the Northern Alliance was [put back] on the table after the embassy bombings in Africa, the senior military leadership refused to consider it . . . They said it was an intelligence operation, not a military mission" (Shultz 2004, 32). Shultz elaborates on this phenomenon:

> Even when events finally impelled the Clinton administration to take a hard look at offensive operations, the push to pursue them came from the civilians of the National Security Council's Counterterrorism and Security Group. One of the hardest of the hard-liners was the group's chief, Dick Clarke . . . but Dick Clarke was attempting to take on a Pentagon hierarchy that wasn't of the same philosophical mindset . . . such measures worried the senior brass, who proceeded to weaken those officials by treating them as pariahs. That meant portraying them as cowboys, who proposed reckless military operations that would get American soldiers killed. (31)

General Shelton unwittingly echoes this sentiment in explaining the military's hesitancy to use force: "All too often, I was forced to add reality to Dick's [Richard Clarke's] ideas. We felt bad because these ideas briefed very well, and frankly you knew some of them were going to catch the attention of the President, but when you got into the details of what it would take to pull them off, they were far more complicated than a military neophyte or wannabe understands" (Shelton, Levinson, and McConnell 2010, 354). This military vs. civilian clash enhanced the Polythink nature of the national security apparatus and meant that every time military operations were brought up as an option, they were immediately discounted by the military elite and excluded from the main policy discussions.

Thus, institutional cleavages triggered a plurality of viewpoints as to the courses of action available to the U.S. in defending itself from the terrorist threat. This plurality of views in turn triggered a limited review of a broad range of alternative policy options and a refusal to revisit the immediately rejected alternatives—particularly the high-risk military options.[6] This hesitancy to respond with military force also provided a false sense of security to the American people, suggesting that terrorism did not present a major threat.

Polythink Symptom #6:
Framing Effects and Selective Use of Information
The number of pressing, time-sensitive issues that elite decision makers face on a daily basis means that, frequently, decisions must be made within very strict time constraints. In situations of Polythink, decision makers are bombarded

with information and intelligence from individuals and organizations suggesting seemingly innumerable and perhaps even contradictory policy prescriptions. This combination of severe time constraints and vast onslaughts of information can cause decision makers to selectively process and present information, relying on heuristics and predispositions in order to make crucial decisions. Moreover, advisors can use this onslaught of information to their advantage—highlighting intelligence that supports their position. In the case of 9/11, selective information processing was amplified by the dynamics of Polythink, as the sheer number and variety of opinions and worldviews espoused in the national security apparatus caused key decision makers to overlook or misinterpret vital pieces of information that warned of the impending al-Qaeda threat (9-11 Comissiom 2004).

In fact, in the years since 9/11, many analysts have pointed out that the problem with the 9/11 attacks was not that there was no information regarding al-Qaeda's intentions, but that there was actually *too much* information, particularly in the final few months leading up to the attack. Thus, although "on 9/11, it was obvious the intelligence community had missed something big" (Bush 2010, 135), the problem was not with the intelligence itself, but rather with the *interpretation* of it by key analysts and policymakers. George Tenet himself declares in the report that "the system was blinking red" and it simply could not "get any worse" (259). Processing this large volume of information was clearly problematic for policymakers. To clarify the difficulty in handling this amount of intelligence, *The 9/11 Commission Report* outlines the basic method by which this intelligence was processed by the President and his team:

> Because the amount of reporting is so voluminous, only a select fraction can be chosen for briefing the president and senior officials. During 2001 . . . George Tenet was briefed regularly regarding threats . . . relating to Usama bin Ladin. He in turn met daily with President Bush, who was briefed by the CIA through what is known as the President's Daily Brief (PDB). Each PDB consists of a series of six to eight . . . briefs covering a broad array of topics: CIA staff decides which subjects are the most important on any given day. There were more than 40 intelligence articles in the PDBs from January 20 to September 10, 2001 that related to Bin Ladin. The PDB is considered highly sensitive and is distributed to only a handful of high-level officials . . . Clarke and his staff . . . did not have access to [this] internal, non-disseminated information. (254–255)

Clearly, this method of processing large volumes of intelligence, though perhaps necessary, can lead to the selective processing of information by key decision makers. This can, in turn, result in sub-optimal decision-making processes, such as the failure to adequately address the bin Laden threat prior to the 9/11 attacks.

On August 6, 2001, President Bush received a now infamous PDB memo from the CIA that described how bin Laden was determined to attack the U.S. and stated that "FBI information . . . indicates patterns of suspicious activity in this country consistent with preparations for hijackings or other types of attacks, including recent surveillance of federal buildings in New York" (PDB, 08/06/2001). However, this explosive memo was in fact "the *only* PDB item that addressed the homeland threat in the 192 PDBs that the President had seen since assuming office . . . a homeland threat was simply not the focus of the myriad intelligence briefings the President received" (Rice 2011, 69). Bush (2004) reiterates this sentiment, describing how "in early August, the Agency delivered a Presidential Daily Briefing that reiterated bin Laden's long-standing intent to strike America, but could not confirm any concrete plans . . . 'We have not been able to corroborate some of the more sensational threat reporting, such as that . . . bin Laden wanted to hijack a U.S. aircraft,' the PDB read" (135).

Given this ambiguity about the specific potential target of terrorist attacks and the sheer wealth of information available on various other important national security concerns, key decision makers in the Bush Administration chose to focus on different aspects of intelligence briefs that reflected their interests in a range of topics, other than the al-Qaeda threat. For example, Dick Cheney and Paul Wolfowitz were often preoccupied with the threat from Saddam Hussein and Iraq; Donald Rumsfeld often focused on the challenges of updating American military capability for the twenty-first century; George Bush and Condoleezza Rice were concerned with the threat of cruise missiles from states such as Iran and North Korea, while Richard Clarke remained primarily concerned with al-Qaeda. These predispositions colored key policymakers' interpretations of the intelligence data and led the Administration to miss warning signs from the CIA and the FBI.

Thus, in the case of 9/11, the phenomenon of Polythink contributed to the misinterpretation and faulty processing of available information concerning the terrorist threat. The President, understandably, received only abbreviated briefings that covered a host of other topics in addition to the al-Qaeda threat, making it difficult to understand the singularity and pressing nature of the threat. The information provided to Bush by his advisors was colored by their own divergent interests and concerns, obscuring the centrality of the danger posed by al-Qaeda. Finally, key figures in the Administration who *were* fundamentally concerned with bin Laden and his organization were not privy to much of the classified information gathered by the various intelligence agencies or were not taken seriously by more-senior officials who downplayed the urgency of this specific threat.

In this context of dissenting interpretations and selective processing of information, the importance of framing also becomes a critical source of biased information processing in decision making. Indeed, leading up to the 9/11 attacks, both Clinton and Bush had to address a key debate in the framing of the danger from terrorism: Were terrorist attacks an act of war or were they simply breaking the law? That is, should terrorists be treated as enemy soldiers to be attacked and neutralized or as lawbreakers to be arrested and prosecuted (Shultz 2004)?

The much-debated answers to this question had important implications for the chosen policy vis-à-vis al-Qaeda. Richard Shultz (2004) examines the Clinton Administration's pre-9/11 hesitancy to use preemptive force in his article "Showstoppers," in which he identifies nine key factors that contributed to keeping "counter-terrorism units on the shelf" (25). One critical factor was the issue of framing. Shultz explains how, despite calls from some to pursue terrorists with aggressive, preemptive military action, many other policy advisors to President Clinton, particularly those in the military, framed the problem of terrorism as a *crime* rather than as an *act of war*. While this view starkly contradicted the views of, for example, Richard Clarke and George Tenet, its elucidation by some members of the advisory team contributed to Clinton's hesitation to use preemptive military force against terrorist groups—if terrorism is a crime, then offenders should be prosecuted and not assassinated. Thus, individuals on the Clinton advisory team had starkly different conceptions of what the threat of terrorism represented—was it war or just lawbreaking?

This problem continued into the Bush Administration and is echoed by Condoleezza Rice's description of the dilemma facing the nation's counterterrorism apparatus in the months prior to 9/11. According to Rice (2011),

> The weakness in our effort was systemic . . . The FBI treated the internal terrorism problem as a law enforcement matter, not an intelligence mission . . . prevention was secondary to punishing terrorists after they were caught committing a crime. Agents had to be careful not to gather evidence in ways that might get a case thrown out of U.S. courts: think Law and Order. This law enforcement orientation led to a wall between criminal and intelligence investigations within the Bureau itself. (68)

This framing issue is even cited by former Vice President Dick Cheney in his memoir as an issue that plagued the Bush Administration in the pre-9/11 period. Cheney (2011) says: "This approach [to terrorism] hadn't stopped the attacks . . . we needed a new way forward, one based on a recognition that we were at war" (330). Bush (2010) echoes this sentiment, arguing that "on 9/11, it was obvious the law enforcement approach to terrorism had failed. Suicidal men willing to fly passenger planes into buildings were not common criminals. They could not be deterred by the threat of prosecution. They had declared war on America. To protect the country, we had to wage war against the terrorists" (154).

Framing issues surrounding the relative *urgency* of the problem also contributed to the advent of Polythink in approaching the problem of the looming al-Qaeda threat. For example, while hawks in the administrations of both Clinton and Bush—most notably Richard Clarke and Mike Sheehan, the State Department Coordinator for Counter-terrorism—argued that there was indeed a clear and present danger from al-Qaeda and that urgent preemptive military action must be taken, many others disagreed. Although it was clear to all that terrorism did represent a threat, many at the Department of Defense felt that the more immediate danger came from governments, rather than stateless terrorist groups. They therefore framed the issue of terrorism as "a distraction that was the CIA's job . . . The Pentagon way to treat terrorism against Pentagon assets abroad was to cast it as a force protection issue" (Mike Sheehan, as quoted in Shultz 2004, 28). This classification severely underestimated the severity of the threat. Thus, while these advisors would advocate the arrest of perpetrators of terrorism and seek to protect their forces and embassies abroad, they did not consider offensive actions against terrorists as a relevant policy option and, in fact, may even have viewed terrorism as "a small price to pay for being a super-power" (Mike Sheehan, as quoted in Shultz 2004, 28).

Framing issues also arose from the State Department. During Clinton's tenure, many in the military sought to treat the Taliban as an arm of al-Qaeda, a precursor to the so-called Bush Doctrine that would be invoked following the 9/11 attacks—that the U.S. would recognize no difference between terrorists and the people that harbor them. However, the State Department hesitated at the idea of treating a sovereign foreign government as a terrorist entity.[7] General Hugh Shelton explains that when he met with Secretary of State Madeleine Albright following the USS *Cole* attacks, he pleaded with her to go after the Taliban, but she "pushed back" and said, "No, the Taliban constitutes a legitimate sovereign government and we need to respect that." Moreover, "according to Albright, what I was suggesting was declaring war on a nation-state, and her position was that despite Tenet's evidence to the contrary, the Taliban weren't the ones who were attacking us, that was bin Laden—and this all played out not ten seconds after George Tenet had tracked through exactly how bin Laden and the Taliban were working hand in hand" (Shelton, Levinson, and McConnell 2010, 359).

These competing frames of al-Qaeda and the Taliban—as lawbreakers, sovereign governments, a sideshow to more-important threats, or unfeasible targets for attack—contributed to the Polythink mind-set of the national security apparatus and made group consensus and the development of a cohesive, comprehensive strategy to tackle bin Laden and his sponsors incredibly difficult to achieve.

Polythink Symptoms #7 and #8:
Lowest-Common-Denominator Decisions and Decision Paralysis
Of course, the most critical negative symptom of Polythink decision making is the defective "bad" policy options that are often chosen as a result of the many factors enumerated above. In hindsight, some claim that the most effective course of action against bin Laden likely would have been preemptive action to apprehend or neutralize leading terrorist figures and defensive measures to prevent infiltration by terrorist elements (e.g., Clarke 2004). Why weren't these strategies implemented before September 11? There are, of course, many important and legitimate reasons unrelated to the actual decision-making process—domestic constraints, risk aversion, budget issues, problems of international law and collateral damage, the prevailing attitudes toward terrorism at the time, and more. However, as the above evidence makes clear, the plurality of opinions and dissent associated with the Polythink phenomenon also played a key role in shelving these types of decisive actions. The decisions taken prior to the 9/11 attacks were passive, lowest-common-denominator decisions that all members of the decision group could agree on—essentially to maintain intelligence operations and wait for the absolutely decisive intelligence that could justify a small operation to capture or kill bin Laden.

This phenomenon of pursuing lowest-common-denominator decision making is repeatedly demonstrated throughout the Clinton and the Bush Administrations. For example, Shultz (2004) describes how, under Clinton, "the possibility of hunting down the terrorists did receive ample attention," yet "somewhere between inception and execution, the options were always scuttled as too problematic" (33). This process continued under Bush. Perhaps understandably due to the newness of the administration and the complexity of the issue at hand, the Bush Administration was slow to set forth a specific policy for the intelligence and military communities to follow with regard to the terrorist threat. George Tenet (2007) describes an early incident in which the Senior Director of the NSC returned to him a draft report he had sent to Deputy National Security Advisor Stephen Hadley regarding the expanded powers that the CIA would need in order to fight the impending terrorist threat. He says, "If you formally submit these to the NSC, the clock will be ticking, and we don't want the clock to tick just now"—in other words, "the new administration needed more time to figure out what their new policies were and did not want to be in a position someday to be criticized for not moving quickly enough on a critical intelligence community proposal" (Tenet 2007, 144).

In the end, both administrations adopted a lowest-common-denominator decision in which intelligence operations would continue unabated, but military action would not proceed in the absence of incontrovertible intelligence and the nearly complete obviation of the risk of collateral damage or troop endangerment. These were two impossible conditions that effectively precluded the choice of military action entirely. This approach satisfied the military, who were loath to put soldiers at risk, particularly for what was perceived as the sideshow of guerrilla terrorism (Shultz 2004, 28). This approach also appeased political advisors at the White House and diplomats at the State Department, who were concerned about the political and diplomatic implications of preemptive military action. Perhaps the only truly dissatisfied executives were George Tenet at the CIA, Mike Sheehan at the Department of State, and Richard Clarke at the NSC.

This sequence of decisions cannot be explained solely by practical and political factors. Rather, it was a consequence of the Polythink group decision-making dynamic within the Clinton and Bush Administrations—in the face of an overwhelmingly diverse set of policy options brought forward by a cacophony of competing voices and perspectives, all of whom see the situation in different terms, the decision-making process is paralyzed. With so many objections to each and every policy option, leaders were unable to make the hard decisions necessary to obviate the impending threat. Instead, they accepted policies with the lowest common denominator, hoping to satisfy as many constituencies of advisors as possible, while at the same time alienating the fewest. The failure of this approach to the terrorist threat would soon become clear in the most horrific of ways: with almost 3,000 dead, the attacks of September 11 were the most deadly assault by foreign enemies on American soil in all of history.

Contrasting 9/11 Decision-Making Processes
with the Characteristics of Groupthink

At first glance, the decision-making process that led to the failure to prevent the 9/11 attacks bears some similarity to the hallmarks of Groupthink outlined by Janis. For example, decision makers were under high stress from external threats and pressures, a characteristic that Janis argues can often lead to Groupthink. In the wake of the USS *Cole* attack in October 2000, fears of an international terrorism threat against the U.S. had starkly increased. Policymakers were under public pressure to prevent additional terrorist attacks and to find and prosecute the perpetrators of the *Cole* attack—namely, bin Laden and his terrorist network.

However, despite these pressures and fears, there was also a widespread belief that a successful terrorist attack on the American homeland—at least, an attack of the magnitude of 9/11—was highly unlikely. *The 9/11 Commission Report* (2004) documented this phenomenon by elucidating the case of the 1993 World Trade Center bombing and the arrest of Mohammed Salameh—a perpetrator of the attack who was caught while attempting to reclaim a $400 truck rental deposit. The report claims:

> An unfortunate consequence of the superb investigative and prosecutorial effort [of the first World Trade Center attack] was that it created an impression that the law enforcement system was well-equipped to cope with terrorism . . . *Although the bombing heightened awareness of a new terrorist danger, successful prosecutions contributed to widespread underestimation of the threat.* (73, emphasis added)

This illusion of invulnerability and the reducing of the enemy to inferior, unthreatening stereotypes are actually characteristics of Groupthink. However, as Clarke pointed out, in the case of 9/11 there was far from consensus in the national security apparatus that the homeland would be attacked from abroad by terrorists. Thus, the case of 9/11 is characterized much more by the symptoms of Polythink, as we have repeatedly shown. Though, a symptom of Groupthink, the optimistic overconfidence in the safety of the homeland described here, was also present.

Triggers of Polythink in the
Pre-9/11 Decision-Making Process

The preceding discussion has demonstrated the ways in which the security and foreign policy decisions prior to 9/11 were plagued by the detrimental symptoms of Polythink. Indeed, nearly all of the symptoms of Polythink fit this case. The many competing voices and perceptions surrounding the same decision problem, the intra- and intergroup rivalry, the poor communication and confusion, a limited review of alternative policy options, a failure to reconsider previously rejected alternatives, and selective processing of information and intelligence all characterized the 9/11 case. The combination of these Polythink symptoms in turn contributed to a key consequence of Polythink, decision paralysis, in which leaders were unable to formulate a proactive, cohesive policy to mitigate the growing risks of the al-Qaeda threat.

Until now, we have explained *how* the 9/11 attacks were characterized by Polythink, but we have not explained *why*. Why was it that federal government officials with a wealth of background and experience in national security and foreign policy issues could be so susceptible to the Polythink phenomenon? There are many triggers, which will be enumerated below.

Institutional Limitations—
The Problem of Turf Wars and Multiple Gatekeepers

To begin, the nature of national security policy formation necessarily involves myriad decision-making groups—from the White House, to the Pentagon, to the CIA, to the FBI. Critical information can get lost or may not even be shared throughout this huge bureaucracy, causing key communication errors that can contribute to the varied viewpoints and sub-optimal decisions we often see in Polythink.

The 9/11 Commission Report (2004) points to a secondary result of this divided bureaucracy—critical issue areas that are left unmonitored and for which no one is responsible. In the commission's words,

> The September 11 attacks fell into the void between the foreign and domestic threats. The foreign intelligence agencies were watching overseas, alert to foreign threats to U.S. interests there. The domestic agencies were waiting for evidence of a domestic threat from sleeper cells within the United States. No one was looking for a foreign threat to domestic targets. The threat that was coming was not from sleeper cells. It was foreign—but from foreigners who had infiltrated into the United States. (263)

Because U.S. national security and foreign policy strategies are developed in consultation with several key centers of power in the federal government, including intelligence and security agencies such as the NSA, the CIA, and the

FBI, military powers such as the Joint Chiefs of Staff and the Department of Defense, diplomatic officials at the State Department, and key political players at the White House, the ultimate policy outcome can be determined by the different ways in which these advisors approach the issue at hand. Namely, advisors from different government institutions will tend to approach the decision problem from their own unique institutional perspective. For example, the CIA will tend to see threats around the world and emphasize the urgent need for covert action abroad; the FBI and the Department of Justice will likely focus on the threat from internal elements and the need for better law enforcement measures; the State Department will often stress the importance of diplomacy and alliances with sympathetic foreign powers; staffers at the White House will usually focus on the political repercussions and domestic audience costs of potential foreign policy options; and the military and Department of Defense will most likely seek to mitigate potential risks to the military and its soldiers in combat situations by advocating for higher troop levels in many military operations.

These competing institutional considerations are one of the most critical factors in triggering the Polythink syndrome between and within decision-making groups, as each advisor brings with him or her his or her own institutional perspective and interpretation of the situation at hand, offering policy prescriptions that are in line with these worldviews and advances the interests of his or her own organization. These viewpoints can in turn lead to chronic misunderstanding between institutions or, conversely, be written off as biased or even obsessive by key decision makers in the Administration. These differing perspectives, *if reconciled*, can often prove to be very helpful for decision makers. For example, General Shelton elaborates on this type of "Productive Polythink": "Your guy is looking at it from a policy standpoint and my guy is looking at it from an operational perspective. Together they help each other—yours helps mine focus on the bigger issue, and mine damn well better help yours track through the operational concerns" (Shelton, Levinson, and McConnell 2010, 408–409). However, more often than not, the chasms in policy prescriptions offered by advisors with different institutional affiliations prove hard to bridge. In his book, former Director of the FBI Louis Freeh (2005) illustrates the paralysis that such adversarial institutional perspectives can cause, complaining:

> We knew what steps to take . . . The Gore Commission [report] . . . issued in
> February 1992, warned that the airline industry and operations were vulnerable

at multiple points to hijacking and terrorist attacks, but basically nothing was done about it. Politicians were worried that the public wouldn't tolerate long lines at security checkpoints. The airlines didn't want to spend the money to beef up their own defenses . . . What should have been a big step forward in the fight against terrorism devolved into the usual inside-the-Beltway brawl. (192)

Another example can be seen in the Department of Defense's unwillingness to execute covert operations against terrorists abroad. Shultz (2004) recounts an interview with one former senior defense official who explained, "A gap exists, they believe, between DOD's *capability* for clandestine operations and its *authority* under the United States Code . . . At the heart of this debate . . . was 'institutional culture and affiliation.' The department took the position that it lacked the authority because it did not *want* the authority—or the mission" (Shultz 2004, 29–30).

These examples demonstrate the way in which institutional affiliation can color the policy prescriptions that individual members of the decision group advocate. In some cases, these separate institutional considerations might have a positive impact on the decision-making process, prompting the President or leader to consider varied perspectives on the issue at hand and the impact that his decision will have on the broad variety of federal agencies for which he is ultimately responsible. In general, this process must be managed by a very effective leader who knows how to integrate the various perspectives into a cohesive policy.

Moreover, bureaucratic divides between government institutions contributed to a phenomenon whereby the federal government "lacked the ability to know what it knew" (*The 9/11 Commission Report* 2004, 77). For example, the report points out that at the FBI "there was no effective mechanism for capturing or sharing its institutional knowledge . . . there were no reports offices to condense the information into meaningful intelligence that could be retrieved and disseminated" (77).[8] This fragmentation is a crucial example of "seeing only part of the problem" within a decision-making unit, a common decision-making bias that impedes informed policy design and can exacerbate Polythink (Mintz and DeRouen 2010).

The related problem of communication (or lack thereof) between key decision-making branches is lamented by Condoleezza Rice. She explains that often the Secretary of Defense and the Secretary of State were not available or did not want to attend daily National Security Council briefings on potential security threats: "A two-hour NSC Principals meeting is core to the national security advisor's mission but a drain on the time of a secretary, who can end up making the trip to the White House two or three times a day" (Rice 2011, 20). These problems continued right up until the day of the attacks and are perhaps best exemplified by the following excerpt from *The 9/11 Commission Report* (2004) regarding the government's response on the day of the attacks. As one witness recalled to the commission, "[It] was almost like there were parallel decision-making processes going on . . . in my mind they were competing venues for command and control and decision-making" (36).

The problem of intergroup miscommunication is often magnified by the presence of "multiple gatekeepers" to the President. These gatekeepers filter and interpret information, providing a pared-down version to the next gatekeeper in line that reflects their own biases and interpretations of the material at hand. For example, as outlined in *The 9/11 Commission Report* (2004, 254–255), CIA and FBI field agents routinely draw up reports based on raw intelligence received from the field. Such reports will then get filtered up through the agency until only the ones deemed most important are compiled into a single report to pass off to the President's office. Often, this report will then be previewed by either the President's National Security Advisor or the Secretary of Defense before it reaches the President's desk. This means that key information has the potential to be inadvertently removed from the reports before the intelligence ever reaches the decision maker's desk.

Thus, in the time leading up to (and during) the 9/11 attacks, the national security apparatus of the federal government was hampered by key communication failures within and between its national security agencies and levels of command that contributed to the phenomenon of Polythink and impeded their ability to work together to form a cohesive policy response to the impending threat (*The 9/11 Commission Report* 2004).

Political Concerns—Domestic Audiences

As discussed in Chapter 2, policymaking can be viewed as a two-level game, as policymakers "play" not only at the international level but also at the national level—to their domestic audiences. While decision makers' primary concerns may be centered around preserving the safety and security of the U.S., many officials must also deal with the impact that the chosen policies will have on public opinion, voting behavior, and popular support. This can lead to Polythink in that appointed professional officials, not subject to the whims of the electorate, may provide perspectives that are completely different from those of elected officials, who have their eye on the next election fight. Security decisions are not always popular decisions, and oftentimes presidents and their advisory teams take significant political risks in supporting, for example, aggressive military action against a potential threat (though the rally-round-the-flag effect may provide short-term bursts in popularity). If the action fails, they will have exhausted significant political capital and potentially alienated key segments of the electorate. Thus, before 9/11 a dichotomy existed whereby appointed officials adopted a more hawkish view than their elected political counterparts. This dichotomy played a prominent role in the fight against terrorism in the 1990s and in 2000–2001.

One particularly illuminating case was the failure of the military strikes on the Al-Shifa pharmaceutical factory in Sudan. The attacks had been planned by the CIA in retaliation for the 1998 U.S. embassy bombings and because the factory had ties to al-Qaeda and was suspected of producing the nerve agent VX. These attacks were launched on tenuous evidence, and their failure was touted by right-wing politicians eager to criticize President Clinton, calling the strikes a "wag the dog" tactic to distract the American public from the explosive Monica Lewinsky scandal. Indeed, *The 9/11 Commission Report* (2004) speculates about the lasting effect of this strike on the psyche of the Clinton Administration moving forward in the fight against al-Qaeda: "The failure of the strikes [on al-Shifa], the 'wag the dog' slur, the intense partisanship of the period, and the nature of the al-Shifa evidence likely had a cumulative effect on future decisions about the use of force against bin Laden" (118).

Varying political considerations were also in play during the Bush Administration. Less than one year after a divisive presidential election in which a Republican challenger succeeding in winning back the White House after eight years of Democratic leadership, there were still many holdovers from the Clinton Administration. This meant that in addition to the obvious divides caused by organizational affiliation, major political lines divided key decision makers in the national security apparatus (for example, both Clarke and Tenet had been Clinton appointees). Moreover, the Bush Administration harbored a deep distrust of any policy that had been pursued by the Clinton Administration (Clarke 2004). This may have triggered a desire to change course and contributed to the subsequent downgrading of Clarke and Tenet to second-tier advisors, thereby limiting their impact in critical national security discussions. These and other actions[9] contributed to a lack of continuity between the two administrations and may have inhibited the development of a cohesive strategy that could run across both Clinton and Bush's terms in office.

Thus, the shift in leadership had critical implications for the ongoing security decisions taken against bin Laden and al-Qaeda. Namely, it exacerbated the already existing Polythink symptoms affecting American national security decisions as new appointees and administrators jostled alongside Clinton appointments to provide their input and place their own stamp on the foreign policy direction of the country. This discontinuity and shifting "lens" through which the problem of terrorism was viewed and then framed by the Clinton and Bush Administrations demonstrates the high potential for Polythink *between* various presidential administrations in a democracy such as the U.S. and not just within one administration, as well as its adverse effects. In essence, "[al-Qaeda] took the long view, believing that their struggle would take decades, perhaps generations. America worked on a four-year electoral cycle and at the end of 2000, a new cycle was beginning" (Clarke 2004, 227).

Normative Differences in Decision-Making Processes

Yet political and institutional concerns are not in and of themselves sufficient to explain the occurrence of Polythink—oftentimes decision makers from the same institution, even from the same political party, can view decision problems in fundamentally different ways with fundamentally different policy prescriptions. This discrepancy occurs because of key normative differences in individuals' decision-making processes. In addition to their formal ideological structures, presidents approach foreign policy decisions utilizing their preexisting belief systems (Edwards 2003). As international relations scholar Charles Kupchan (1994) explains, "Beliefs interact with external conditions and events to provide an explanation of foreign policy behavior" (491). In other words, understanding leaders' operational codes and belief systems can be critical to understanding foreign policy decision making (Kupchan 1994). This is because beliefs and worldviews often "provide comfortable anchors for decision making and act as expressions of social identities and personal idiosyncrasies that shape the definition of national interests" (Walker, Schafer, and Young 1999, 612). These subjective perceptions differ from person to person, leader to leader, and can thus be a major contributing cause of Polythink.

It is therefore important to recognize that the "national behavior [of decision makers is] a product of the subjective perception and interpretation of a situation . . . their expectations from various courses of action, and their choice processes" (Snyder, Bruck, and Sapin 1962, cited in Taber 1992). These worldviews include beliefs about the ways in which government should be run and decision-making processes undertaken. Taber (1992) summarizes this normative issue in his discussion of leaders' "operational codes," emphasizing that "decision makers' operational codes consist of their fundamental beliefs about the dynamics of international relations and about the efficacy of human action, coupled with their simplifying images of salient international actors (as, e.g., friendly or un-friendly) . . . These beliefs enable decision makers to process information and examine potential courses of action efficiently" (889). As a result, beliefs can have an impact on a decision maker's subsequent decision and can vary widely across different decision makers, both within and between presidential administrations.

Another crucial normative concern is the way in which individuals process information. Some prefer to see the world in binary terms, "with us or against us," while others like to take a more nuanced "gray" approach. This difference can influence interpretations and policy prescriptions for a given decision problem. For example, there were key differences between Clinton and Bush in terms of their decision-making styles: "Bush wanted to get to the bottom line and move on. Clinton sought to hold every issue before him like a Rubik's Cube, examining it from every angle to the point of total distraction for his staff" (Clarke 2004, 243–244). It is important to point out that neither process is necessarily normatively "better" than the other. Rather, it is the differences in processes between decision makers that can be problematic by causing confusion and lack of understanding between and within administrations tackling a decision problem. There are also obviously differences between hawkish and dovish or conservative and liberal approaches to foreign policy-making.

Essentially, these normative differences—in worldview, in belief systems, and in methods of information processing—between advisors or other decision makers who must work together on the same decision problem can exacerbate the problem of Polythink. It can cause key members of the same decision-making team to view the decision problem in starkly different terms and impede successful coordination and understanding of the other's vision of the situation. As we will see in Chapter 4, it can also lead to Groupthink if members of the decision-making team all have a tendency to see issues in similar ways.

Security Experts and Novices—A Divide

Another contributing factor to Polythink in the context of national security and foreign policy decision making is the difference between so-called "experts" and "novices." They tend to make decisions in different ways, see situations differently, and recommend different policy options as a result. In the case of 9/11, the key divide was between the military "experts" at the Joint Chiefs and the Department of Defense and the "novices" in the politically oriented White House and the intelligence-focused CIA. This distinction is critically important in the case of 9/11 because there was a unique situation in which civilian advisors—such as George Tenet and Richard Clarke—were recommending military action while military officials were opposing it, a situation that in and of itself provided clear evidence of Polythink. In addition, this created a problem of credibility, whereby military officers were more trusted to recommend military options than civilians were. If the military was against it, the thinking went, it must not be a good idea.

This dynamic is highlighted by Richard Shultz (2004) as he recounts a meeting with one former defense official who recalled a briefing on counterterrorism options given to the Secretary of Defense by senior civilians and military officers:

> The civilian, a political appointee with no military experience, says, "As your policy adviser, let me tell you what you need to do militarily in this situation." The chairman sits there, calmly listening. Then it's his turn. He begins by framing his sophisticated PowerPoint briefing in terms of the "experience factor," his own judgment, and those of four-star associates. The "experience factor" infuses the presentation. Implicitly, it raises a question intended to discredit the civilian: "What makes you qualified? What makes you think that your opinion is more important than mine when you don't have the experience I have?" "Mr. Secretary," concludes the chairman, "this is my best military advice" (31).

Shultz (2004) concludes that this dynamic continued throughout the Clinton and Bush Administrations (until 9/11): "During the 1990s, the 'best military advice,' when it came to counterterrorism, was always wary of the use of force. Both risk-aversion and a deep-seated distrust of Special Operations Forces traceable all the way back to World War II informed the military counsel offered to top decision makers."[10] Thus, others in the Administration who recommended more-militant action were often stymied by the qualms of the military toward undertaking these missions.

This divide existed for several reasons. For one thing, the military would almost always recommend missions with large numbers of forces to serve as protection against potential attack. These large numbers would scare policymakers in the White House, since they went far beyond the small tactical assaults initially recommended by the CIA, which would then shelve the mission completely. Clarke (2004) explains, "Whether it was catching war criminals in

Yugoslavia or terrorists in Africa and the Middle East, it was the same story. The White House wanted action. The senior military did not and made it almost impossible for the President to overcome their objections" (145). Second, the military tended to believe that threats to the security of the U.S. came from rogue states, rather than from the stateless entities epitomized by al-Qaeda. *The 9/11 Commission Report* (2004) points out that before 9/11, when discussing the problem of terrorism,

> NORAD perceived the dominant threat to be from cruise missiles. Other threats were identified during the late 1990s, including terrorists' use of aircraft as weapons . . . [However,] exercise planners assumed that the aircraft would originate from outside the United States, allowing time to identify the target and scramble interceptors. The threat of terrorists hijacking commercial airliners within the United States—and using them as guided missiles—was not recognized by NORAD before 9-11. (17)

In other words, fighting terrorism was a somewhat new, complex, and difficult type of warfare with no clear enemy or declaration of victory, and this may have been something that the Joint Chiefs of Staff were not willing or ready to address before the 9/11 attacks. This under-attribution of the options open to one's enemies contributed to increasing Polythink within the Administration by further confusing the security picture and leaving room for doubt in each advisor's interpretation of the situation.

The Leader and the Followers

Polythink can also exist between a leader and his team of advisors. Due to the nature of leadership positions, leaders often process information differently (for example, they will receive compressed intelligence briefs rather than access raw intelligence reports from the field). The intelligence briefs received by the President can be biased, faulty, overly dense, or overly cursory, and can therefore color his viewpoint in a way that is much different from his advisors on the ground, who process tons of raw intelligence daily. These differences in information processing between the President and his advisors affected policy formation up until 9/11, as field officers at the CIA and FBI were routinely more alarmist in their reactions to intelligence than were the higher echelons of political advisors and the President himself.

A second potential decision-making problem stems from the leadership style of a particular leader vis-à-vis his advisory team. Though the President's staff plays a crucial role in decision-making processes, "extending his capabilities by increasing his 'available attention, knowledge, and expertise' and by coordinating the behavior of the other units involved in making and implementing foreign policy" (Feldman 1990, 17, as cited in Hermann and Preston 1994, 76), leaders maintain incredible power to shape the advisory groups themselves and, therefore, the subsequent substance of their discussions and policy considerations. Leadership style thus has a critical impact on the quality of group decision-making processes—whether they will be plagued by Polythink or Groupthink or take on a more optimal approach somewhere between the two. As Hermann (1980) explains, a leader's foreign policy choices are affected by four key personality characteristics: beliefs, motives, decision style, and interpersonal style. A leader's decision style includes components such as openness to new information, preference for certain levels of risk, complexity in structuring and processing information, and ability to tolerate ambiguity (Hermann 1980). These decision-making styles can affect foreign policy choices. For example, the competitive advisory system is most likely to be selected by presidents who have a high tolerance for internal conflict.[11]

In line with their distinct leadership styles, Clinton and Bush shaped their presidential advisory systems in distinct but, in hindsight, similarly problematic ways that hindered the fight against al-Qaeda. For example, Clinton "exhibited little interest in foreign policy in his initial months in office and even after his aides began to describe his foreign policy as one of 'enlarging' the global range of democracy his actions in the international arena were cautious and largely ad hoc" (Greenstein 1993, 593). He also possessed an "intrinsic interest in the detailed rationales for alternative policies," a characteristic that may exacerbate Polythink among an advisory group (594). In contrast, George W. Bush's advisors tended to "shield [him] from potentially valuable debate" about the course of action to take following the 9/11 attacks (Greenstein 2003, 20–21), a characteristic that may exacerbate Groupthink.

Thus, a leader can go a long way toward structuring decision-making processes in his government that lead to Polythink or Groupthink and that may promote or impede optimal policy choices. In other words, a leader can (inadvertently or purposefully) "manufacture" a Groupthink or Polythink dynamic. If a leader can absorb and integrate the varying perspectives of different advisors, institutions, and groups, then Polythink can be a beneficial process. This is the case with Productive Polythink (see Chapter 8). However, in the case of pre-9/11, this formidable task was not accomplished effectively by either President Clinton or President Bush. Rather, the discordant voices surrounding the President impeded optimal policy formation on the part of the executive and reduced the government to near inaction in the face of the growing terrorist threat.

Conclusion

The 9/11 attacks were not solely the result of Polythink in the Clinton and Bush Administrations. However, it is clear that faulty decision-making processes and symptoms such as lack of sharing of information and intelligence warnings, the limited review of options, and other symptoms of Polythink did play a key role in preventing effective action to counter the threat of al-Qaeda terrorism. Likewise, 9/11 was not the fault of any one person, but rather the fault of a system, where each branch charged with protecting the American homeland failed in some way, failing to work together, share information, adjust its viewpoint to new intelligence reports, and develop a plan for cohesive action in the face of the impending threat. After September 11, inquiries were launched, changes were instituted, and promises made for the future. However, the pattern of faulty decision making caused by the plurality and polarization of viewpoints within the American defense apparatus continued after the attacks. In Clarke's (2004) words, "After September 11, I thought that the arguments would be over, that finally everyone would see what had to be done and go about doing it . . . The people trusted, as I did, that the mechanisms of government, now awakened, would deal with the terrorist threat completely and systematically. We were wrong" (239–240).

4 Polythink and Afghanistan War Decisions
War Initiation and Termination

Leaders around the globe routinely make critical war and peace decisions. As citizens, we hope and believe that these leaders are engaging in thorough, careful, systematic, and thoughtful decision-making processes, rationally weighing the costs and benefits of each potential action. However, as we saw in Chapter 3, group decision-making dynamics and processes at the highest level of government are prone to sub-optimal, defective decision making. Whether it be the extreme cohesiveness of Janis' (1982a) Groupthink or the pluralism of group members' opinions and the rampant divisiveness of Polythink decision-making groups, such "defective" processes can lead to foreign policy and national security fiascoes. Such fiascoes can severely damage the credibility, interests, and security of the U.S.

In this chapter, we analyze the group dynamics in the Bush and Obama Administrations that fundamentally shaped their policy decisions regarding the entrance to and exit from the Afghanistan War, respectively. While the initial invasion period was characterized by a deeply ingrained Groupthink mentality that had been shaped by the traumatic and devastating September 11 attacks, the decision to withdraw from the war was fraught with internal divisions and discordant worldviews of the national security policymaking complex—a Polythink process that deeply inhibited the development of a cohesive strategy for the successful conclusion of the war.

After more than a decade of war, the loss of 3,259 coalition soldiers (iCasualties 2013), the deaths of an estimated 15,000 to 17,000 Afghani citizens (Costs

Of War 2013), and a financial toll of nearly $7 billion (Costs of War 2013), it is clear that decisions made in Washington, even those of a self-described group of experts with "decades of crisis management experience" often exact a heavy price (Bush 2010, 185). It is thus critical that we delve into the "black box" of decision-making processes to ascertain exactly how group dynamics influenced these monumental decisions of war and peace.

Using the wealth of declassified information, biographies, and memoirs of key decision makers and recently published reports on the Afghanistan War, this chapter will scrutinize the complex group decision-making structure responsible for the war's successes and failures, identifying symptoms of Groupthink and Polythink in two critical U.S. policy choices—the decision to enter Afghanistan and the decision to exit it.

The Entrance to Afghanistan: Groupthink or Rational Consensus?

Labeled by President Obama as the "war of necessity" during his 2008 campaign, the Afghanistan War has been widely accepted as a necessary response to the attacks on September 11, 2001. Indeed, "any leader whom one can imagine as President on September 11 would have declared a 'war on terrorism' and would have ended the Afghan sanctuary by invading" (Clarke 2004, 244). However, the soundness of a policy *decision* is not necessarily always the product of a sound decision-making *process*. Thus, while the "quality of the process in decision making is likely to be connected to the quality of the outcome associated with the decision . . . the quality of the decision-making process certainly is not the only explanation for poor outcomes," or for positive outcomes (Schafer and Crichlow 2010, 9–10).

In other words, while the decision to enter Afghanistan is widely accepted as a necessary policy choice, the process by which that decision was made was not necessarily as positive. Indeed, President Bush's decision-making team has often been characterized as suffering from a deep Groupthink mentality that harmed the pursuit of crucial foreign policy goals (Badie 2010; Houghton 2008; Kaufmann 2004; Mintz and DeRouen 2010; Pfiffner 2009; Schafer and Crichlow 2010). Thus, the potential Groupthink mentality of the Bush Administration in invading Afghanistan perhaps deserves additional scrutiny.

This paradox of a flawed decision-making process leading to a positive decision outcome is explained in Steve Yetiv's work on non-fiasco theory (2003, 2004). He explains that the stress triggered by an external threat may lead to overestimation of that threat, but, in the intervening time, if that threat does indeed become greater, then the policy path chosen will be productive, even if the initial assessments that led to that policy were flawed (Yetiv 2004, 187). And indeed, after the 9/11 attacks, a Groupthink "siege mentality" was particularly pervasive in the Bush Administration. This led to enhanced perceptions of threat and an aggressive pursuit of al-Qaeda and the Taliban in Afghanistan. However, it also impeded the thorough consideration of foreign policy options, planning for contingencies, and long-term policy development.

Numerous examples document the Groupthink mentality that existed in the Bush Administration's decision calculus surrounding Afghanistan. For example, only eighteen days into the Afghanistan War, Bush, already facing criticism from the media for the "slow pace of operations," determined that "any indication of doubt from the president [would] ripple throughout the system and, so, he sat his national security team down asking 'I just want to make sure that all of us did agree on this plan, right?' - They all agreed" (Bush 2010, 199). This failure to tolerate ambiguity and nuance and to adequately map out a long-term strategy that would recognize and plan for foreseeable risks is a hallmark of Groupthink. It also left a lasting legacy on the effectiveness of the Afghanistan War.

Indeed, beyond the initial military takeover, planning was minimal. On the eve of the war, Bush met with CIA Director George Tenet and General Tommy Franks and asked, "So who's going to run the country?" In response, "there was silence" (Bush 2010, 197). This focus on the invasion at the expense of the reconstruction illustrated the overreliance of Bush's decision-making unit on the military brass, whose "dress uniforms with the rows of ribbons highlighted their military expertise, which was a whole lot more extensive than [Bush's],"[1] at the expense of external experts in and outside the State Department, who would have provided a different perspective and contribution to the deliberations (Bush 2010, 193).

False Comfort

The emphasis of the Administration on best-case scenarios and the overconfident view of the costs of the conflict were exacerbated by the early success of the military phase of the war. Bush acknowledges this fault, recognizing that "in retrospect, our rapid success with low troop levels created false comfort, and our desire to maintain a light military footprint left us short of the resources we needed. It would take several years for these shortcomings to become clear" (Bush 2010, 207).

It is interesting to note that in many ways, these early failures to question assumptions, hear various perspectives, and explore alternative policy options during the initial *entrance* into the war spurred the Polythink group dynamic that would mark the decision-making process surrounding the subsequent U.S. *withdrawal* from Afghanistan. In an effort to avoid the Groupthink mistakes of his predecessor, President Obama's national security team would spend months divisively debating minute details of the Afghanistan withdrawal plans, finally developing a compromise "mini-surge" option that has been critiqued from both the left and the right as a satisficing choice with questionable strategic merit.

Identifying Symptoms of Polythink in the Afghanistan Withdrawal

As discussed in Chapter 2, Polythink symptoms include intragroup conflict, confusion and lack of communication, a paradoxically limited review of policy options, a failure to reappraise previously rejected alternatives, biased information processing characterized by framing effects, and most importantly, lowest-common-denominator decision making or even decision paralysis. Nearly all of these key symptoms were present, to varying degrees, in the early years of the Obama Administration's national security team.

Polythink Symptom #1:
Intragroup Conflict—Infighting and Turf Battles

Perhaps the most well-known Polythink symptom, at least in the press and in the public's mind, may have been the inner turmoil and infighting of Obama's foreign policy team. Deftly alluded to in the double entendre title of Bob Woodward's book *Obama's Wars*, this "team of rivals" remained sharply divided along institutional, ideological, and generational lines that proved hard to overcome. In the words of former Obama Deputy National Security Advisor Douglas Lute's staff (in Woodward 2010),

> Tribes populated the presidency, reflecting its divisions—The Hillary [Clinton] tribe lived at the State Department. The Chicago tribe occupied [David] Axelrod's and [Rahm] Emanuel's offices. The campaign tribe was at the NSC—led by chief of staff Mark Lippert and strategic communications director Denis McDonough, both former Obama campaign aides—[who] seemed to flaunt their personal relationships with the president and often circumvented [James] Jones as the national security adviser. (144)

Relations between White House advisors and the Department of Defense were also often fraught with tension. This "deficit of trust," as former Commander of U.S. Forces in Afghanistan General Stanley McChrystal (2013) termed it, "appeared unintentional on both sides . . . but over time, the effects were costly" (284). McChrystal's memoir and other recently published insider memoirs have cast into sharp relief the internal divisions in the Obama Administration, suggesting that "they were even more intense and disparate than previously known" (Baker 2010). In reviewing *Obama's Wars* for the *New York Times*, Peter Baker (2010) summarizes the divisive portrait that Woodward presents of the U.S. national security apparatus during the Afghanistan War review process:

> Mr. Biden called Richard Holbrooke "the most egotistical bastard I've ever met," although he "may be the right guy for the job." A variety of administration officials expressed scorn for James L. Jones, the retired Marine general who is national security adviser, while he referred to some of the president's other aides as "the water bugs" or "the Politburo." Adm. Mike Mullen, chairman of the Joint Chiefs of Staff, thought his vice chairman, Gen. James E. Cartwright, went behind his back, while General Cartwright dismissed Admiral Mullen because he wasn't a war fighter. Defense Secretary Robert M. Gates worried that General Jones would be succeeded by his deputy, Thomas E. Donilon, who would be a "disaster." Gen. David H. Petraeus, who was overall commander for the Middle East until becoming the Afghanistan commander this summer, told a senior aide that he disliked talking with David M. Axelrod, the president's senior adviser, because he was "a complete spin doctor." General Petraeus was effectively banned by the administration from the Sunday talk shows but worked private channels with Congress and the news media.

In other words, infighting among various members of the Obama Administration was rampant. Turf battles between the White House and the State Department were also prevalent. Vali Nasr, former Senior Advisor to Richard Holbrooke during his tenure as U.S. Special Representative for Afghanistan and Pakistan, chronicles the discord and dysfunction between the State Department and the White House on end-of-war and postwar planning in Afghanistan. Nasr (2013) claims, "The truth is that his administration made it extremely difficult for its own foreign-policy experts to be heard. Both Clinton and Holbrooke, two incredibly dedicated and talented people, had to fight to have their voices count on major foreign-policy initiatives."[2]

Polythink Symptom #2: Leaks and Fear of Leaks

This infighting was expressed throughout the Afghanistan War review process by a series of *leaks* that often undermined the internal review process. President Obama and his White House team repeatedly felt that the military was leaking their preferences to the media "to trap" and force the Democratic President to fall in line with military advice (Woodward 2010, 195). Baker (2009) points out that throughout the policy review process, "the White House suspected the military of leaking details of the review to put pressure on the president . . . The military and the State Department suspected the White House of leaking to undercut the case for more troops . . . The president erupted at the leaks with an anger advisers had rarely seen, but he did little to shut down the public clash within his own government." Indeed, it deeply angered Obama that "Petraeus was publicly lobbying and prejudging a presidential decision" (Woodward 2010, 158). He felt that Petraeus' public comments to the media amounted to "a preemptive strike in the public relations war" and that it was unhelpful "to have the combatant commander pontificating in a newspaper about what the strategy must be and the certainty of defeat without the addition of a lot more troops" (Woodward 2010, 158) when the troop numbers were precisely the issue the President wanted to debate.

Under McChrystal's tenure, leaks were also rampant. While McChrystal (2013) calls the leak of his strategic assessment on Afghanistan "frustrating" and describes it as "creating pressures for each of the players that wouldn't help the subsequent decision-making process" (344), he nonetheless spoke often with the press and was chastised often by Chairman Mullen and others. In fact, McChrystal's tenure as Commander of the U.S. Forces in Afghanistan came to an abrupt end after senior members of his staff publicly disparaged Vice President Biden and other members of Obama's Cabinet in a now infamous *Rolling Stone* interview written by Michael Hastings (2010). Ultimately, McChrystal acknowledged that he was too slow to recognize "the extent to which politics, personalities, and other factors would complicate a course that, under the best of circumstances, would be remarkably difficult to navigate" (McChrystal 2013, 350).

McChrystal was not the only advisor to butt heads with the President. In his newly released memoir, *Duties: Memoirs of a Secretary at War*, former Defense Secretary Robert Gates also expresses discontent with Obama's handling of the Afghanistan drawdown. He writes: "All too early in the [Obama] administration, suspicion and distrust of senior military officers by senior White House officials—including the president and vice president—became a big problem for me as I tried to manage the relationship between the commander in chief and his military leaders" (excerpt printed in the *Washington Post* on January 7, 2014). Indeed, "their different worldviews produced a rift that, at least for Gates, became personally wounding and impossible to repair" (Woodward 2014), a hallmark of Polythink.

Polythink Symptom #3: Confusion and Lack of Communication

The many competing voices and conflict within the foreign policy decision-making unit of the Obama Administration in turn led to gaps in communication and confusion regarding the execution of war strategy and even extended to perceptions of the overall policy goal in Afghanistan. Was the goal to leave a functioning democracy? To eradicate the Taliban? Or was it the more moderate goal of simply "limiting" the Taliban's ability to operate? In fact, "eight years into the war, [the principal foreign policy decision-making officials] were struggling to refine what the core objectives were" (Woodward 2010, 185). For instance, McChrystal (2013) states,

> Confusion arose almost immediately between the White House and Department of Defense over the exact numbers involved, and the specific makeup of the forces. Not long after President Obama approved sending the seventeen thousand troops, the military reported back that an additional four thousand troops were needed. From a White House perspective it surely appeared as though the Department of Defense hadn't done enough detailed staff work or, worse, that the military was playing games with the numbers. (285)

Moreover, while there was distrust between the White House and the military regarding the *number* of troops needed (many White House officials were assuming that the Pentagon was trying to "force the president's hand" [Woodward 2010, 124]), the White House largely assumed that the military knew *where* those extra troops should go. Thus, important questions about deployment locations and troop concentrations went unasked, leading to additional confusion during the actual execution of the additional troop deployments. Rajiv Chandrasekaran (2012b) reports that one "senior White House official involved in war policy" claimed that nobody at the White House bothered to say, "Tell us how many troops you're sending here and there . . . We assumed, perhaps naively, that the Pentagon was sending them to the most critical places." This confusion over where, when, and how many troops would actually be deployed was rampant throughout the decision-making process. In many ways, it was caused by the Polythink dynamic, which potentially encouraged military decision makers and politicians to capitalize on such confusion in the negotiations process (Woodward 2010).

Polythink Symptom #4: Limited Review of Policy Alternatives, Objectives, Risks, and Contingencies

In another hallmark of Polythink, the internal Obama Cabinet discussions surrounding the Afghan War had the illusion of an expansive review process, but nonetheless centered on a small number of actual policy options. Despite Obama's insistence that the team would "need to come to this with a spirit of challenging assumptions" and being "a big believer in continually updating our analysis and relying on a constant feedback loop," the review was surprisingly limited (Woodward 2010, 161). Indeed, the bulk of the Afghanistan policy review focused on three pseudo "options" presented to President Obama by the military: 85,000 troops for a full counterinsurgency, 40,000 troops as a more fiscally and politically feasible option for counterinsurgency, and 20,000 troops for a plan that would focus mainly on counterterrorism operations (Woodward 2010, 272). To these options Defense Secretary Robert Gates added a fourth, a "compromise" option that was essentially the 40,000 troop number minus one brigade of 5,000 to 10,000 soldiers that would be held in abeyance, pending necessity. However, these many options in fact presented only the illusion of choice to the young president. Obama himself was aghast (as quoted in Woodward 2010):

> The president took another look at Mullen's four options. "So let me get this straight, okay?" Obama asked. "You guys just presented me four options, two of which are not realistic"—the 85,000 dream and the 20,000 hybrid. Of the remaining two—the 40,000 and Gates's 30,000 to 35,000—he noted their numbers were about the same. "That's not good enough." And the way the chart presented it, the 30,000 to 35,000 option was really another way to get to the full 40,000 because there would be a decision point for the fourth brigade in a year, December 2010. So 2A is just 2 without the final brigade? he asked. "Yes," said McChrystal. Two and 2A are really the same, Obama said. "So what's my option? You have essentially given me one option." He added sternly, "You're not really giving me any options. We were going to meet here today to talk about three options." (278)

Many of Obama's non-military advisors expressed a similar sentiment. Obama's Special Assistant and Senior Coordinator for Afghanistan and Pakistan, General Douglas Lute, particularly felt that Chairman Mike Mullen of the Joint Chiefs "had failed to maintain the integrity of the process, which required the serious presentation of something other than the one recommended option. He adamantly wouldn't budge and give a hard look at alternatives" (Woodward 2010, 322). Lute also felt that Defense Secretary Robert Gates "had failed to expand the horizon of alternatives for the president . . . The secretary was supposed to give his own advice and bottom-line recommendation, but he was also supposed to be the final window into the larger world of choice for a president" (Woodward 2010, 322). Ambassador to Afghanistan Karl Eikenberry expressed additional reservations, stating that "we have not fully studied every alternative" and that "we underestimate the risks of this expansion," by relying on "forecasts that are imprecise and optimistic," potentially adopting a strategy that would "increase Afghan dependency and deepening military involvement in a mission that most agree cannot be won solely by military means" (Eikenberry 2009).

Vice President Joe Biden, for his part, was a staunch advocate of an alternative plan that he termed "counter-terrorism plus," the addition of 10,000 to 20,000 troops that would focus mainly on counterterrorism measures and abandon Petraeus's "protect the people" counterinsurgency strategy (Eikenberry 2009). Throughout the decision-making process, he attempted to introduce this additional, conceptually different, policy option. According to political scientist Stephen D. Biddle, Biden, like Obama himself, had "always believed that the only reason to be in Afghanistan is al-Qaeda" (Gwertzman 2013). This led to a debate very early on "between the vice president and people aligned with him[3], who asked why the United States was messing around with the counterinsurgency in Afghanistan if the real problem is al-Qaeda and counterterrorism" (Gwertzman 2013). Though the President often asked Biden to present these ideas in principal-level meetings, the option could not gain traction because of staunch opposition by the military. Thus, though "a president did have choices, in this case his had been significantly limited . . . to the disadvantage of all" (Woodward 2010, 322).

Moreover, the discussion on end-of-war and postwar planning in Afghanistan was limited almost exclusively to the *military* dimension of planning. For example, Obama decided early on not to seriously consider an immediate withdrawal of the U.S. forces in Afghanistan (Pfiffner 2011). Indeed, he explicitly stated: "I just want to say right now, I want to take off the table that we're leaving Afghanistan" (Woodward 2010, 186). Communication with the State Department on diplomatic courses of action was also minimal, and suggestions for diplomatic and political solutions were quickly discarded. Objections raised by Karl Eikenberry (2009) regarding the feasibility of working with Afghan President Hamid Karzai were largely ignored. Richard Holbrooke, a staunch advocate of a more diplomatic process, was also generally silenced throughout his term as Special Advisor on Pakistan and Afghanistan. For example, as reported by Nasr (2013), on Holbrooke's last trip to Afghanistan, in October 2010, he pulled aside Petraeus and said, "David, I want to talk to you about reconciliation." "That's a 15-second conversation," Petraeus replied. "No, not now." Throughout the review process "there was no discussion at all of diplomacy and a political settlement . . . The military wanted to stay in charge, and going against the military would make the president look weak" (Nasr 2013). In many ways, the personal dislike many of Obama's advisors felt (another key characteristic of Polythink) toward Holbrooke's eccentric and idiosyncratic style further limited his success in advocating for negotiations with the Taliban and so shelved an important policy alternative without seriously airing its possibilities for success. In fact, "the White House never issued a clear policy on reconciliation during the administration's first two years" (Chandrasekaran 2012b).

According to Chandrasekaran (2012a), this failure had "profound consequences: The Obama White House failed to aggressively explore negotiations when it had the most boots on the battlefield. Promising leads were left to wither. And the military once again capitalized on civilian disunity to pursue its maximalist objectives."

Polythink Symptom #5:
Failure to Reappraise Previously Rejected Alternatives

One symptom of Polythink that was, however, strikingly *absent* during the Obama Administration's review of the Afghanistan War strategy and plans for the eventual troop drawdown was the failure to reappraise previously rejected alternatives. Indeed, everything from tactics to overall strategy to even the mission itself was constantly reexamined and questioned by the president's decision-making unit. General McChrystal (2013) explains,

> I was a commander focused on explaining the mission I understood I'd been given and the strategy currently being prosecuted . . . a counterinsurgency campaign. . . . I should have better understood that the president's review pro-

cess . . . was not just evaluating my strategy and force request to accomplish a counterinsurgency mission but *was reevaluating the mission itself.* (349, emphasis added)

Indeed, in his recently released memoir, McChrystal (2013) repeatedly claims, "It was clear to me that the mission itself was now on the table for review and adjustment" (352). Importantly, it was not just Bush's policies that were reconsidered, but even Obama's personal preference (and campaign message) not to increase already soaring troop levels in Afghanistan. By 2011 there were 101,000 American soldiers serving in Afghanistan, more than double the number of troops that had been there during the Bush Administration (CNN 2011). This willingness to reappraise, reconsider, and reevaluate cherished assumptions was in part driven by Obama's appreciation for the book *Lessons in Disaster* about the Vietnam War. Thus, basic goals, ideals, and strategies surrounding the war effort, from both the Bush years and Obama's tenure, were fundamentally reconsidered throughout President Obama's strategic review process on the Afghanistan War.

In many ways, however, this constant reappraisal was a reaction to the perceived Groupthink decision-making process regarding the entrance to the war. The main conclusion the President and his team drew from the book was that "both President John F. Kennedy and President Lyndon B. Johnson failed to question the underlying assumption about monolithic Communism and the domino theory," and this "clearly [drove] the Obama advisers to rethink the nature of Al Qaeda and the Taliban" (Baker 2009). At the same time, Obama often needed to reconsider his own views on the issues due to the constraints on his authoritative power. As a newly elected first-term, Democratic president continuing a Republican-initiated war effort, President Obama was politically limited in the policies that he could realistically execute in Afghanistan.

This constant reappraisal process illustrates a fundamental dilemma of *Polythink*. While reappraisal and reconsideration of previously rejected alternatives can be critical to ensuring a comprehensive, fully informed policy formation process, it can also lead to excessive hesitancy and decision paralysis (see Polythink Symptom #7 below). Under Polythink, group leaders will often tamp down this reappraisal process in order to avoid the paralysis that would result from a diverse, myriad group of advisors constantly reconsidering each potential consideration and policy option voiced by themselves and other group members. However, in the case of the Afghanistan War review, the perceived Groupthink processes of the previous administration prevented at least most military options from being permanently shelved and off-limits for further discussion.

Indeed, the collective trauma felt by the foreign policy community in the wake of the Bush Administration's approach to Afghanistan and Iraq and Obama's own personal decision-making style and ideology led to a boomerang effect in which the decision unit swung in the opposite direction—examining and dissecting each aspect of the war strategy, leading to what some called "dithering" (Cooper 2009). In a scathing critique of the Obama Administration's lengthy review process, former Vice President Dick Cheney claimed, "In the fall of 2008 . . . we [the Bush Administration] dug into every aspect of Afghanistan policy, assembling a team that repeatedly went into the country, reviewing options and recommendations, and briefing President-elect Obama's team . . . They asked us not to announce our findings publicly, and we agreed, giving them the benefit of our work and the benefit of the doubt" (as quoted in Cooper 2009), implying that the additional lengthy Obama review was unnecessary. Obama's aides shot back, "What Vice President Cheney calls 'dithering,' President Obama calls his solemn responsibility to the men and women in uniform and to the American public" (as quoted in Cooper 2009), thereby demonstrating the difficulty of striking a balance between a thorough review (and re-review) process and the need for quick, decisive action in war and foreign policy decision-making choices.

Polythink Symptom #6:
Framing Effects and Selective Use of Information

Just as in the failure to reappraise previously rejected policy alternatives, in situations of Polythink a leader may choose to limit collective review of *information* in order to manage the myriad viewpoints and avoid endless discussion and rehashing of policy options by bickering advisors. Individual advisors in Polythink groups may also possess an incentive for processing or presenting information in a biased manner, using selective pieces of information and favorable framing tactics to strengthen their specific perspective regarding the policy issue at hand. Indeed, in the case of the Afghanistan War review, different advisors framed the war—and potential U.S foreign policy options regarding it—in a variety of discordant ways, using accurate but incomplete information to bolster their perspectives.

For example, the military and the Department of Defense framed the war as a battle necessary for the security of the U.S., both as a way to decimate extremists bent on attacking the U.S. and as a deterrent for future would-be terrorists. Secretary of State Robert Gates even declared in one strategy meeting, "I'd like to think about broadening the top priority beyond the homeland to include our interests abroad, key allies, partners, and our forces around the world. The focus is al Qaeda and the degree to which al Qaeda would be empowered by a Taliban success. If the Taliban make significant headway, it'll be framed as the defeat of the second superpower" (as quoted in Woodward 2010, 189).

On the other hand, members of the State Department[4] (as well as Vice President Biden) framed the conflict as a liability to America's diplomatic interests abroad and believed that al Qaeda could be contained without the counterinsurgency (COIN)-style campaign advocated by the military. For example, Biden felt that "Afghanistan only had to be a slightly more hostile environment for al Qaeda than Pakistan ("one Predator tougher") for [al Qaeda] to choose not to return [to Afghanistan]" (as quoted in Woodward 2010, 160).

However, these various frames and differential uses of information actually proved helpful to President Obama in his decision-making process. Rather than tamp down information processing and discussion in order to move the decision-making process forward, Obama, a voracious consumer of intelligence, often "peppered advisers with questions and showed an insatiable demand for information, taxing analysts who prepared three dozen intelligence reports for him and Pentagon staff members who churned out thousands of pages of documents" (Baker 2009). Thus, in this case, the particular decision-making style of the chief decision maker led to *increased* information processing and helped unify the competing frames presented by advisors. This is one example of how leaders can channel Polythink in productive ways.

Polythink Symptoms #7 and #8:
Lowest-Common-Denominator Decisions and Decision Paralysis

The most consequential symptom of Polythink is, of course, the quality of the final policy decision as formulated by the decision-making unit. In the case of the Afghanistan War review process, Obama's ultimate choice was made after more than a year of paralyzing back-and-forth discussions and debates and a three-month extended war review process. Ultimately, he elected to deploy 30,000 additional troops in a form of counterinsurgency "light." This was basically a satisficing, lowest-common-denominator decision that sought to bridge the gaps between his military commanders' insistence on high troop numbers and counterinsurgency strategy and his civilian advisors' preferences for counterterrorism, diplomacy, or withdrawal. Essentially, it was a decision made in order to "keep the 'family' together" (Woodward 2010, 309). This policy option was engineered by Defense Secretary Robert Gates in an attempt to straddle the military and civilian components of the decision-making unit, "seeking what he called the 'sweet spot'" that would satisfy both the military and the White House (Woodward 2010, 250). Thus, though "the McChrystal team had won on troop strength, Obama and Biden won on narrowing the mission" (Alter 2010, 388).

However, many political analysts have argued that the policy chosen ran the risk of achieving *neither* a successful military counterinsurgency *nor* a successful drawdown and diplomatic solution to the conflict. For example, the *Wall Street Journal* characterized the move as "a high risk political and military strategy" that "risks angering critics on the left wing of the Democratic Party, as well as national-security-minded Republicans" (Spiegel, Weisman, and Dreazen 2009). Moreover, the one-year timeline for beginning troop withdrawals specified in the final plan was criticized by Arizona Senator (and former presidential rival) John McCain as "emboldening al-Qaeda and the Taliban, while dispiriting our Afghan partners and making it less likely that they will risk their lives to take our side in this fight" (Spiegel, Weisman, and Dreazen 2009). Obama's own advisor, Douglas Lute, wondered how the president had "packaged this for himself," surmising that (as quoted in Woodward 2010),

> The president had fast-forwarded and figured it would most likely be ugly following July 2011. Obama had to do this 18-month surge just to demonstrate, in effect, that it couldn't be done. . . . Obama would have given the monolithic military its day in court and the United States would not be seen as having been driven off the battlefield . . . the president had treated the military as another political constituency that had to be accommodated. (338)

Triggers of Polythink in the Afghanistan Withdrawal Decision

As in the case of September 11, there are multiple causes of Polythink in the Afghanistan withdrawal case that we will now turn to examine.

Institutional Limitations and Turf Battles— The Problems of Communication and Multiple Gatekeepers

The necessity of coordinating war strategy among several different departments, with personnel often scattered across several different countries, led to some communication problems and confusion during the Afghanistan War review. This problem was perhaps compounded by the Obama Administration's need to act expediently, soon after taking office—"Staffs need time to conduct due diligence on issues before recommending long-term projects or commitments. But in 2009, with the development of events and the approaching Afghan elections, President Obama's new administration quickly found itself faced with important decisions" (McChrystal 2013, 284). However, perhaps more importantly, the necessity of inter-agency cooperation combined with President Obama's reliance on his inner circle of political advisors led to a unique situation in which approval from multiple political advisors was often necessary for other advisors—be they from State, Defense, or the military—to maintain access and a direct line of communication with the President.

This trigger of Polythink, termed "multiple gatekeepers," often frustrated key advisors and increased group conflict within the Administration, impeding the cooperation necessary to develop cohesive war policies. For example, National Security Advisor Tom Donilon was known to run a "tight process" at the NSC and was said "to have been peeved, for example, when a Chairman of the Joint Chiefs of Staff insisted on delivering a dissenting view to the president" (Ignatius 2013b). Secretary of State Hillary Clinton also at times found it difficult to overcome the bureaucracy and get around the so-called "Berlin Wall of staffers" who "shielded Obama from any option or idea they did not want him to consider" (Nasr 2013). She did, fortunately for her, prove more adept at this challenge than, for example, the late Richard Holbrooke, who often felt that his access was completely cut off and never quite found a place in the Administration's foreign policy bureaucracy. Former National Security Advisor Jim Jones suffered similar trials before he found himself replaced by Tom Donilon. Referring to Obama's political advisors as "water bugs," he claims that his "access [to Obama] was cut off" (Woodward 2010, 139).[5]

In the case of the withdrawal from Afghanistan, the idea of "where you stand depends on where you sit" also proved to be a key trigger of the Polythink dynamic. Members of Obama's political team expressed starkly different viewpoints than both the State Department, the military, and the Department of Defense. This divide stemmed from the different frames, bureaucratic roles, and interests through which each group viewed the Afghanistan War (Marsh 2013). While the military viewed the Afghanistan War as an important, and very public, display of America's military power, members of the State Department (though Hillary Clinton is an exception) viewed the war as a potential drag on diplomatic overtures to other predominantly Muslim countries, which resented the U.S. involvement there. Meanwhile, the political advisors saw the war as a quagmire that would cost Obama and the Democrats domestic support and risk the rest of the president's domestic and international agenda. In Jim Jones's words, "there were people whose background is politics, so they look at everything in political terms . . . The hard part was to not let the political interpretation of everything we decide drive the train: If you can't sell it politically, you can't do it" (quoted in Woodward 2010, 332).[6]

Thus, though "Obama made the final decision, his decision was constrained by the menu of choices presented to him by his advisers . . . This menu of choices was in itself the product of bureaucratic politics" (Marsh 2013, 285). In sum, the institutional lens through which the Afghanistan War was seen was a critical factor that divided the decision-making unit. This increased Polythink and inhibited consensus and cooperation on one overarching policy objective.

Political Concerns—A Democrat Seeking to End a Republican War

In the case of the Afghanistan War withdrawal, political divides were truly at the forefront. Despite Obama's insistence that as Commander in Chief he must continue to responsibly carry out the Afghanistan War to a successful conclusion, the discomfiting fact that Obama owed his meteoric career rise to his opposition to overreliance on the use of force to achieve national security ends could not be avoided: "Obama had campaigned against Bush's ideas and approaches. But . . . Obama had perhaps underestimated the extent to which he had inherited George W. Bush's presidency—the apparatus, personnel and mind-set of war making" (Woodward 2010, 281). What's more, the political "loyalty" of many members of his advisory team in the first term was unclear. For example, Secretary of Defense Robert Gates was a Republican from the Bush Administration, Richard Holbrooke was close to the Clintons, the military brass often appeared to tacitly support Republican candidates and officeholders, and Obama's political team still deeply distrusted Secretary of State Hillary Clinton's motives. Indeed, "those in Obama's inner circle, veterans of his election campaign, were suspicious of Clinton. Even after Clinton proved she was a team player, they remained concerned about her popularity and feared that she could overshadow the president" (Gordon 2013a).

And in fact, a major critique of Obama's handling of the Afghanistan War centered on his habit of inserting political considerations into troop decisions (Lubold 2013). One commentator claims, "The president had a truly disturbing habit of funneling major foreign-policy decisions through a small cabal of relatively inexperienced White House advisors whose turf was strictly politics" (Lubold 2013). Others argue that the president really had no choice but to consider the political ramifications of his actions in Afghanistan: "If he sped up this timetable and America's Afghan allies began to go down the drain, it would surely become a major line of attack by Republicans. They would charge that he ordered the drawdowns for this September for purely political reasons, just to help boost his reelection prospects. They'd charge that U.S. generals in the field warned against this 33,000 withdrawal package and stressed its dangers" (Gelb 2012). General McChrystal laments this perhaps unavoidable, but nonetheless problematic, emphasis on political concerns in foreign policy decision making. He reflects on Daniel Ellsberg's book, *Secrets: A Memoir of Vietnam and the Pentagon Papers*, implicitly but directly paralleling the failures in Vietnam and Afghanistan (McChrystal 2013):

> Many of the failures in Vietnam owed not to flawed analysis but to politically driven decisions to ignore the difficult conclusions the analysis offered. The Pentagon Papers, which he famously leaked, convinced him that decision makers had not been misled into disaster by ignorance or bad advice. Rather, faced with two politically toxic but militarily sound options—withdrawal or full escalation—they chose to pursue other policies for political reasons, even though analysis told them these policies were likely to fail. It was a chilling thought. (352)

Thus, the focus on political concerns deeply divided the decision-making unit, increasing Polythink and leading to sub-optimal policy choices that may have been partially based on over-weighted, non-compensatory political factors.

Normative Differences in Decision-Making Processes

As in many group decision-making units, decision-making worldviews differ among group members. The Afghanistan War review was no exception. President Obama, famous for his cool, deliberative, and "professorial" decision-making style, needed to effectively manage a decision-making unit made up of individuals with disparate worldviews, integrating each advisor's input into the group's internal discussions and ultimate policy proposals. For example, institutional divides in normative decision-making processes existed between the military and the State Department. Indeed, one expert explains that "in most administrations, an inevitable imbalance exists between the military-intelligence complex, with its offerings of swift, dynamic, camera-ready action, and the foreign-policy establishment, with its seemingly ponderous, deliberative style" (Nasr 2013).

However, some members of the decision-making unit found themselves excluded from the deliberation process due to their particular worldview and decision-making style. For example, Richard Holbrooke, "with his frequent references to Vietnam and flair for the dramatic," found himself "the odd man out with White House advisers—He spoke like a man who just left talking to Kennan—and walked into 2009, still in black and white, with his hat on . . . if you were this young crowd that came in with Barack Obama, it seemed cartoonish. . . . They weren't able to hear what he was saying because they were distracted by the mannerisms and the way he did things—and he couldn't figure that out" (Chandrasekaran 2012c). Ultimately, the differing worldviews and styles of information seeking, deliberation, and decision making within the decision unit would become a major obstacle in the Obama Administration's attempts to find consensus. Though "good people [were] all trying to reach a positive outcome, [they were] approaching the problem from different cultures and perspectives, often speaking with different vocabularies" (McChrystal 2013, 287).

Security Experts and Novices—A Crucial Divide

As in 9/11, the main divide in the president's foreign policy advisory team was between the career military and the civilian advisors. This divide between security experts and novices is a noticeable pattern in foreign policy decision making and is strongly related to the two groups' differential institutional affiliations and disparate normative worldviews. Indeed, advisors and members of decision-making units bring not only expertise and experience to the decision problem, but also their personal histories, beliefs, and life experiences, which color their advice and policy proposals. Thus, throughout the Afghanistan War review "the president was struggling with the different points of view . . . The military was unified supporting McChrystal's request for 40,000 more troops. His political advisers were very skeptical" (Woodward 2010, 311). Many political advisors felt that the president was "being screwed by the senior uniformed military" who were "systematically playing him, boxing him in" (173). These discordant perspectives fueled "a growing divide between the White House and the Pentagon" very early on in the review process (143). When the famed Eikenberry cables were released, this divide became almost cavernous—"The top American diplomat in Afghanistan had just isolated himself from the military and alienated his counterpart—McChrystal. One of the essentials in counterinsurgency was cooperation between the civilian and military leadership. That had just been blown to pieces" (262).

While these divides between security experts and novices are to some extent explained by their different institutional affiliations and ideological worldviews, their divergent opinions also highlighted key distinctions in their relative areas of expertise. For example, while political advisors clamored for troop reduction timelines so that Obama would have time and resources to devote to his domestic agenda, military advisors attempted to explain the complexity of such a withdrawal and why the military often failed to come up with concrete numbers and time frames. In the words of McChrystal (2013),

> In truth, suddenly cutting a chunk out of a larger force package was complex business . . . Ensuring that the reduced force has all the necessary capabilities, yet stays within a specified number, is more difficult than it would appear . . . Yet to those unfamiliar with the arcane system and often complicated math, it would seem like a basic, fair request to ask the military to tell exactly how many soldiers it was deploying, and what each of them would do . . . As I confided in Charlie Flynn that spring, "This is, after all, our profession—they have a right to be upset." (285)

On the side of the White House, Obama's limited foreign policy experience also affected his relationship with the military, for both political and practical reasons. For example, the military's paradoxically heavy deployment early in Obama's term to Helmand Province, the least populous area of Afghanistan, to engage in a "protect the people" COIN strategy, was a key illustration of how political figures could fail to provide adequate oversight to the military's choices. As Chandrasekaran (2012b) writes,

> The Helmand deployment exposes the limits of [Obama's] understanding of Afghanistan—and his unwillingness to confront the military—early in his presidency. In more than two hours of discussion, the 14-member war cabinet—which included Vice President Biden, Defense Secretary Robert M. Gates and Secretary of State Hillary Rodham Clinton—never asked McChrystal why he wanted so many more Marines in Helmand. The civilians didn't know enough about Afghanistan to focus on that issue. They were also concerned about micromanaging the war, of looking like President Lyndon B. Johnson picking bombing targets in North Vietnam.

On the other hand, however, many civilian advisors, particularly in the State Department, felt that the president's military advisors lacked a *different* type of expertise on the complex cultural and governmental history of Afghanistan.

For example, many non-military, civilian experts on Afghanistan's social, cultural, and political history "feel quite the opposite [of the military]—They see few gains in fighting the Taliban that can outlast a U.S. pullback and fewer hopes in the future viability of the corrupt and highly inefficient Afghan political regime" (Gelb 2012).

In the case of the Afghanistan War review, this expertise gap—on both military and social/diplomatic matters—between the uniformed military and the civilian advisors and leaders was further exacerbated by the need for the young President to make critical, time-sensitive war decisions very early in his term. In other words, "this compressed decision-making timeline on Afghanistan [occurred] before people had been able to develop mature relationships and trust to go at this as effectively" as could otherwise have been done (Gordon 2013b).

The Leader and the Followers—
The Relationships within the Decision Unit

Ultimately, the leader bears responsibility for ensuring that foreign policy decision-making processes are conducted thoroughly and completely but nevertheless result in clear action and relative consensus. Striking a Con-Div balance between Polythink and Groupthink in group decision-making processes is thus a central challenge for leaders. In fact, "the growth in the power of the presidency, the reach of a president's decisions and actions, and the impact they can have all over the world make it essential to examine character and the ways in which it can and does influence policy making and implementation" (Wayne 2011). Reviewing Obama's personal leadership style is thus an important step in understanding the decision unit's group dynamic.

To begin with, Obama's relationship with his advisors was very cerebral, rather than warm. This was very different from Bush's relationship with his advisors. He even wanted his National Security Advisor, a person who is typically extremely close to the President, not to be "perceived as his guy," and he reached the "baffling conclusion that the lack of a personal relationship [with NSA Jim Jones] could be an asset," an ill-fated idea that led to Jones' resignation after only a year and a half in the position (Woodward 2010, 38). Second, Obama's approach to decision making about the war "contrasted clearly with the approach of President George W. Bush . . . the decision-making process in the Bush White House was often marked by secrecy, a lack of deliberation, and the exclusion of members of the administration and the career services who ordinarily would have been consulted on important decisions" (Pfiffner

2011, 259). Obama's approach was instead "inclusive and more consistent with scholarly conclusions that 'multiple advocacy' would best inform presidential decision making" (Pfiffner 2011, 259). This style, however, was also conducive to creating a Polythink dynamic.

Obama also clearly embraced a competitive advisory system whereby "he invited competing voices to debate in front of him, while guarding his own thoughts" (Baker 2009). Obama himself acknowledged that he, for example, "encouraged the vice president to be an aggressive contrarian" and asked him to "say exactly what you think [and] ask the toughest questions you can think of" (as quoted in Woodward 2010, 160). He felt that "the American people are best served and our troops are best served by a vigorous debate on these kinds of life-or-death issues. [He] wanted every argument on every side to be poked hard. And if we felt a little give there, we wanted to keep on pushing until finally you hit up against something that was incontrovertible and something that we could all agree to" (as quoted in Woodward 2010, 160).

However, given the divisive infighting of his Cabinet and the overly extended nature of his policy review, this multiple advocacy and competitive model were not effective and quickly led to Destructive Polythink—stirring even more group conflict, triggering confusion, and nearly resulting in decision paralysis at critical moments in the Afghanistan War. As a result, during President Obama's entire first term, "there was hidden friction between powerful Cabinet secretaries and a White House that wanted control over the foreign-policy process" (Ignatius 2013b). Recognizing the difficulties that this advisory format had caused, Obama completely reorganized his Cabinet for his second term. For his second term, "Obama has assembled a new team that, for better or worse, seems more likely to follow the White House lead . . . The first term featured the famous 'team of rivals,' people with heavyweight egos and ambitions who could buck the White House and get away with it . . . The new team has prominent players, too, but they're likely to defer more to the White House" (Ignatius 2013b).

Conclusion

The Afghanistan War review process undertaken by the Obama Administration provides perhaps the best-documented case study through which to analyze Obama's decision-making style and the dynamic of his foreign policy decision-making unit. The many published memoirs by former Obama Administration officials provide firsthand accounts that, taken together, supply a very full picture of the decision-unit dynamic in the Afghanistan policy review. Over the course of three months, President Obama met with his full national security team for a series of ten in-depth strategy meetings to determine the fate of the U.S. war effort in Afghanistan. Throughout the review process, Obama demonstrated a commitment to a competitive advisory system, whereby multiple advocacy would be encouraged. Indeed, "Obama wanted to encourage frank disagreements about policy, but he also valued consensus once he made final decisions, [saying], 'I welcome debate among my team, but I won't tolerate division'" (Pfiffner 2011, citing Woodward 2010, 374). However, Obama's commitment to debate, combined with the strong internal divisions among his diverse "team of rivals," often veered into a more destructive and divisive Polythink dynamic.

Perhaps the strongest evidence demonstrating Polythink in President Obama's first term is the reshuffling of his advisory team for his second term. As journalist David Sanger reports, "With the selection of a new national security team deeply suspicious of the wisdom of American military interventions around the world, President Obama appears to have ended, at least for the moment, many of the internal administration debates that played out in the Situation Room over the past four years" (Sanger 2013). Wary of the internal rifts and divisions that plagued his first Administration—resulting in only one foreign policy advisor remaining in her same position for the entire four-year period (Hillary Clinton)—Obama constructed a much more insular Cabinet for his second term:

> Gone for the second term are the powerful personalities, and more hawkish voices, that pressed Mr. Obama to pursue the surge in Afghanistan in 2009, a gamble championed by Secretary of State Hillary Rodham Clinton and Robert M. Gates, the former secretary of defense. Gone from the C.I.A. is the man who urged Mr. Obama to keep troops there longer, David H. Petraeus (Sanger 2013).

Instead, his new Cabinet was made up of individuals more likely to "toe the party line." "They share his commitment to ending the war in Afghanistan and avoiding new foreign military interventions, as well as his corresponding belief in diplomatic engagement . . . They have independent views, to be sure, but they owe an abiding loyalty to Obama" (Sanger 2013).

Obama's experiences of division and plurality of national security opinions from his first-term foreign policy advisory team thus deeply affected the architecture of his second-term Administration. "In Obama's nomination of people skeptical about military power, you can sense a sharp turn away from his December 2009 decision for a troop surge in Afghanistan . . . Clearly, he doesn't intend to repeat that process" (Ignatius 2013b). The fear now is that in his efforts to gain Cabinet consensus and avoid dissent, and given the vagaries of Polythink that plagued his first Administration, Obama's second-term Administration may well come "perilously close to Groupthink" (Ignatius 2013b). And indeed, this changed decision-unit architecture had a clear impact on subsequent foreign policy challenges in the Obama Administration, as will be discussed in Chapter 7 of this book.

5 Decision Making in the Iraq War

From Groupthink to Polythink

In this chapter we continue our analysis of the detrimental effects of flawed group decision-making processes surrounding decisions of war and peace. Specifically, using the Iraq War as a case study, we analyze the implications of Groupthink and Polythink for decisions made by the U.S. government in this controversial theater.[1] Breaking down the group dynamics in the Bush and Obama administrations, we demonstrate the effects of the decision-unit group dynamic on the decisions to initiate the war, to undertake the Surge, and ultimately to withdraw from Iraq.

On December 18, 2011, all U.S. combat troops officially left Iraq. After almost nine years of war, the American combat role there had come to a close.[2] However, the full legacy of what many label a mismanaged decision-making process in a "war of choice" (Haass 2009) has yet to be fully determined. As this chapter demonstrates, after a widely criticized Groupthink decision-making process (Badie 2010; Schafer and Crichlow 2010) regarding the Bush entry to the war, the successful decision-making surrounding the Bush Administration's Surge, orchestrated by General Petraeus, was characterized by a more balanced, Con-Div decision-group dynamic. We will show that beginning in 2008 with the election of President Obama—a staunch critic of the war—the new Administration exhibited Polythink, especially at the tactical level, as competing voices within the Administration diverged on the wisdom, pace, and levels of troop drawdowns in Iraq.

By contrasting the early Groupthink decision-making processes with regard to the U.S. entrance to the war with the later Con-Div decision-making processes regarding the Surge and then with the Polythink dynamic that characterized the withdrawal from Iraq, we will demonstrate the detrimental effects of Groupthink or Polythink in the U.S. national security apparatus. These three decisions—the Groupthink decision to invade, the Con-Div balanced Surge decision, and the Polythink decision to withdraw—also reveal the ways in which decision-making processes can be placed at different points on the Groupthink-Polythink continuum and applied to decisions regarding war and peace.

The Decision to Invade Iraq in 2003: A Classic Groupthink Dynamic

In the months prior to the U.S. invasion of Iraq, the small group of decision makers in the Bush Administration exhibited a pattern of Groupthink. There was a clear consensus within the decision-making unit that American forces would be greeted as liberators by the Iraqi people. The backgrounds, worldviews, beliefs, and mind-sets of the group's members were not completely similar. However, the universal opinion of the neoconservatives who dominated Bush's Cabinet in the post-9/11 environment with respect to removing Saddam Hussein from power represents a typical Groupthink syndrome in which "the decision processes and norms within that structure (or lack of structure) worked to reinforce existing biases and stereotypes more than to raise questions about how workable the strategies and tactics stemming from those stereotypes really were" (Schafer and Crichlow 2010, 235).

Other symptoms of Groupthink were also evident in this phase: for example, the Administration often focused only on the short-term results of the military campaign while ignoring the longer-term problems of insurgency and political violence in Iraq (Mintz and DeRouen 2010, 41). Whereas the "shock and awe" air campaign at the start of the war was well planned and successful, the occupation of Iraq was a nightmare, leading to 4,485 Americans killed and tens of thousands of Iraqi casualties over the course of the war (News Research Center 2009). Just as in the classic Groupthink syndrome, group members:

1. Locked in on their preferred alternative course of action, ignoring the risks of this chosen policy and failing to consider what could go wrong in Iraq, instead focusing only on what could go right (Hersh 2004, 168–169, as cited in Schafer and Crichlow 2010, 223)

2. Did not seriously evaluate different alternatives or contingency plans for dealing with Iraq (Yetiv 2004, 230) and failed to reevaluate policy options that had previously been rejected

3. Engaged in biased, selective information processing, ignoring critical information that contradicted their views and preferences

4. Engaged in poor information search, overestimating the group's ability to correctly estimate their rival's capabilities on WMD and failing to trust or seek out external counsel or intelligence (Badie 2010)

5. Framed and portrayed their views, goals, and the invasion in a way that supported their position and overall preference, while discounting competing assessments and descriptions

6. Rejected the advice of those who did not share the same worldview as the majority of the group, leading to a nearly unanimous group recommendation to attack Iraq

A review of the classic symptoms of Groupthink that were present in the Iraq invasion decision illustrates that the Groupthink dynamic of the decision-making unit was a clear contributor to the faulty policy planning that characterized the early war years (Badie 2010; Schafer and Crichlow 2010).

The Surge and the Con-Div Group Dynamic

In 2006, the Administration began discussing a possible troop surge in Iraq to stem the rampant violence that was quickly leading the country down the path to civil war. During this period, the decision-making processes inside and outside Washington became much more balanced, careful, and comprehensive—perhaps as a result of the lessons learned from the calamitous first three years of the war.

The Surge in Iraq, often referred to as the "New Way Forward," was a reinforcement of U.S. forces by 20,000 (and ultimately close to 30,000) additional troops, which began in spring 2007 (Boot and Simon 2008). The Surge was announced in January 2007 by President Bush during a television speech, in which he outlined the U.S. strategy in Iraq, articulating the goals of the Surge and its key objectives (as transcribed in the *Washington Post*, January 10, 2007):

America will change our strategy to help the Iraqis carry out their campaign to put down sectarian violence and bring security to the people of Baghdad. This will require increasing American force levels. So I have committed more than 20,000 additional American troops to Iraq. The vast majority of them—five brigades—will be deployed to Baghdad. These troops will work alongside Iraqi units and be embedded in their formations. Our troops will have a well-defined mission: to help Iraqis clear and secure neighborhoods, to help them protect the local population, and to help ensure that the Iraqi forces left behind are capable of providing the security that Baghdad needs. . . . A successful strategy for Iraq goes beyond military operations. Ordinary Iraqi citizens must see that military operations are accompanied by visible improvements in their neighborhoods and communities. So America will hold the Iraqi government to the benchmarks it has announced.

Some saw the Surge as a dramatic policy change from that of a "small footprint" to a more public embracing of the counterinsurgency strategy championed by General Petraeus. However, others claimed that it was simply a continuation of the path-dependent, flawed U.S. strategy in Iraq. These opposing voices claimed that the Administration had no clear exit strategy from the war. Whereas the military campaign at the beginning of the war was successful, once the U.S. actually invaded Iraq and became embroiled in the war, all the sunk costs incurred in terms of casualties, money, and reputation may have led to a process to "stay the course" in Iraq, a process that was extremely difficult to reverse. This often led to post-hoc rationalization of the invasion, its causes, and its explanations. Not surprisingly, considerable debate preceded the Surge decision in 2006–2007.

Unlike the pre-invasion period, however, at this point the Administration's decision makers strongly benefited from the diverse and conflicting points of view regarding the best strategy for moving forward in the Iraq War. The Administration reviewed various viewpoints when considering the Surge, such as the one presented by the bipartisan Iraq Study Group, which actually recommended a steady reduction in troop levels (Baker and Hamilton 2006). Then House Speaker-elect Nancy Pelosi also very publicly opposed the Surge proposal in an article titled "Bringing the War to an End Is My Highest Priority as Speaker" (Pelosi 2006). On the other hand, after the 2006 U.S. midterm elections, in which the Republicans lost control of the House and the Senate, a Heritage Foundation conference chaired by Republican whip Congressman Roy Blunt (R-MO) under the title "The New Way Forward: Refocusing the Conservative Agenda" (Blunt 2006) supported a surge in U.S. forces in Iraq, albeit not exactly in the way it was ultimately carried out. President Bush recognized these many conflicting viewpoints in his speech (as transcribed in the *Washington Post*, January 10, 2007):

> Many are concerned that the Iraqis are becoming too dependent on the United States and, therefore, our policy should focus on protecting Iraq's borders and hunting down Al Qaida. Their solution is to scale back America's efforts in Baghdad or announce the phased withdrawal of our combat forces . . . *We carefully considered these proposals.* And we concluded that to step back now would force a collapse of the Iraqi government, tear that country apart, and result in mass killings on an unimaginable scale. (Emphasis added)

Thus, the decision to undertake the Surge exhibited strong characteristics of a balanced decision that took into account the views of several players: experts, think tanks, opposing groups (e.g., Democrats in Congress), policy groups (such as the ten-person bipartisan Iraq Study Group), military leaders, Senator John McCain (R-AZ and a strong advocate of the Surge), the Iraqi government, and many others.

As a classic Con-Div decision, the Surge policy was not rushed or conducted with shortcuts that limited information review and assessment of policy alternatives. In fact, President Bush waited for the results of three other studies, conducted at the Pentagon, the State Department, and the National Security Council, before making the decision. The president echoed this idea, stating (as transcribed in the *Washington Post*, January 10, 2007):

> My national security team, military commanders and diplomats conducted a comprehensive review. We consulted members of Congress from both parties, allies abroad, and distinguished outside experts. We benefited from the thoughtful recommendations of the Iraq Study Group . . . In our discussions, we all agreed that there is no magic formula for success in Iraq. And one message came through loud and clear: Failure in Iraq would be a disaster for the United States.

Overall, the Surge has been largely credited as a success by many experts, as evidenced by a *New York Times* report that states: "The surge, clearly, has worked, at least for now . . . The result, now visible in the streets, is a calm unlike any the country has seen since the American invasion" (Filkins 2008). Clearly, the Con-Div group dynamic of President Bush and his national security team at the time benefited the decision-making process, leading to a carefully considered policy review process. Despite this, however, many have continued to criticize the Surge for the damage it brought to Iraq, and for not ending the war sooner and more decisively (Kingsbury 2014; McIntyre and Ure 2008; Ricks 2009).

Most of the Con-Div symptoms characterized the Surge decision. Though it took the President a few months to consult relevant groups, organizations, and influential individuals about the wisdom and consequences of this decision, there was clearly no deadlock or paralysis in the decision-making process. There was also less likelihood that the President would ignore critical information than if the decision had been made under a Groupthink dynamic. Less group information-processing bias was evident in the Surge decision as well; for example, the President did not plunge into the decision or "shoot from the hip." As expected from a Con-Div decision, there was little confusion about direction and action items.

However, not all Con-Div symptoms fit the Surge decision. There was no real harmony among the groups and individuals consulted, many of whom disagreed on the potential efficacy of the Surge policy, and they did not always speak with one voice when addressing the Surge policy in public and in the press. Overall, however, five of the seven symptoms of Con-Div fit the Surge decision. Thus, the decision process for the Surge was very different from the one to invade Iraq. The Surge decision is also an example of purposeful decision-unit design being utilized by a leader attempting to avoid the more homogeneous, Groupthink-like mode that had led to problematic policy choices earlier in his Administration. We now turn to another key decision on Iraq.

The Withdrawal from Iraq—A Polythink Process

The withdrawal from Iraq, unlike the early periods of the war and the Surge, was characterized by Polythink. There were divergent policy opinions about the speed and character of the withdrawal process and disagreements about the overall wisdom of the withdrawal decision. However, at the same time, the decision to withdraw from Iraq provides an example of a Polythink dynamic that was, relatively speaking, managed and controlled by the policymaker (with some notable exceptions, as will be detailed below).[3]

Polythink Symptom #1:
Intragroup Conflict—Infighting and Turf Battles

During the first term of the Obama Administration, group disagreement and conflict were important problems to overcome. This situation, however, was not caused by the ostracizing of one discordant group member or institution (as had been the case with Colin Powell and the State Department in the Bush Administration). Rather, the conflict was attributable to the large variety of viewpoints among members of the decision-making unit regarding the Iraq troop drawdown. One foreign policy analyst went so far as to claim, "A man who advertised himself as 'No Drama Obama' . . . in reality . . . presides over an administration pulsing with internecine conflict and policy disarray" (Karl 2012). While Obama's Administration was not necessarily as fractious as this statement suggests, many battles did indeed take place between Obama's inner circle of political staffers and his military advisors.[4]

Thus, the Polythink atmosphere in the Obama Administration, composed of Obama's political advisors who were very much against the war, Democratic holdovers from the Clinton Administration who were moderate in their advocacy for a troop drawdown, and more-conservative military leaders who had previously served in George Bush's Republican Administration, created fertile ground for intergroup turf conflict. This at least partially impeded the close cooperation necessary to ensure not just a stable drawdown of troops but also a lasting plan for the survival of Iraq's fledgling democracy. The rise of the ISIS terrorist group in Iraq a mere two years after the final withdrawal of U.S. troops there underscores the serious consequences of this failure.

Polythink Symptom #2: Leaks and Fear of Leaks

Much of this internal decision-unit conflict was manifested by a series of leaks to the press (as well as a profound concern within the Administration regarding *potential* leaks). For example, Mark Lippert was forced out of his position as Deputy Assistant to the President amid internal friction with National Security Advisor General James Jones (as reported in Woodward 2010), with Jones accusing Lippert of "leaking negative stories about him" (139). Perhaps the most famous example of airing negative stories to the press was General Stanley McChrystal's *Rolling Stone* interview, in which he and his advisors express derisive opinions about Vice President Joe Biden, Special Advisor on Afghanistan Richard Holbrooke, U.S. Ambassador Karl Eikenberry, and even President Obama himself (Hastings 2010). These past experiences with leaks led many in the Obama Administration to attempt to tamp down the dissent. For example, when General Mike Mullen, Chairman of the Joint Chiefs, sent a confidential letter to National Security Advisor Thomas Donilon (who had replaced Jim Jones) expressing concerns that a residual force in Iraq was necessary after the end of combat operations (Hastings 2010), it upset many of Obama's political advisors. They felt that the military was boxing the White House in and creating a potential political liability if the letter leaked (Gordon and Trainor 2012).

Polythink Symptom #3: Lack of Communication and Confusion

A lack of communication and subsequent confusion within the decision-making apparatus often relate directly back to the Polythink phenomenon. The size and heterogeneity of the group of policymakers and advisors that compose the federal security and defense apparatus can naturally lead to interagency competition and concerns about security leaks and subsequently heightened bureaucratic issues of access to information. This problem is particularly prevalent in situations of group conflict within the decision unit.

In the Obama Administration during the 2009–2011 withdrawal from Iraq, communication among agencies was much stronger than during the early Bush years, largely because of bureaucratic changes that were implemented after the interagency communication failures of 9/11. However, communication between civilian advisors and the military remained problematic, and not simply because of bureaucratic challenges or a lack of technological ability. Rather, it was the result of the conflicting worldviews of the two groups of advisors. For example, Obama and his close political advisors generally regarded America's involvement in Iraq as a potential "minefield" rather than as an opportunity to advance American interests, and thus sought to chart a way out of Iraq as quickly as possible—a view that was at odds with the desire of many military commanders to preserve hard-fought gains in the field (Gordon and Trainor 2012).

The reasons for these institutional battles have their origins in Graham Allison's (1971) famed observation that "where you stand depends on where you sit." Thus, members of the military have their own institutional goals and agendas that may not meld well with the goals and agendas of political advisors or White House staff.

In the withdrawal from Iraq, these institutional considerations clearly contributed to the communication barriers and growing sense of policy confusion about the plans for troop withdrawal. Moreover, communication with the

Iraqi government—a key player in the ultimate decisions about a U.S. troop presence in Iraq—remained incredibly problematic. This symptom of *inter-state* Polythink was a critical factor in the Obama Administration's failure to secure a second Status of Forces Agreement (SOFA) that would have enabled a small contingent of U.S. troops to remain in Iraq after the 2011 withdrawal. For example, while President Bush held a weekly teleconference with Iraq Prime Minister Nouri al-Maliki, President Obama spoke to Maliki only a handful of times during his entire first term in office. This greatly hampered communication between the two sides at a very sensitive period.

Moreover, the Obama Administration, in its negotiations with the Iraqis, often "negotiated against themselves more than it negotiated with the Iraqis," demonstrating the competing viewpoints and perspectives within the Administration (Pollack 2011). This confusion and lack of communication within and between the American and Iraqi administrations severely hampered efforts to work out a long-term solution to the U.S. troop levels in Iraq that would have enabled a sustained U.S. presence to support Iraq's democracy and temper the influence of Iran over the long term. And indeed, in hindsight, achieving a second Status of Forces Agreement with the Iraqis may have been critical in preventing the growth of the ISIS terror organization in Iraq, which now threatens to draw the U.S. back into prolonged conflict in the region. Former Secretary of Defense Leon Panetta sharply criticized President Obama in his 2014 memoir, stating, "It was clear to me—and many others—that withdrawing all our forces would endanger the fragile stability then barely holding Iraq together ... Those on our side viewed the White House as so eager to rid itself of Iraq that it was willing to withdraw rather than lock in arrangements that would preserve our influence and interests" (Panetta 2014). Essentially, Panetta links the 2014 rise of ISIS with the power vacuum that was created in part by the lack of a small, enduring U.S. military presence in that country.

Polythink Symptom #4: Limited Review of Policy Alternatives, Objectives, Risks, and Contingencies

Interestingly, the limited review of policy alternatives conducted by the Obama Administration with regard to the Iraq War was, in this case, more symptomatic of Groupthink than Polythink. In other words, the limited review of alternatives was *not* due to a cacophony of options that were simply too voluminous to be included in the choice set. Rather it resulted from President Obama's (and the country's) incredible fatigue with the Iraq War. There was actually a strong *consensus*, especially among the President's constituency, that the Iraq War should end, and end quickly. Even the "once-ardent opponent of a firm departure date from Iraq," Secretary of Defense Robert Gates, announced in 2008 that "a bridge had been crossed" and the "debate in Iraq was no longer over when to leave, but rather how to do this in a responsible way" (Bruno 2009).

Thus, almost immediately after President Obama was elected on a campaign promise to bring troops home from Iraq, discussions began on how to fulfill that promise. Except for some minimal lip service to the dangers of "cutting and running," options *other* than a "timely withdrawal" were reportedly never seriously considered by anyone in the decision-making unit. War fatigue combined with turning public opinion and the President's own distaste for the war ensured that the debate would center only on the *pace* of the withdrawal, rather than on the *principle* of it. In terms of the specific speed and tactics of the troop drawdown, there were several different camps. On the one hand, the Iraq Study Group advocated that U.S. troops be shifted from combat to training and that combat troops be withdrawn from Iraq over a relatively short period of time. Obama and his political advisors had also made a campaign promise that all troops would leave Iraq within sixteen months. In contrast, the U.S. military, including Iraq commander Ray Odierno,[5] generally advocated a withdrawal timetable of twenty-three months, stressing the importance of not withdrawing many troops in the early months before the Iraqi elections scheduled for January 2010—much longer than Obama's campaign promise. Thus, the divide between military and civilian advisors became apparent once more.

To bridge this divide, Defense Secretary Robert Gates advocated a nineteen-month timetable that would enable the White House to say that the combat mission in Iraq had come to a close at the politically opportune moment—right before the midterm elections (Gordon and Trainor 2012). Moreover, Obama would specify a date for ending the American "combat mission" in Iraq, but would not remove all of the brigades at that point; those that remained would simply be renamed "advise-and-assist units" (Gordon and Trainor 2012). This satisficing plan enabled Obama to keep his campaign promise while also incorporating advice from the military and is a key example of lowest-common-denominator decision making. However, this minor debate over numbers was the only real consideration of policy alternatives that took place and paled in comparison to the fierce debate about troop numbers in Afghanistan that was chronicled in Chapter 4.

Polythink Symptom #5:
Failure to Reappraise Previously Rejected Alternatives

Indeed, the Obama Administration's very public and steadfast commitment to the policy of speedily withdrawing from Iraq was never fully reconsidered—the Obama Administration maintained its pledge to draw down troop forces and shift resources to domestic concerns and the War in Afghanistan. Though this policy was perhaps warranted, the Administration's singular focus on withdrawal did hamper U.S. efforts to ensure political stability and security in Iraq. Many felt that the Obama Administration, by publicly signaling a "pivot" toward Afghanistan, or even the Far East, had taken irreversible steps that sent Iraq "beyond America's influence" (Pollack 2011). According to the testimony of Iraq expert Kenneth Pollack before the U.S. Senate Committee on Armed Services, "There is no turning back the clock, even if Washington suddenly had a change of heart. The decisions that have been made are now virtually set in stone. There will not be a significant American military presence in Iraq in the future. That train has left the station and it cannot be recalled or reboarded at some later stop" (Pollack 2011).[6] Many also blame Obama's hastiness to withdraw from Iraq for the Administration's failure to secure a second Status of Forces Agreement. Such an agreement would have enabled a small number of soldiers to remain in Iraq and guard America's interests there (for example, preventing arms flow from Iran).

Thus, the government's public commitment to one course of action—troop drawdown—hindered, according to the President's critics, the U.S. goals of providing long-term political stability and security in Iraq. However, though the withdrawal itself was never reconsidered, the Obama Administration did reconsider some of the specific details of its war plans, particularly its sixteen-month troop drawdown policy in Iraq.

Polythink Symptom #6:
Framing Effects and Selective Use of Information

Elite decision makers inherently work within time constraints stemming from the sheer enormity of pressing political issues that they must address. In situations of Polythink, the number of these competing information streams is often exacerbated.

In the case of the Afghanistan War review, President Obama was able to effectively integrate these competing information streams, limiting the potential paralyzing impact of conflicting information. In the Iraq troop debate, however, additional information problems arose. Namely, while available information and analysis were indeed voraciously, and less selectively, consumed by both administrations in the later years of the war, *availability* of information and intelligence remained a stubborn problem, particularly as the number of forces in Iraq shrank from 2009 onward. Political scientist Michael Gordon explains how a key consequence of the military's departure from Iraq was that the U.S. had a vastly diminished capacity to monitor violent incidents in a critically strategic country, which undermined the credibility of its claims that violence had diminished (Gordon and Trainor 2012). In other words, according to Gordon, documented attacks may have gone down because documentation went down, not because attacks did. The frosty relationship between President Obama and Iraqi Prime Minister Maliki further inhibited the Administration's understanding of the on-the-ground issues facing Iraq as the number of American troops diminished (Panetta 2014). Indeed, an analysis conducted by Michael Knights (2012) at the Washington Institute for Near East Policy has shown that Iraqi-on-Iraqi violence actually *increased* in the wake of the U.S. withdrawal:

> Analysis of general incident levels across the country is a better means of tracking these trends, but it is precisely this kind of data that the U.S. government no longer receives due to its military disengagement in Iraq. In effect, the U.S. government is slowly going blind in Iraq due to the military drawdown and the U.S. embassy's inability to get out and about. According to Washington Institute for Near East Policy metrics derived from ongoing security-liaison relationships in Iraq, there were 561 reported attacks in January 2012, an increase from the 494 in December 2011 and well above the 302 incidents in November.

With the rise of ISIS in Iraq, this analysis appears prophetic—nearly eight thousand Iraqis were killed in 2013, a return to 2008 levels of violence (Fox News, January 2, 2014).

Polythink often also results in the development of competing frames to present the same issues—clearly demonstrated by the Bush and Obama administrations' fundamentally different framing of the Iraq War. While the Bush Administration focused on the potential benefits of nation-building in Iraq for the spread of democracy in the Arab world, President Obama introduced a loss-aversion framework that portrayed the decision to continue the war as a potential loss on numerous dimensions (e.g., economic, reputation costs, and loss of life). However, even *within* the Obama Administration, the decision to end the war in Iraq was framed in several ways. This phenomenon occurs frequently in presidential advisory groups (Garrison 2001). Instead of talking about a lack of success in establishing democracy in Iraq and about the numerous casualties of the war, or even the growing influence of Iran in Iraq, the Administration often framed the decision to exit the war as an economic decision and as the result of a fear of overextending U.S. commitments abroad. However, the decision to exit Iraq was also often framed as a redoubling of the U.S. commitment to Afghanistan—namely, in order to do a better job in Afghanistan, we must withdraw from Iraq. Thus, the Obama Administration advanced both a thematic framing strategy and evaluative framing mechanisms in shaping the withdrawal policy (Geva and Mintz 1997).

Polythink Symptoms #7 and #8:
Lowest-Common-Denominator Decisions and Decision Paralysis
Finally, and perhaps most importantly, Polythink can lead to paralysis of the decision-making unit, resulting in a failure to implement policy or the implementation of short-term "Band-Aid" satisficing policies for which approval can be gained. The postwar withdrawal plan in Iraq is a key example of this phenomenon, as it was tailored to fit lowest-common-denominator compromises that could achieve the broadest coalition of support from the discordant national security, diplomatic, and political teams.

A key example of this type of satisficing decision making can be seen in the decisions on troop levels and withdrawal pace in the early stages of the Obama Administration. In essence, the timeline for troop withdrawals that was eventually chosen "split the difference between the sixteen months he promised as a candidate and the twenty-three-month timeline favored by his commanders" rather than representing the optimal military strategy (Bruno 2009). The search for "balance" among various viewpoints has characterized much of the Obama Administration, and this "sometimes awkward attempt to accommodate both sides of the political spectrum, deemed insufficient by critics and infuriating by allies" has also included "his plans to withdraw troops from Iraq and Afghanistan" (Parsons and Hennessey 2012).

Triggers of Polythink
Thus, the decision-making processes of the Obama Administration were once more affected by the Polythink dynamic. However, Groupthink elements were present as well, as evidenced by a general consensus within the decision unit that withdrawal was the only policy option that would receive serious attention.

In this case, the Polythink debate centered more on *tactics* (i.e., the pace of withdrawal) than on *strategy* (i.e., the long-term mission), a somewhat common phenomenon in U.S. defense policymaking. These symptoms were triggered by fundamental structural and individual processes within the national security apparatus that hampered the ability of the U.S. government to approach the Iraq drawdown with a clear plan and vision for Iraq's long-term stability.

Institutional Explanation and Turf Wars— Problems of Communication and Multiple Gatekeepers

As discussed earlier, the unwieldy size of the federal government often leads to bureaucratic confusion, miscommunication, and the problem of "multiple gatekeepers" to the President, all of which inhibits the development of a cohesive policy, leads to mismanagement, and exacerbates the problem of Polythink in decision making. This bureaucratic theme recurs because, in many ways, the structure of the American government itself is problematic for foreign policymaking and war planning. For example, while the U.S. Constitution "delineates the powers and responsibilities of the government for making and implementing American foreign policy—Article I grants the Congress some specific powers, and Article II grants the executive branch the principal responsibility for foreign policymaking[—]the references to foreign policymaking are general and brief, and because of this, one scholar characterized constitutional provisions concerning foreign policy as 'an invitation to struggle' between the congressional and executive branches" (Caldwell 2011, 189). This inherent ambiguity within the Constitution has meant that "various presidential administrations have developed differing conceptions of presidential control over foreign policy" (Caldwell 2011, 189).

Thus, even in Groupthink situations such as the Iraq invasion, bureaucratic battles and failures of communication between institutions with overlapping mandates can exacerbate the poor group decision-making processes that often lead to negative policy outcomes. For example, immediately after the Iraq invasion, major sites throughout Baghdad were looted. This widespread mayhem happened despite the fact that "Tom Warrick, the director of the State Department's Future of Iraq Project, had provided ORHA [the Office of Reconstruction and Humanitarian Assistance] a list of the vulnerable sites to be secured after the invasion." The problem was simply that "either this list was not passed on to the military field commanders, or it was ignored." The result of this failure was the strengthening of the negative preconceptions of most Iraqis that the U.S. was most interested in Iraq's oil and not the security of its citizens (Caldwell 2011, 176–177). Likewise, battles between the Departments of State and Defense over postwar planning also reflected the bureaucratic clashes in Washington. Secretary of Defense Donald Rumsfeld insisted that the DoD be placed in charge of postwar planning, while Secretary of State Colin Powell insisted that the role had historically been played by the State Department. Thus, postwar planning itself became a bureaucratic battle within Washington.

Similar bureaucratic failings continued throughout the Obama Administration, and tensions and miscommunication between the military and civilian advisors to Obama often flared, inhibiting full cooperation on issues related to the Iraq drawdown. These problematic inter-agency relations are symptomatic of many national security and foreign policy processes and seem to illustrate a fundamental problem of the military-industrial establishment in addressing national security issues. Some critics even argue that "the entire system for managing national security affairs is broken and needs to be revamped" (Dobbins 2007). In Polythink situations such bureaucratic hurdles can be particularly problematic, as they magnify the number and severity of the already existing plurality of viewpoints.

Ongoing Divides between Civilian "Novices" and Military "Experts"

Institutional considerations also exacerbate Polythink in the decision-making processes of the federal government. This problem is particularly pronounced when the decision group is made up of representatives of various agencies. Each representative feels that he or she needs to staunchly defend the interests, perspectives, and worldview of his or her own agency and therefore he or she may make more extreme policy recommendations than if he or she were not acting as an official representative of that "group." In the withdrawal from Iraq, these institutional considerations were clearly exhibited in the decision-making process. The novices of President Obama's political inner circle routinely pushed for a quick drawdown of troops, emphasizing Obama's campaign promise to withdraw all troops from Iraq within sixteen months. They viewed the Iraq War in the context of Obama's larger national agenda, framing the opportunity-costs of troops in Iraq in the context of pressing domestic issues, limited budgets, and the ongoing recession. Thus, they argued that "the war had to be viewed in the context of a weakened economy at home. The collapse of the housing and financial markets had created constraints. The lawmaker's job was to assess Iraq through the lens of finite resources" (Gordon and Trainor

2012, 535). In contrast, veterans of the State Department, including Secretary
Clinton, who had also supported ending the war during her campaign but had
refused to set a concrete timeline as Obama had, took a more cautious view of
troop withdrawal, emphasizing the need to leave behind a stable political system in Iraq that would protect the fragile gains made during the past few years.

However, the most contradictory perspective came from the U.S. military leaders, who feared that Obama's withdrawal policy would threaten the
hard-won gains of the 2007 Surge. Many analysts proclaimed that "if the decision on American troops had been left up to the American and Iraqi militar-
ies, some sort of continued United States military presence would have been
agreed upon without much controversy or fanfare. But the decision was one
the politicians in each country had to take on" and so became much more controversial (Gordon and Trainor 2012, 657). And indeed, military leaders such
as Iraq Commander Ray Odierno routinely asked Obama "to stretch out the
timetable he had proposed as a candidate and, above all, not to withdraw too
many troops in the early months, before the Iraqi elections scheduled for January 2010" (Mann 2012, 118). President Obama acknowledged both the validity
and the institutional nature of this request, reportedly saying, "I have no problem with you guys . . . I'd advocate the same if I was in your shoes" (Gordon
and Trainor 2012, 536). According to Obama, his job was "to look at the whole
picture. I expect you [Petraeus], as the commander of our forces in Iraq, to ask
for everything you need and more to ensure your success. That's what you owe
the troops who are under your command. My job, then, which in some ways
is more difficult, is I've got to choose. Because I don't have infinite resources"
(Woodward 2010, 14–15).

However, the unified position of the military against his sixteen-month
timetable did place the Democratic President in a difficult political position.
He was extremely susceptible to claims that he was "weak" on national security;
if the military was unified in its recommendation, he could hardly be seen as
defying military advice. Thus, Obama needed to search hard for a compromise
position that would "strike a balance between satisfying his commanders and
placating the antiwar wing of his party" (Gordon and Trainor 2012, 574).

Political Concerns

Political concerns were also evident in the decisions about the Iraq War and
often exacerbated the plurality of opinions within the Obama Cabinet on the
drawdown plans. The withdrawal from Iraq had been a major campaign issue

and American public opinion had long since turned against the war, meaning that elected members of Congress were also pushing for an end date to the war. There was thus a key divide in the government between elected officials, answerable to a public who overwhelming supported withdrawal, and appointed officials, who felt responsible for ensuring that the hard-fought military gains of the past several years would be sustained. As Gordon and Trainor (2012, 653) explain:

> Obama, Biden, and Clinton were all former senators who had wrestled with policy in the Congress and were attuned to the public mood. Their aides, by and large, were former congressional staffers or politicos. The team's sensitivity to the public mood was arguably an asset in building support for a foreign policy doctrine. But it also raised the question of whether politics played too large a role in formulating policy—whether the tail was wagging the dog.

Another key issue was the Polythink that existed *between* the Republican and Democratic administrations. Switching administrations in the midst of war can be problematic, as the continuity of government is often at least partially disrupted by the changeover of leadership and department staff. Moreover, as political scientists Kurt Campbell and James Steinberg point out, new administrations have an inherent tendency to write off the policies of the outgoing administration while also failing to appreciate the differences between campaign promises and policy realities (Campbell and Steinberg 2008). Obama tempered this effect somewhat by retaining the previous administration's Secretary of Defense. He argued, "Retaining Gates at the Pentagon might make sense . . . Continuity during the wars could be essential. And it might be helpful as U.S. troops pulled out of Iraq to have at the Pentagon someone who had overseen the stabilization and reduction of violence there" (Woodward 2010, 19).[7]

However, this decision did not change the inconvenient fact that after eight years of Republican leadership, Obama had inherited a war that he famously and fundamentally opposed, yet was nonetheless tasked with successfully carrying out. Carryovers from the Bush Administration such as Secretary of Defense Robert Gates and military leaders such as General David Petraeus needed to adjust to the changed reality of a president who did not support the rationale for the war and was desperately seeking an exit. According to Bob Woodward, "Opposing the Iraq War had been central to Obama's rise, causing some members of the Bush Administration, including Gates, to fear what the new president might do (Woodward 2010, 75). General Petraeus in particular saw "Obamaland as potentially hostile" (as cited in Woodward 2010, 16):

> When candidate Obama had visited Iraq over the [previous] summer, the conversation between the two had not gone well . . . Obama, an outspoken, acerbic opponent of the Iraq War, said he still wanted to withdraw and would have to consider Iraq in the context of all the other pressing national security concerns, including Afghanistan. The Obama presidency was going to dramatically alter Petraeus's status. He had direct access to President Bush, and his mentor, retired General Jack Keane, the former vice chief of staff of the Army, had an extraordinary pipeline to both Bush and Vice President Dick Cheney.

This would no longer be the case under the Obama Aadministration; this shift in political leadership thus had a noticeable impact on the decision-making processes surrounding the Iraq War planning and increased the level of Polythink in the decision-making group as new perspectives and opinions were added to the mix.

Normative Differences in Decision-Making Processes
Normative differences in decision-making processes contributed to Polythink in both the Bush and the Obama Administrations. In the Bush Administration there were competing worldviews, but the neo-conservatives were largely dominant. Dan Caldwell (2011) references Ivo Daalder and James Lindsay's work in the book *America Unbound*, in which they identified three distinct groups within the Bush Administration: assertive nationalists (Dick Cheney, Donald Rumsfeld), neoconservatives (Paul Wolfowitz, John Bolton, Richard Perle), and pragmatic internationalists (Colin Powell, Richard Haass). They explain that

> each of these three groups had a distinctive world-view and preferred means of dealing with international relations in general and Afghanistan and Iraq in particular. The attacks of September 11 reduced the significance of these differences as the nation rallied to defend itself against the clear and present danger of terrorism, and when the United States attacked Afghanistan in October 2001, there was substantial bipartisan support. However, as the Bush administration moved toward a decision to attack Iraq, these differences became more important and pronounced. (195–196, as cited in Caldwell 2011)

These normative differences fundamentally shaped the way different members of the Bush decision-making unit processed information and made decisions. They were a fundamental reason for some of the major conflicts within the Bush Cabinet—a hallmark of Polythink—and the ultimate reason that half of these individuals did not make it through both terms, either quitting or being forced to resign. This demonstrates how a Polythink atmosphere can shift as one more powerful group imposes its ideas on the others, even forcing them out of the decision unit.

Obama's first Administration also possessed a decision-making group with an even broader diversity of worldviews and perspectives, shaped by fundamentally different formative political experiences and famously known as "a team of rivals." Tensions between the worldviews of this diverse Cabinet deeply influenced the policy decision-making process. For example, "Obama's views of the world and of America's role in it were shaped to a far greater extent by his age and by the times in which he came to national prominence . . . Obama was the first president since Vietnam whose personal life and career were utterly unaffected by that war" (Mann 2012, 73). He and his close political staffers "self-consciously thought of themselves as a new generation in American foreign policy . . . they were post–baby-boomers, born in the 1960s and 1970s; they were infants or in elementary school (or, in one case, not yet born) during the Vietnam War . . . [and] had not yet started their careers in government at the end of the Cold War . . . [when] the United States no longer had as much money to spend overseas as it had a decade earlier" (Mann 2012, xix).

In contrast, the political views of other members of the Administration, such as Clinton and Gates, had in many ways been shaped by the Vietnam War and the Cold War. Secretary of Defense Robert Gates once commented, "Jim [Jones] and Hillary and I have joked that we're of a different generation than those in the White House. While they're texting, we're on the cell phone or even a landline" (Mann 2012, xix). Citing one high-ranking Administration official, scholar James Mann (2012) explains,

> You can divide up this town into people who believe that the world revolves around the United States—that other countries wake up in the morning thinking about the United States—and other people who don't think that . . . Hillary Clinton thinks of the United States as the world's indispensable nation, as the world's leader. She's still rooted in the Clinton administration of the 1990s. And fundamentally, Barack Obama doesn't think that way. That's the difference between them. (252–253)

The Cold War mentality had also been typical of many members of the Bush Administration, many of whom had served in government in the Reagan and Bush Senior administrations. These divides, along with many others (such as the tendency to see the world in gray vs. black and white, the preference for processed information vs. raw intelligence, etc.), both between the Bush and Obama administrations and within the two administrations, are some of the most fundamental contributors to Polythink. This explains how trained individuals, assessing the same intelligence and policy options, can draw fundamentally different conclusions regarding the decision-making problem, the relevant policy options, and the strengths and weaknesses of each potential course of action.

The Leader and the Followers

Finally, the relationship between the leader and the followers may also exacerbate Polythink, as the decision problem is viewed in fundamentally different ways, depending on one's position within the decision-making unit. For example, Obama has relied heavily upon his own small, informal network of close aides. These aides did not hold Cabinet-level positions, but in most cases worked closely with him during his 2008 presidential campaign. As Mann (2012) explains,

> They had no previous experience in carrying out foreign policy at the State or Defense Departments, although some had worked on Capitol Hill. Obama installed these aides primarily on the National Security Council, and he often worked with and through them in formulating ideas and dealing with the foreign policy bureaucracies. The effect of these personnel decisions was that Obama had only distant relationships with those who held formal responsibilities for foreign policy, such as the Secretary of State and the National Security Adviser, but he was extremely close to the former campaign aides on the National Security Council staff. (10)

Bush also lacked experience and background in international relations, and so he "essentially handed the administration's foreign policy portfolio to Cheney, who had both substantial background and interest in these issues" (Caldwell 2011, 190). In another example of Bush and Obama's contrasting relationships with their subordinates, George Bush had talked weekly to General Petraeus in Monday morning teleconferences and had "even gone on a spirited mountain bike ride with Petraeus in the Virginia countryside." Obama, on the

other hand, "was more cerebral and distant in his dealings with top commanders. An attorney at heart, Obama did not want to be swamped with briefing
charts or one-upped on the strategy" (Gordon and Trainor 2012, 561). These differing strategies in dealing with advisors demonstrate the important role that
leaders can play in influencing the decision-making process. Namely, a leader's
relationship with his followers can result in Groupthink spurred on by a deep
sense of group cohesiveness and closeness. Or it may trigger Polythink, brought
on by the confusion and discord generated by keeping advisors at arm's length
and not revealing one's own policy preferences. It can also lead to Con-Div, if
the goals, vision, and philosophy are spelled out by the leader but there remains
disagreement within the group for achieving these common goals.

Conclusion and Policy Implications

The Iraq War has been the most divisive U.S military conflict since the Vietnam War. With an estimated 4,485 Americans (News Research Center 2009)
and 110,991 to 121,182 Iraqis ("Iraq Body Count" 2013) killed, and at a direct cost
of more than $800 billion as of 2011 (Francis 2011), the expense of this conflict
in blood and treasure has been immense. These costs underscore the critical
importance of understanding and optimizing foreign policy decision-making
processes before, during, and after the conflict. The growth of ISIS in Iraq and
the renewed U.S. involvement in the region mean that addressing the role of
elite group dynamics in affecting these crucial national security decisions is
more important than ever. The structure and composition of the decision unit
that is charged with making war and peace decisions and the group dynamics within this unit affect the choices it makes. Appreciating these dynamics is
key to understanding, predicting, and improving national security and foreign
policy decisions.

6 Polythink in the Iranian Nuclear Dispute

Decisions of the U.S. and Israel

In the previous chapters, we demonstrated the ways in which Polythink can be detrimental to formulating cohesive, effective policies on critical issues of national security, such as entry to and exit from wars. This chapter expands on the range of national security decisions that can be affected by Polythink, examining its impact on diplomacy, strategy, and negotiations. Specifically, we will assess the Obama Administration's 2009 Iran Policy Review concerning the Iranian nuclear program and Israel's 2012 decision not to attack Iran's nuclear facilities.

We begin with the U.S. Administration's decision-making dynamic in addressing the Iranian threat during President Obama's first two years in office. This period was characterized by an early attempt to restart relations and engage in diplomacy, but ended with the Obama Administration passing the Comprehensive Iran Sanctions, Accountability, and Divestment Act in July 2010 through the UN Security Council—the most restrictive economic sanctions on the Iranian regime to date.[1] Why did the renewed push for negotiations at the outset of Obama's first term so quickly end in a 2009 decision to pursue a far-reaching, punitive sanctions policy at both the national and the international levels?

Essentially, despite Obama's campaign promise to reset relations with the Iranian leadership and "talk directly to Iran" (Obama 2007), his Administration quickly found itself plagued by many symptoms of Polythink that led to a least-common-denominator, path-dependent march toward sanctions.[2] What's more, the symptoms of Polythink present *within* the first Obama Administration with regard to Iran were compounded by Polythink at the *international* level as the major international players developed competing interpretations of the decision problem and dissenting prescriptions for how to collectively solve it. As one commentator put it, "Obama discovered during his first two years in office . . . [that] hoped-for partners often disagreed on *the nature of the problem, what constituted the proper solution and who should bear the burden of implementing it.* They had their own interests and priorities, and often they were not looking to Washington for direction" (Lindsay 2011, 765–766, emphasis added)—a key indication of Polythink. The crisis has demonstrated how Polythink can be particularly detrimental to situations of negotiation and mediation, delicate diplomatic processes that often require patience and political room to maneuver and compromise, both of which are deeply limited by the presence of Polythink.

In the second section of this chapter, we will analyze the decision-making processes that occurred in the Israeli government regarding the Iranian nuclear program in 2012 as the government weighed a military strike on Iran's nuclear facilities. Interestingly, we find that in the Israeli case the Polythink dynamic was triggered mainly by disagreement among three sub-decision-making groups: Israeli political leaders, the Israeli military establishment, and the U.S. Administration.

The Situation in Iran

Since the 1979 overthrow of the Shah in Iran, Iran's relationship with the West, and the U.S. in particular, had been fraught with conflict: "Administration tensions, varying levels of dysfunction and wider governmental conflict [all] affected policy formulation and execution by producing different agendas, and, occasionally, a range of different assessments of U.S. policy" (Murray 2010, 211). These characteristics are all hallmarks of the Polythink dynamic. In the post-9/11 years, tensions had increased. Iran's aggressive pursuit of nuclear technology under the leadership of President Ahmadinejad, and growing concern of the U.S. about the advent of radical political Islam and terrorism in the Middle East had driven this historically divisive relationship to new heights of antagonism and urgency.

Indeed, at that time, the common narrative of the American-Iranian relationship was that there had been "an exhaustion of diplomacy" that had repeatedly failed to make any progress, and therefore an Iranian nuclear capacity was potentially setting the stage for another nuclear standoff, reminiscent of the cold war. In 2006, for example, political scientist Efraim Inbar argued, "In all probability, the West has nothing to offer that can dissuade Iran from going nuclear, particularly since the nuclear program is viewed as the best insurance policy for the current leadership and is probably the single most popular policy associated with this regime" (93). A U.S. official in the executive branch echoed this sentiment, anonymously telling the *New York Times* in March 2006, "The reality is that most of us think the Iranians are probably going to get a weapon, or the technology to make one, sooner or later" (as quoted in Sagan 2006, 46). Some scholars even argued, at that time, that Iran's acquisition of nuclear capability would not be an altogether bad outcome, asserting that "it would probably be the best possible result: the one most likely to restore stability to the Middle East" because of the nuclear balancing it would achieve by making Iran feel more secure and therefore behave less volatile (Waltz 2012).

However, this position has been widely challenged, mainly because these "nuclear stability" narratives in many ways fail to account for the demonstrated power of forceful diplomacy (or military threats) to prevent aspiring nuclear powers from proceeding with their nuclear programs (Albright and Shire 2009). As political scientist Scott Sagan (2006) argued, "The lesson to be drawn from the history of nonproliferation is not that all states eyeing the bomb eventually get it but that nonproliferation efforts succeed when the United States and other global actors help satisfy whatever concerns drove a state to want nuclear weapons in the first place" (47). According to these analysts, Iran, in 2009, was not necessarily on some inevitable march toward nuclear proliferation. This position has, of course, been disputed by others who emphasize deterrence and the use of force. However, as we explain below, sub-optimal group decision making triggered by Polythink in the 2009 Obama Administration and the international community (specifically the P5+1 powers) contributed to the 2010 decision.

President Obama Takes Office—
The 2009 Iran Policy Review

In January 2009, President Obama came into office, stating that "our policy of issuing threats and relying on intermediaries to curb Iran's nuclear program, sponsorship of terrorism, and regional aggression is failing" (Obama 2007, 6). Jonathan Rynhold (2008) explains:

> One of the main themes of Obama's campaign was "change," including a rejection of George W. Bush's "ideological" approach to foreign policy, in favor of

"pragmatism." Whereas Bush viewed the world in terms of good and evil and asked countries to choose sides, Obama speaks in terms of bridging divides. In contrast to Bush's unilateralism, Obama has emphasized the importance of American leadership acting multilaterally, in concert with allies. The Bush Doctrine called for the preventive use of force, while Obama has stressed diplomatic engagement, viewing the use of force as a last resort. (1)

And indeed, the first measure of the Obama Administration was to begin a comprehensive review of the Iran policy and develop a strategy that could fulfill Obama's promise for diplomacy (Parsi 2012). This review examined all the elements of America's Iran policy and utilized the expertise of various organizations within the federal government, even recruiting outside experts to hear their opinions. This essentially provided the White House with an opportunity to demonstrate that "the Obama administration would listen to its friends and take their concerns into consideration, in contrast to the modus operandi of the Bush administration" (Parsi 2012, 44). Unfortunately, however, Obama's deliberative decision-making style often steered his decision unit into a Polythink dynamic that was exacerbated by the existing international Polythink on this issue.

Symptoms of Polythink in the Obama Administration's 2009 Iran Policy Review

The 2009 U.S. decision on Iran exhibited a number of Polythink symptoms: disagreements and dissent within the decision unit, lack of communication, confusion, limited review of alternatives, failure to reappraise previously rejected alternatives (at that time), selective use of information, framing, lowest-common-denominator decisions, and decision paralysis.

Polythink Symptom #1:
Intra-Group Conflict—Disagreement and Dissent

Like the U.S. Iran policy for decades before, in Obama's 2009 Iran Policy Review, there was no shortage of competing voices on his advisory team and within the larger national security community whether to use force, impose sanctions, or advance diplomacy. Some analysts argued that "a military strike intended to destroy Iran's nuclear program, if managed carefully, could spare the region and the world a very real threat and dramatically improve the long-term national security of the United States" (Kroenig 2012). Others claimed that "military action against Iran would be a profound strategic miscalculation" (Debs and Monteiro 2012) that would "not achieve the goal of eliminating or significantly delaying Iran's nuclear ambitions" and would only "drive underground a program that is already lacking in sufficient transparency" (Albright and Shire 2009, 5).[3] The powerful and conflicting voices within the U.S. Congress also seriously constrained Obama's maneuverability with regard to Iran. Indeed, for decades, "conflicting agendas" across the wider U.S. government had deeply affected policy as "a Congress with greater assets at its fingertips, wider oversight capacity, less party discipline and more exposure to lobby groups, frequently traduced presidents' policies" (Murray 2010, 212).

The debate over the use of diplomacy was also heated within Obama's Cabinet. Frequent "expressions of uncertainty—or outright opposition—toward the engagement strategy raised questions about . . . whether Obama had surrounded himself with advisers who did not share his foreign policy vision" (Parsi 2012, 61). The President's political advisors were often against his early diplomacy push, arguing that "opposing sanctions might have been good policy, but it was bad politics . . . It would cost the president tremendous political capital in Congress and could come back to haunt the administration in the midterm elections" (Parsi 2012, 110). In essence, there was deep contention over the question of "when to talk, with whom and about what" (Murray 2010, 217). For example, most in the State Department (such as Hillary Clinton, William Burns, and Jim Steinberg) opposed the Tehran Declaration (the diplomatic push led by Turkey and Brazil), while a smaller, minority faction led by Deputy Assistant Secretary of State John Limbert favored an exploration of the deal. His argument, however, "did not have any takers at the top" (Murray 2010, 195).

Moreover, the question of whether talks should be "incremental" or "substantive" also divided the decision unit (Murray 2010, 218). This disagreement among Obama's top advisors over his foreign policy proved detrimental to the engagement process. Indeed, "while Obama's extended hand to Iran had encountered outside opposition, the last thing the president could afford was opposition from his own immediate circle of advisers" (Parsi 2012, 62). Engagement had simply become too risky politically.

Unlike the military or diplomatic options, the preference for sanctions in Obama's Cabinet was relatively universal, despite the failure of previous efforts to effect much change in Iran's behavior. However, this widespread support for sanctions may have itself derived from the Polythink dynamic surrounding the other two options—in the absence of broad support for either a military option or direct diplomacy, sanctions seemed to be a satisficing middle-ground outcome.[4] As Sagan (2006) puts it, "As Washington learned with India and Pakistan in the 1980s and 1990s, sanctions only increase the costs of going nuclear; they do not reduce the ability of a determined government to get the bomb" (45).[5] Moreover, "the divergence between the terms of the UN sanctions and the harsher measures adopted by the U.S., Europe, and several other countries" was strong evidence of Polythink at the international level. These divergent sanctions policies "created an uneven playing field in Iran's energy sector that profoundly advantaged China, which may prove unsustainable over the long term" (Maloney 2011).

Polythink Symptom #2: Leaks and Fear of Leaks

In the 2009 Iran Policy Review, leaks of classified information were relatively limited, but still occured, due in part to the Polythink dynamic that characterized the decision unit. The reason was most likely because the President had publicly declared that the military option against Iran was still "on the table." The specifics of this military option would, for national security reasons, obviously need to be kept top secret. On the other hand, there was a real fear that Israel would become frustrated with the lack of action by the U.S. and would move closer to attacking Iran if it was leaked that the U.S. had definitively decided to refrain from using force. There had also been growing anxiety among U.S. allies in the Gulf (Saudi Arabia and other Gulf states) about U.S. overtures to Iran.

Though leaks were not rampant during the review process, there were nonetheless some leaks that had major effects on the formation of the U.S. Iran policy during this time. For instance, in one International Atomic Energy Agency (IAEA) report leaked to the New York Times in October 2009, IAEA inspectors concluded that Iran had acquired "sufficient information to be able to design and produce a workable" atomic bomb. This conclusion went far beyond the public position of the U.S. government at the time, which was that Iran had stopped work on a nuclear bomb in 2003 (Broad and Sanger 2009). U.S. allies such as Israel and the Gulf states pointed to the IAEA report as evidence of the ongoing military dimensions of Iran's nuclear program. Staffers within the Obama Administration have also leaked intelligence on Iran's nuclear program to the press. In one particularly famous incident, an Obama official approached *New York Times* journalist David Sanger at a G-20 Summit dinner and took him to view satellite images that confirmed the existence of a previously secret nuclear plant in Iran that the Iranians had kept hidden from IAEA inspectors (Gerstein and Gavin 2010; Sanger 2012). According to Sanger, this leak was meant to be used as "long-sought leverage against Tehran," so that the U.S. could demand that the country allow "highly intrusive international inspections" and "propel the confrontation with Tehran to a new and volatile pitch" (Broad and Sanger 2009).

However, leaks over the Iran Policy Review also originated from sources outside the White House. In 2009, excerpts of a secret three-page memorandum sent by Defense Secretary Robert Gates to White House officials leaked to the press. In this memorandum, Gates claimed that the White House did not have "an effective long-range policy for dealing with Iran's steady progress toward nuclear capability" (Sanger and Shanker 2010). The leaking of the memo's contents could be viewed as an attempt by the Pentagon to pressure the Obama Administration into pursuing (or at least more deeply considering) more-aggressive strategies for containing Iran's nuclear ambitions.

Polythink Symptom #3: Confusion and Lack of Communication

Confusion and lack of communication among the various bureaucracies involved in constructing foreign policy vis-à-vis Iran were rampant. The White House's waffling on how best to approach the Iran nuclear problem was a main source of confusion. In truth, the White House was "not unified in its position on this issue" and so was sending "mixed messages" to Congress throughout the first year of Obama's term (Parsi 2012, 109). As Murray (2010) demonstrates, "the fact that both [the U.S. and Iranian] governments spoke in manifold and contradictory voices only enhanced the potential for misunderstanding and deepened suspicions" (215). This confusion became particularly pronounced following the June 2009 elections in Iran, as the White House found itself caught off guard by the post-election protests and widespread accusations of election fraud. Thus, perhaps the most important part of the Obama Iran Policy Review was not the policy ultimately decided upon by the Administration but rather "what it kept ambiguous, unstated, or undecided" (Parsi 2012, 58) through its "ambiguous phrases about how close the United States was willing to allow Iran's program to proceed" (Sanger and Shanker 2010).[6]

Polythink Symptom #4: Limited Review of Policy Alternatives,
Objectives, Risks, and Contingencies

In early 2009, Secretary of Defense Robert Gates sent a secret cable to the Administration detailing "concerns in the Pentagon and the military that the White House did not have a well prepared series of alternatives in place in case all the diplomatic steps finally failed" (Sanger and Shaker 2010). This cable came despite the fact that in 2009 the Institute for Science and International Security (Albright and Shire 2009) released a "road map" of recommendations containing no fewer than *nine* policies that the Obama Administration could potentially utilize to restrain Iran's nuclear ambitions: increasing sanctions, holding direct talks, recommitting to an incentives package, seeking improved transparency from Iran, taking steps toward diplomatic relations, engaging Russia and China, supporting regional arms control and security arrangements, establishing regional constraints on nuclear energy, and opposing a military solution (Albright and Shire 2009). However, most of these suggestions were either ignored or implemented only briefly and halfheartedly by the Administration, an outcome that resulted from a host of practical and political reasons. However, Polythink—and the implicit desire to avoid it—surely played a role in this limited review of alternatives. Finding consensus on each of these policies individually within the national security apparatus was difficult. Reaching consensus on all of these strategies together would have appeared to be nearly impossible, with the potential to open a divisive policy debate.

Moreover, the discussion on U.S. policy toward Iran centered almost exclusively on its nuclear program. While some scholars felt that more soft-power issues should be included in the Iran policy and that even a new "Marshall Plan" for Iran should be developed—"the goal would be to more effectively contend with Iran's supply of ideological radicalism by attempting to mitigate popular demand for it"—these views were not widely shared (Sadjadpour and de Gramont 2011, 162). The negotiations thus took on a zero-sum quality. Any gain for the Iranians became an automatic loss for the Americans, making compromise solutions even more difficult to find. By narrowing the negotiations parameters and alternatives, the U.S. Administration developed a "singular focus on the nuclear issue . . . [and] turned the negotiations into single variable bargaining" reducing maneuverability and potential broad compromise solutions (Parsi 2012, 220).

This zero-sum quality of the negotiations was to some extent understandable; the Obama Administration sought to limit the negotiations to the issue they found most pressing—Iran's growing nuclear program. This strategy would deliberately limit the likelihood for Polythink, by tempering dissent from those in the Administration, Congress (and other governmental units) against the negotiations and reducing time-consuming debates within the Cabinet regarding the terms of any potential negotiation outcome.

Finally, even the fundamental goals and objectives of the U.S. vis-à-vis Iran were often unclear and scarcely reviewed. Was the ultimate goal the abolishment of the Iranian nuclear program? Or were there more moderate aims of a "freeze" or the admission of IAEA inspectors? Should the U.S. use force? If debate in the Obama Administration about *tactics* (diplomacy, sanctions, or military action) was this difficult, opening a debate on the *goals themselves* may well have led to even more paralysis within the decision unit. This type of discussion was conspicuously avoided. Fundamental questions such as "what end state in U.S.-Iran relations was Washington seeking, and what form would it have to take to be acceptable to both countries as well as to Washington's regional allies" never received a full airing in the Cabinet at that time (Parsi 2012, 59–60). Thus, Polythink—or the desire to avoid it—triggered a focus on short-term tactics, rather than long-term strategy and goals. This focus on satisficing short-term solutions is a key, recurring theme in Polythink groups and is particularly detrimental to the process of negotiation, which is a long-term, painstaking process fraught with setbacks.

Importantly, at that time this limited review of alternatives contributed to a "false narrative of exhausted diplomacy and painful but insufficient sanctions" (Parsi 2012, 229), which increased the relative attractiveness of two other policy positions: (a) the position that the only remaining option is a military strike on Iran's nuclear facilities; and (b) the position that Iran's possession of nuclear weapons is an approaching inevitability and so we should turn to focus on post-nuclear deterrence.

Polythink Symptom #5:
Failure to Reappraise Previously Rejected Alternatives

Deeply tied to the limited review of alternatives is the failure to reappraise any alternatives that have been previously rejected. Thus, Polythink triggers a double problem—various alternatives do not receive a full airing the first time they are brought up, and then once these alternatives are rejected, they tend not to be reconsidered later in the decision-making process, unless the decision unit is substantially changed, as was the case with Obama's second term administration. This is due to the desire to avoid reopening debate on a heretofore arduously decided issue. In the case of Iran, this process manifested itself in the constant shortchanging of the diplomatic option for the threat of military force against Iran's nuclear facilities.[7] Indeed, the option of military force had remained perennially "on the table," at least in rhetoric. Many scholars and pundits point to its continuous presence as a key reason for the West's slowing of Iran's nuclear efforts in 2009. Since one of the main reasons states seek nuclear weapons is to increase security and deter would-be attackers, some now view taking force off the table as a "necessary and acceptable price for the United States to pay to stop Tehran from getting the bomb" (Sagan 2006, 59). Advocates of this position argue that the U.S. should have instead "been open to re-examining proposed incentives with an eye to Iran's economic and security needs" (Albright and Shire 2009, 4).

However, while those in the U.S. who argued for an imminent attack on Iran's nuclear facilities were still small in number (see Kroenig 2012), many others wanted to see the credibility of this option *bolstered*, and few advocated its removal from the table, arguing that credible threats of force were critical to Iranian compliance. This debate on whether to rely on hard power or diplomacy is as much a reflection of the Polythink dynamic in the U.S. government as it is of tangible strategic calculations. In the words of Iran scholar Trita Parsi (2012),

> A mixture of political factors, management of relations with other permanent members of the council, and prestige made serious diplomacy a non-option by the time Washington had committed itself to the sanctions track. First, the political investment in the sanctions track was immense . . . Second, the heavy investment in the sanctions process helped to turn the matter into one of prestige . . . *Third, moving forward with the sanctions in a swift manner was necessary in order to sustain consensus among the P5 + 1* . . . Fourth, and perhaps most importantly, the Obama administration had simply run out of political space domestically to accept the Tehran Declaration. (207–209, emphasis added)

Thus, once diplomacy was "tried and failed," this narrative resulted in the "limiting of Washington's options on Iran to various forms of confrontation—that is, either continued sanctions and containment or military action" (Parsi 2012, preface). By 2013, the international picture and the decision makers involved (in both the U.S. and Iran), had changed significantly, with the West becoming more and more concerned by the instability caused by uprisings throughout the Arab world. This granted the Obama Administration additional flexibility to strike a deal with the Iranians, essentially mitigating, in Obama's view, concerns about Iran at a time when U.S. attention had shifted to new civil conflicts in Libya, Egypt, and Syria and the rising threat from ISIS.

Polythink Symptom #6:
Framing Effects and Selective Use of Information

U.S. reluctance to enter another regional conflagration in the Middle East has been a dominant theme of the Obama Administration since taking office. This disinclination, alongside the disagreement over which policy options to pursue in response to the Iranian problem, may have led the Obama Administration to frame the Iranian nuclear program in a skewed manner. The Israelis have often submitted intelligence reports with "worst-case scenarios" that encouraged a sense of urgency in the international community. The American intelligence services, on the other hand, typically offered a much longer time frame before Iran would get the bomb, and the "window of opportunity" to attack would close.[8] However, in keeping with Obama's tendency to request reams of information on pressing policy issues, selective information processing was, once again, less of a problem during the Iran Policy Review, despite the prevalence of Polythink in the decision-making unit.

Polythink Symptoms #7 and #8:
Lowest-Common-Denominator Decisions and Decision Paralysis

The Polythink surrounding the Iranian nuclear problem—at both the domestic and the international levels—led the Obama Administration, in 2009, to espouse a lowest common denominator strategy of adopting additional economic sanctions.[9] In the push to satisfy international allies (such as Israel, Saudi Arabia, and other Gulf states) and a hawkish Congress at home while also gaining the support of major international players (such as China and Russia) that were more sympathetic to Iran, the Obama Administration constantly balanced the competing interests and perspectives of key international players within the unique global decision-making unit of the United Nations.

Essentially, in containing Iran's nuclear ambitions in 2009, the Obama Administration faced a situation with few good options, and even fewer options for which consensus could be gained domestically and internationally. This may be an explanation for why "Cold War–style containment emerged as the default option for the United States; because it worked against the Soviet Union, many simply assume that it will work against Iran" (Adamsky 2011, 168). Just as in the case of the Iraq and Afghanistan troop drawdowns, a hybrid lowest-common-denominator option was selected—a "dual-track" strategy of "simultaneously offering Tehran engagement without preconditions while ratcheting up sanctions in case Iran did not yield to American demands" (Parsi 2012, 54–55).

The Polythink dynamic surrounding the Iranian nuclear issue has in many ways triggered a reliance on "old think" (Parsi 2012, 222) that stems directly from the disjointed nature of Polythink decision-making units. When a group is characterized by Polythink, the development of new policies, particularly bold or innovative ones, will be exponentially more difficult than continuing on an already existing policy path, due to disagreements within the decision-making group. This dynamic is clearly represented in the Iranian case during the first term of the Obama presidency. Resetting relations and engaging in direct diplomacy or using force represented bold and risky policy options that were not fully considered or implemented during the first term of the Obama Administration because the dissension within the Cabinet, the U.S. political system, and the UN made such a choice controversial. The same holds true for the reverse side of the coin—military action against Iran was not undertaken at the time because consensus was simply too difficult to obtain.[10]

What's more, planning new, farsighted, *long-term* policies in this situation can become very difficult. Diplomatic processes in particular can be painstakingly slow and experience frequent setbacks. Furthermore, if a decision-making unit is characterized by Polythink, each setback makes it increasingly difficult to sustain consensus unless there is a drastic change in the situation (as was the case in mid-2013). Wracked by Polythink, the first Obama Administration found it much easier to continue on the already existing sanctions path simply because it was the path of least resistance, though it may not have represented the most optimal strategy.

International Polythink on the Iranian Nuclear Program

Thus far, we have examined the role of Polythink within the Obama Administration. However, the Iranian nuclear program has truly been an issue of *international* concern. Thus, exploring the ways in which different states attempted to work together to address this problem is of chief importance. The West, led by the U.S., wanted to stop Iran from developing nuclear weapons. In fact, Bowen and Kidd (2004) claimed that "in contrast to the recent controversies over Iraq, America and Europe share the same concerns about Iran's ambitions and both want to prevent Tehran from acquiring nuclear weapons . . . There is also agreement that a concerted and unified international effort is required to address the Iranian challenge . . . In this respect there is a consensus" (267).

Despite this veneer of agreement, however, in 2009, a Polythink environment influenced deliberations of the international players involved in this global issue on how best to achieve this goal.

Polythink at the international level is perhaps best characterized by the group dynamics of the UN Security Council on the Iranian issue at the time. The U.S., France, and the UK were vocal in their opposition to the Iranian nuclear program. These veto-wielding countries, plus Germany, advocated strong sanctions against Iran. At the same time, Russia and China opposed military intervention in Iran but were slow to adopt tough sanctions. In the words of former Israeli Defense Minister Moshe Arens (2013), "Who invented this forum of nations, *a group with differing interests in Iran*, and who deemed them the ones to confront Tehran?" (emphasis added).

These differing interests are driven primarily by security and economic concerns. Israel is a nation repeatedly and directly threatened by the Iranian leadership. The U.S., also concerned about Iran's nuclear program, the potential for a nuclear arms race in the Middle East, and proliferation of nuclear material in the region, but weary of new Middle Eastern wars, takes a more cautious perspective than Israel, yet nevertheless often also takes a somewhat alarmist stance in its intelligence reports (Hymans 2013). In contrast, states like China and Russia, with large economic and strategic interests in Iran, do not express as much concern about Iran's continued nuclear development, despite evidence of Iranian intransigence such as its kicking out nuclear inspectors and making inflammatory speeches against Israel. China, for example, is a big consumer of oil from Iran, and its trade with Iran is in the tens of billions of dollars (Downs and Maloney 2011).

Russia also has economic and financial interests in Iran—having supplied the Iranians with much of their nuclear technology and material (Shleifer and Treisman 2011). By supporting and protecting the Iranian program from a military attack by the U.S. and its allies, both China and Russia also challenge the U.S. and the West geostrategically in one of the most important places in the world—the Middle East. In fact, the China-Iran nexus potentially threatens U.S. hegemony in the region (Donig and Sussman 2011).[11]

This case represents a prime example of the framing effects of Polythink— in an attempt to sway other members of the international decision unit, advocates of one policy direction typically use framing tactics to advance their position and counter-framing to downplay the position of their rivals.

Consequences

This multi-tiered Polythink dynamic—within Obama's Cabinet, throughout the broader U.S. government, and within the international community—ultimately led to adoption of the lowest-common-denominator policy decision of international sanctions early on in Obama's first term in office. In 2009, it meant that "despite extensive outreach, clear strategic benefits, and an unprecedented opportunity for engagement, Obama found himself stuck in the same confrontational relationship with Iran as that of other American presidents before him" (Parsi 2012, 210). Obama was limited by the hostility of Congress to negotiations and by the skepticism and dissent within his own Cabinet in the first term of his presidency about the diplomatic process. The U.S. and its allies were further constrained by the opposition of some members of the Security Council to take military action against Iran on the one hand and, on the other, stymied by allies such as Israel and the Gulf states from taking a more conciliatory approach. These divergent viewpoints and dissent effectively froze, delayed, or diminished diplomatic resolutions and military actions to stop the Iranian nuclear project during the first term of the Obama Administration. Paradoxically, this situation developed despite the fact that there was nearly unanimous consensus against the prospect of an Iranian nuclear state. Interestingly, during the second term of the Obama Presidency, when the "team of rivals" advising the President was redesigned as a team that would be more likely to follow the White House's lead (Ignatius 2013b), the Administration was able to pursue the policy of negotiation with Iran, within the framework of the P5+1 Geneva talks. This shift was, of course, spurred primarily by simultaneous changes in the Iranian leadership and composition of the Iranian decision unit with the election of Rouhani that drastically altered the Iranian negotiation position as well.

In the next section of this chapter, we will turn to examine a Polythink decision-making dynamic outside of the U.S. context—the Israeli government's debate over the Iranian threat.

The 2012 Debate in Israel on a Preemptive Strike

The 2012 debate on whether Israel should attack Iran's nuclear facilities is an important example of Polythink at the highest echelon of political and military decision making. It also is a prime example of the ways in which subgroups can contribute to the Polythink syndrome.

The Israeli debate on the Iran nuclear program positioned current and former top brass of the Israeli defense establishment against the Israeli Prime

Minister (Benjamin Netanyahu) and then–Defense Minister (Ehud Barak). In addition, the Obama Administration opposed an attack on Iran. Indeed, "while Washington and Jerusalem [had] the same stated goal of stopping Iran from developing a nuclear weapon, there [was] a growing chasm over what might be the acceptable terms for an agreement" (Rudoren and Sanger 2013). The three subgroups—the Israeli political leadership, its military leaders, and the U.S. Administration—and the dynamic among them affected and shaped the Israeli decision on Iran.

Among top defense establishment officials opposing the attack were the former head of the Israeli Mossad, the former head of the Israel Security Agency, and both the former and then serving Chiefs of Staff of the Israel Defense Forces (IDF), as well as the serving Israeli President, Shimon Peres. All vocally campaigned against such an attack. In contrast, Netanyahu and Barak vehemently supported an attack to stop the Iranian nuclear program. The end result of this debate was that Israel did not attack Iran in 2012.

Subgroups in the Iran Decision

There were three key subgroups in the debate on whether Israel should attack in Iran: the Israeli political establishment (primarily Prime Minister Netanyahu and Defense Minister Barak), leaders of the Israeli military establishment, and members of the U.S. Administration. Evaluated separately, each group exhibited strong tendencies of Groupthink, but for different reasons, as will be explained below. Due to disagreements among these subgroups, the *overall* dynamic on Iran corresponds to Polythink.

Whereas the U.S. view was largely leader-driven and, as such, a by-product of the position of the President and his advisors on Iran before the U.S. election, the opposition of IDF and other Israeli military agencies to the attack was based on their (shared) professional opinion that an effective plan was not in the works and that Israel was vulnerable to counter rockets and missile attacks from surrounding states and terrorist groups. It is known that the Chief of Staff of the IDF had not advocated, at that time (2012), an attack on Iran. The former Chiefs of Mossad and the Israel Security Agency both warned of the overall threat to Israel from such an attack and the uncertainies surrounding it ultimate success. Others (e.g., President Shimon Peres) argued that since the Iranian nuclear program is a global problem and not only an Israeli one, Israel should not take the lead on Iran and instead should let the U.S. deal with the Iranian threat to its interests and security.

There is no doubt that the 2012 debate in Israel about Iran exhibited patterns of Polythink. Interestingly, however, in both the civilian and the military echelons, each of the subgroups involved exhibited clear patterns of Groupthink. The chiefs of the Israeli intelligence agencies (such as Mossad and Shabac) and leaders of the Israeli Defense Forces (IDF) largely share the same political socialization patterns and worldviews. They thus espoused similar positions on Iran. They urged the political echelon not to disobey the U.S. position and argued that there was still time to see how the sanctions would work.

On the other hand, in the subgroup that consisted of top politicians, Barak and Netanyahu shared the same opinion, advocating an attack on Iran's nuclear facilities. However, this view was in the minority in the Israeli security cabinet. Netanyahu and Barak had both served previously as Prime Ministers and had served in the same elite commando military unit, Sayeret Matkal. They saw eye to eye on issues regarding Iran (at that time), and, apparently, their assessment of costs and benefits led them to a different conclusion than that of the defense establishment. The political subgroup ultimately makes the final decision on such issues in Israel. However, given the opposition to an attack from the other two subgroups, they decided in 2012 to refrain from an attack.

The boundaries between military and civilian sectors in Israel are ambiguous, vague, and permeable. Top military officers such as Barak, Mofaz, and Yaalon (and previously Moshe Dayan and Yitzhak Rabin, to name a few) advanced to serve as Prime Ministers or held important cabinet positions. Few Defense Ministers (Arens, Peretz) came from the civilian world. The military has been very influential in making national security decisions in Israel. Without the support of the defense establishment, it was virtually impossible for the Prime Minister to order an attack.

Indeed, it might be that any other combination of two out of the three subgroups (for example, the political echelon plus the military or the political plus the American government) would have led to a different outcome. In other words, had two of these three groups (one of which must have been the political echelon) supported an attack, Israel most likely would have chosen to do so. However, because the political echelon in fact found itself in the minority, with both the other groups against its position, it was reluctant to order such an attack. Specifically, at the time of the 2012 debate, members of the Israeli military establishment and most of the security cabinet opposed the attack. The U.S. Administration has also opposed the attack. In other words, two of the important gatekeepers opposed the attack, while one (the top political leadership, in this case the Prime Minister and the Defense Minister) favored an attack. In an article in the *New York Times*, Graham Allison and Shai Feldman (2012) even argued that the defense establishments in the U.S. and Israel have worked together to successfully block an attack by Israel on Iran's nuclear facilities.

Symptoms of Polythink in the Israeli Decision on Iran

Most of the symptoms of Polythink were present in this case, as follows.

Polythink Symptom #1:
Intragroup Conflict—Disagreement and Dissent

The editor of the Israeli newspaper *Haaretz*, Aluf Benn (2012), claimed that the public and media debate in Israel on whether to attack Iran was a sign of "democracy in its best." On the one hand, Netanyahu and Barak tried to persuade the Israeli public and the world that such an attack was necessary. On the other hand, opponents of an attack were using all channels at their disposal: the Knesset, the media, demonstrations, petitions, etc. (Benn 2012). The newspaper *Israel Hayom*, which is close to the Netanyahu regime, was cheering for an attack, whereas its rival *Yedioth Aharonoth* "highlighted the reasons why not to attack Iran, the U.S. pressure not to attack and the exposure of the home front to an attack" (Benn 2012).

Whereas all players in the vocal debate in Israel on what to do about Iran were against Iran acquiring nuclear weapons, there were numerous accusations by opponents of an attack claiming that supporters of such a move were irresponsible, even motivated by messianic considerations. This may have been part of their quest to influence policymakers and public opinion in both Israel and the U.S..

The military establishment highlighted the opposition to an attack by the IDF Chief of Staff, top generals, and the chiefs of the various intelligence agencies, if the attack could not be coordinated a priori with the U.S. (Benn 2012). The IDF even disclosed its forecast of the number of Israeli civilian casualties that would result from a counterattack by Iran and its regional allies, and the length of time such an attack would delay the Iranian nuclear program, without the military censor intervening in the process. Prime Minister Netanyahu, on the other hand, called the Iranian threat a "second Holocaust." The debate set a new standard in Israel for discussion on the merits and costs of war initiation. For example, sources reportedly close to Prime Minister Netanyahu accused Israeli President Shimon Peres of stepping beyond his authority in lobbying the public against such an attack, with a Knesset member of the ruling Likud Party, Miri Regev, going so far as to describe Peres as "coward and hesitant"[12] (Bender 2012). Others have accused key opponents of the "attack Iran now" doctrine of being politically motivated and/or thirsty for media attention.

In an interview published in *Yedioth Aharonoth* (a leading Israeli newspaper) less than three weeks before Israel's 2013 national elections (Moreh 2013), Yuval Diskin, former head of Israel's Internal Security Service accused Prime Minister Netanyahu of "placing his 'personal, opportunistic and current interests' over those of the state when making crucial policy decisions regarding the Iranian nuclear program" (Rudoren 2013). Diskin, who had resigned eighteen months earlier as head of the internal security service, said other prime ministers he had worked closely with—both conservative and liberal—"came from this place in which the interests of the state stand above all else" (as quoted by Rudoren 2013). Diskin made headlines in April 2012 with these public comments accusing Netanyahu and Barak of "misleading the public" regarding the likely effectiveness of an attack on Iranian nuclear facilities.

The Prime Minister's office issued a statement calling Diskin's accusations "groundless" and "motivated by his personal frustration" that Netanyahu did not choose him to head the Mossad, Israel's international intelligence agency. The statement also said the critique was being "recycled for political reasons" (Rudoren 2013). Barak's office called the claims "astonishing, both in content and in their timing," given that elections were scheduled for January 22 (Rudoren 2013). In the interview in *Yedioth Aharonoth*, Diskin recounts a particular high-level meeting on Iran in which Netanyahu, Barak, and Avigdor Lieberman, then the Foreign Minister, smoked cigars during the discussion. Diskin describes the scene as "a kind of total disregard for all the people" (as quoted by Rudoren 2013). However, despite these protestations, many viewed Netanyahu's speech at the fall 2012 UN General Assembly meeting on the timeline for an Israeli strike on Iranian nuclear facilities as a direct result of "a long-building revolt by Israel's professional security establishment against the very idea of an early military attack, particularly one without the approval of the United States" (Allison and Feldman 2012). There is no question that intragroup conflict, which is a key symptom of Polythink, was at work in this case.

Essentially, advocates of an Israeli attack claimed that a nuclear Iran would: (a) be a direct threat to Israel, as Iran's leaders have repeatedly claimed that they will wipe Israel off the map and have publicly denied the Holocaust; (b) lead to a nuclear arms race in an already unstable and dangerous Middle East; (c) grant terrorist organizations a nuclear umbrella under which to pursue attacks on Israel; (d) greatly increase the likelihood of a transfer of nuclear material to terrorist organizations and other countries, resulting in nuclear proliferation; and (e) lead to Iranian control of the Gulf and oil supplies to the West, Japan, and other countries.[13]

Opponents of an Israeli attack on Iran had a different opinion. They claimed vocally that although they also did not want to see Iran going nuclear, a military attack on Iran was a much more complicated and risky decision with short-term and long-term negative consequences and implications. Specifically, opponents of an attack claimed the following:

A. Israel could not fully destroy Iran's nuclear program. Israel could only delay it. Moreover, the day after an attack on Iran's nuclear facilities, there would be a need to continue the military, economic, and political pressure on Iran so that it would not go back and continue to develop the nuclear program. Opponents claimed that Israel would not be able to carry out an attack by itself, without the help of the U.S. Moreover, without the U.S., there would be little chance that such pressure would yield long-term productive results. China and Russia would be likely to assist Iran in rebuilding its nuclear program if and when Israel or the U.S. attacked them. Therefore, attack opponents claimed that Israel should coordinate its activities with the U.S. Administration and not act alone.

B. Another argument advanced by those against an attack was that Israel could not fully defend its home front against retaliatory attack. Though in recent years, the Israel Defense Forces has greatly improved Israel's defensive capabilities with the development of the Iron Dome, various Arrow systems, and other defensive systems, such systems did not provide a bulletproof response to an attack of multiple warheads coming from Hezbollah, Hamas, and Iran. Just as one cannot play soccer with only great offense but no defense, Israel could not attack Iran with the Israeli home front exposed and vulnerable to a missile attack, including one on the densely populated center of the country. Others, such as then–Defense Minister Barak, estimated Israeli casualties from counterattacks as "only" 500 (Oren 2011).

C. Opponents also argued that an attack on Iran would only encourage the religious clerks in Iran to develop a nuclear bomb with greater motivation and intensity. Their argument was that an Israeli attack would give the Iranians legitimacy to build nuclear bombs. Indeed, although Iran has been racing to build the bomb, as of spring 2013 the Iranian leadership had also been careful not to cross the critical red line in developing its program, especially vis-à-vis the U.S. Going nuclear would be crossing that line, and the Iranians know it. Attack skeptics argued that an attack by Israel on Iran could actually motivate the Iranian leadership to build nuclear weapons with greater determination. They also believed that it could accelerate the transfer of centrifuges to less-vulnerable facilities and areas. An attack on Iran, according to this view, would only strengthen the leadership in Iran and help them escape the blame for the very difficult economic situation they faced as a result of the tough international economic sanctions.

D. A fourth argument advanced was that an Israeli attack on Iran could lead to an Iranian counterattack on U.S. forces in the Gulf and in the region and to the loss of life of American soldiers. This is despite the fact that the Iranians appeared unlikely to drag the U.S. into a war that they would not otherwise want.

E. Moreover, attack opponents argued that an attack on Israel would have significant economic and financial consequences. It would raise oil prices to a high level, and the blame would be on Israel. The tough economic situation in the U.S. and Europe (at that time) would worsen due to such an attack.

F. A final argument was that the U.S. Administration has committed publicly to preventing Iran from going nuclear. They believed that Israel should not ignore Secretary of State John Kerry and Secretary of Defense Chuck Hagel's declaration that Iran will not become nuclear. The opponents of an Israeli attack thus said that Israel should let the U.S. lead the campaign against Iran. Only if such efforts fail should Israel attack. Their argument was that if the U.S. showed greater determination against Iran, this might lead to a peaceful solution. In contrast, those who support an attack claimed that they do not know for sure if Iranian leaders would operate in a rational way as manifested in the MAD strategy of the Cold War or if they are willing to launch a "suicidal" nuclear attack on Israel. According to proponents of an attack, Israel would be better off eliminating or at least delaying the Iranian nuclear threat due to this risk.

Polythink Symptom #2: Use of Leaks

A result of the intra-group and inter-group rivalry and dissent has also been a tremendous series of leaks. Indeed, such leaks of national security and war plans have no precedent in Israel's history. These leaks included the potential attacker's route, tactics, and technologies. This was the case both for opponents and for supporters of the attack option, as predicted by the Polythink syndrome. This led chief *Haaretz* military correspondent Amos Harel to title his 2012 report in *Haaretz*, "The Less Likelihood for an Attack, the Greater the Intensity of Leaks." As the debate intensified, the frequency of leaks intensified as well, culminating in a story on Israeli TV detailing what actually happened in the most crucial meeting when the Israeli decision on whether to attack Iran had taken place.

Polythink Symptom #3: Confusion and Lack of Communication

The vocal public debate on whether to attack Iran was the first time there had been such a debate in Israel on whether to launch war (Benn 2012) with the pros and cons of each alternative discussed and evaluated again and again by politicians, journalists, and analysts. Benn (2012) points out that such a debate did not occur prior to the 1956 war, the 1982 First Lebanon War, the 2006 war with Hezbollah, or when Israel destroyed the nuclear reactor in Iraq. He claims that such debates and criticism are more typical of situations where there was lack of success or a blunder after the action had taken place, not before.

The lack of consensus, the presence of frequent leaks, and the opposing views of Israeli leaders on the Iran decision have all confused the IDF, the public, and the international community. Though the Israeli public did not take warnings of an imminent Israeli attack on Iranian nuclear weapons seriously in the spring of 2012, by the summer of 2012 the situation had changed. Prime Minister Netanyahu declared that the costs of allowing Iran to possess nuclear weapons were much higher than would be the damage to Israel stemming from an attack on Iran's nuclear facilities. Defense Minister Barak added that the danger stemming from Iran's being nuclear was bigger than the corresponding danger that Israel faced even prior to the Six-Day War of 1967. At the same time, U.S. officials and members of the Israeli military establishment have repeatedly presented the view that there is still time to stop the Iranian nuclear program. These contradictory views on Iran have clearly confused the public.

Polythink Symptom #4: Limited Review of Alternatives

Multiple alternatives have been evaluated by the top Israeli political and military echelon in a very comprehensive assessment of policy options. The Polythink symptom of limited review of potential courses of action has not characterized the Iran decision, perhaps because of the Iranian nuclear program's critical importance and centrality to the State of Israel.

Another factor influencing the very thorough review of alternatives on Iran by the political-military echelon has been the investigation by the Winograd Commission of the decision-making process of the Israeli government leading to the Second Lebanon War and the lack of careful and comprehensive review of alternatives during the 2006 war. The commission's recommendation that a comprehensive, systematic analysis of alternative courses of action be part of the process leading to any national security decision of this caliber has definitely had an effect on the policymakers in Israel who dealt with the Iran decision.

Polythink Symptom #5:
Failure to Reappraise Previously Rejected Alternatives

Interestingly, the Polythink symptom of failure to reappraise previously rejected alternatives was also not present in the discussion on what to do about the Iranian nuclear program. Thus, the option of attacking Iran's nuclear facilities—which was not adopted—has emerged, been assessed, and even reemerged and been reassessed at later stages of the crisis. The comprehensive review of alternatives, including their costs and benefits, led to the careful assessment of each policy option. Parsi (2012, 30) enumerates five major pillars describing Israel's approach to Iran: "(1) Efforts to isolate Iran internationally; (2) Covert actions; (3) Counter-proliferation actions to prevent Iranian access to know-how and technology; (4) Efforts to secure international sanctions; and (5) Promotion of regime change through support for political and ethnic groups opposing the Iranian regime." However, the decision to attack Iran has been on the table throughout the crisis.

Polythink Symptom #6:
Framing Effects and Selective Use of Information

Proponents of the attack Iran policy framed the Iranian nuclear program as an existential threat to the survival of the State of Israel, portraying it as another Holocaust. Others countered that such words and threats do not portray a realistic threat, are counterproductive, and were damaging Israel's position in the international community. Both supporters and opponents of use of force against Iran used framing and counter-framing tactics, openly and vocally.

In contrast, in an appearance in the "Iran—The Day After" simulation conducted at the Lauder School of Government at IDC-Herzliya in 2011, both member of Knesset (Israeli Parliament) Tzipi Livni, who at the time was Head of the Opposition, and Lieutenant General (Res.) Dan Haloutz, who had been the Chief of Staff of the IDF, warned that portraying a nuclear Iran as the pre-cursor to a second Holocaust was counterproductive and misleading. Professor Yehezkel Dror has also pointed out that such a portrayal was not beneficial for the public and cautioned against the use of such language and threats.

In addition, counter-framing efforts came from top U.S. officials and ad-visors. For example, Chairman of the Joint Chiefs of Staff General Martin Dempsey argued that Israel did not have the military capabilities to destroy the Iranian nuclear sites and therefore a strike would not be in its interest. Dempsey argued that Israel could only postpone Iran's nuclear development in the short run. Others in the Administration made sure that the Israeli public knew that the U.S. opposed such an attack.

Prime Minister Netanyahu framed the opponents of an attack on Iran as soft, uninformed, and damaging, arguing that they engage in cheap talk (Benn 2012). Some of the Prime Minister's supporters even portrayed President Peres, who had advocated restraint, in these terms. According to Benn, opposition to Peres was not just a media manipulation, but also a political tactic. If op-ponents of an attack would be portrayed as anarchists and as Oslo support-ers, members of the security cabinet and the government would have difficulty voting against an attack, since Likud cabinet members would not want to be viewed as partnering with the left in Israel. According to Benn (2012), the fram-ing attacks and counter-framing by Netanyahu supporters as a left-right issue actually helped the Prime Minister in potential government votes on the issue.

Polythink Symptoms #7 and #8:
Decision Paralysis and Lowest-Common-Denominator Decision Making

The 2012 debate on whether to attack Iran resulted in a deadlock and decision paralysis. It is safe to say that if the U.S. would have supported an Israeli attack on Iran in the fall of 2012, it is very likely that Prime Minister Netanyahu and his security cabinet would have ordered such an attack. But the U.S. Admin-istration's vocal opposition to an attack, coupled with the opposition of very important members of the Israeli military establishment made it difficult, if not impossible, for Prime Minister Netanyahu to order an attack. Despite the Prime Minister's desire to stop the Iranian nuclear program by attacking Iran's nuclear facilities, he was in the minority vis-à-vis his top military advisors and his security cabinet. He also may have come to the conclusion that pursuing an attack option would severely damage the U.S.-Israel strategic relationship. Thus, the result of the disagreement between these subgroups was a decision paralysis, one of the key hallmarks of Polythink.

7 Recent Challenges

The Syria Debate, the Israeli-Palestinian Peace Negotiations, and the ISIS Decision

Groupthink or Polythink?
Examining Obama's Second-Term Foreign Policy Team

Beginning in President Obama's second term, his foreign policy team had become concentrated more in the White House than in his Cabinet, populated by Obama "loyalists" whose worldviews were closer to that of the President himself (Ignatius 2013b). As political analyst and editor of *Foreign Policy* magazine David Rothkopf explained, in Obama's second term in office, "the true believers—as one first-termer called McDonough, Rice, Deputy National Security Advisor Ben Rhodes, and U.N. Ambassador Samantha Power, among others—have moved up and gained power, . . . many of the powerful people who often offset their views—such as Hillary Clinton, . . . Leon Panetta, and former Defense Secretary Robert Gates—have moved on" (Rothkopf 2014b).[1] In other words, in Obama's second term, foreign policy decisions have funneled more often to the President through key loyalists and gatekeepers such as Chief of Staff Denis McDonough, Senior Advisor Valerie Jarrett, and National Security Advisor Susan Rice.[2]

Key other players in the Obama Administration, such as Secretary of Defense Chuck Hagel, lacked the proximity to the President that White House staffers possessed, and therefore frequently found themselves precluded from the informal, chance meetings between Obama and his White House staffers that proved instrumental in forming Obama's policy positions (Ignatius 2013b; Landler 2014b).

The President's second-term decision-unit dynamic thus became much more conducive to Groupthink, in contrast to the Polythink dynamic that had plagued Obama's first-term "team of rivals." This second-term dynamic has not escaped the view of media pundits and Democratic Party strategists, many of whom began clamoring for a shake-up of Obama's advisory team for his final two years in office (Ignatius 2014; Landler 2014b). One strategist (Sink 2014) went so far as to argue that "the general consensus [was] that the president is surrounded by people who do him more harm than good because they are more focused on pleasing him than they are challenging him or proposing a different course." Indeed, the November 2014 announcement of Secretary Hagel's "resignation" was interpreted by many as a sign of the growing insularity of the Obama Administration, whereby Obama "has neutered his cabinet secretaries on foreign policy, forcing all decisions through an intelligent but too-small team in the White House" (Fisher 2014). With the departure of Hagel, a key contrarian voice on ISIS (and Syria) in the Administration was gone. Other analysts, however, have staunchly disagreed with this characterization, claiming that Obama has been unfairly critiqued and that he could "propose what the country wants, succeed at it and still get hammered as a failure" (Ignatius 2013a).

However, as in the earlier Afghanistan and Iraq Policy Reviews, those at the Department of Defense and top brass of the military leadership such as Chairman of the Joint Chiefs of Staff General Martin Dempsey continued to represent a contrarian perspective within the Obama Administration, well into its second term. This was demonstrated by the frequent leaks and "off-message" comments reportedly made by these individuals (Whitlock 2014b). Indeed, the DoD and the military's frequent questioning of the President's policies often led to a decision-making dynamic whereby the *overall team* responsible for national security and foreign policy execution (including the military) was characterized by Polythink, even though Obama's *core* foreign policy team was characterized by Groupthink. This meant that, once again, President Obama appeared to have taken what some critics have called "a Goldilocks approach"—whereby he knows military intervention is required to address a dangerous and growing threat but is unwilling to devote *enough* military strength to achieve his stated goals (Logiurato 2014).[3] In many ways, these compromises resulted from the constraints the President faced within his own Administration, from other lawmakers on the Hill, and from American public opinion (Krugman 2014). However, the change in the decision-unit dynamic from President Obama's first term to his second also illustrates the critical importance of a leader's role in designing his or her decision unit and influencing whether this unit will have a Groupthink, Con-Div, or Polythink dynamic.

In the next sections, we provide three examples of the application of Polythink to recent decisions and events in the international arena. Specifically, we analyze three recent developments in the Middle East: the tragedy in Syria and the UN and U.S. 2012 debate about sanctions against the Assad regime, the 2013–14 peace negotiations between Israelis and Palestinians known as the "Kerry Peace Process," and the summer 2014 U.S. decision to attack ISIS targets in Iraq and Syria.[4]

The United Nations Decision
Not to Sanction Syria in Summer 2012

In the summer of 2012, the question of what to do about the civil war in Syria reached a tragic level when close to 19,000 people, including many women and children, lost their lives (*The Guardian* 2012).[5] There was little doubt that the situation in Syria was approaching the magnitude of a humanitarian catastrophe. However, the United Nations Security Council was wracked by Polythink, as the divergent interests and preferences of its veto-wielding permanent members rendered the council paralyzed and unable to act (Manor 2014). Indeed, while the Security Council has been "dismissed as toothless before, precisely over the right of its five permanent members to block any measure with a veto, the paralysis over Syria marked a new level of dysfunction, experts say, and has given a fillip to those who call for a fundamental shake-up of the Council's composition and rules of engagement" (Sengupta 2014). In part, this dysfunction at the international level was a product of the Polythink dynamic that existed *within* many of the permanent members' home countries as well.

Polythink in the U.S.:
Use of Force, Sanctions, or Support for the Rebels?

The Polythink dynamic was particularly prominent in the U.S. In the face of a growing humanitarian crisis in Syria, the U.S. expressed support for the rebel fighters and decried what it deemed to be excessive violence on the part of the Syrian government in attempting to suppress the rebellion. As the conflict deepened in the summer of 2012, Obama's advisors debated two potential courses of action—whether to arm and train the Syrian rebels or to stay out of the conflict and focus on pressuring Assad through the use of economic sanctions.[6] The dividing line in this Polythink debate was essentially Obama and his closest aides (such as Chief of Staff Denis McDonough) on one side, and Obama's Cabinet officials (such as Clinton, Panetta, and Petraeus[7]) plus the military leadership on the other. Indeed, "throughout 2012, as signs mounted that militants in Syria were growing stronger, the debate in the White House followed a pattern. In meeting after meeting, as officials from agencies outside the executive residence advocated arming pro-Western rebels or other forms of action, President Barack Obama's closest White House aides bluntly delivered the president's verdict: no" (Rohde and Strobel, 2014). Furthermore, the close political aides on Obama's side of the debate often framed discussion in terms of the costs of the U.S. intervening in Syria, while downplaying the many risks associated with *not* intervening—demonstrating the role of framing in Polythink debates. These advisors emphasized the large number of weapons already on the ground in Syria and the risk that they might end up in the hands of extremists (Entous 2013). Others, such as CIA Director General Petraeus, framed the decision in terms of loss—the potential loss of the hard-fought gains of the Iraq War as extremists from the Syria conflict spilled over into neighboring countries (Entous 2013).

In many ways, the discussion in the Obama Administration about what to do about Syria became a debate between bad options, with Hillary Clinton calling the Syria War a "wicked problem" where "none of the approaches offered much hope of success" (Clinton 2014, 460). Secretary Clinton describes the options facing the U.S. as essentially: "Do nothing, and a humanitarian disaster envelops the region. Intervene militarily, and risk opening Pandora's Box and wading into another quagmire, like Iraq. Send aid to the rebels, and watch it end up in the hands of extremists. Continue with diplomacy, and run headfirst into a Russian veto" (Clinton 2014, 460). Alongside Secretary of Defense Leon Panetta and CIA Chief General David Petraeus, Clinton became one of the advisors recommending the option of arming the Syrian rebels. She explains, "The risks of both action and inaction were high. Both choices would bring unintended consequences. The President's inclination was to stay the present course and not take the significant further step of arming rebels . . . In this case, my position didn't prevail" (Clinton 2014, 464). Obama chose to continue attempting the path of sanctions.[8]

Thus, after much internal Polythink debate and dissent, the U.S. became one of the strongest supporters on the Security Council for sanctions against the Syrian regime (Manor 2014). Representing the U.S. position at the UN, Secretary of State Hillary Clinton argued that "for a new agreement actually to be implemented, it would need a UN Security Council resolution 'imposing real and immediate consequences for non-compliance'" (Clinton 2014, 457). However, U.S. efforts in this regard were repeatedly stymied by an obstinate Russia. The U.S. was also wary of becoming mired in another sectarian Middle East conflict after its experience in Afghanistan and Iraq. Concerns about Iran were also central.[9] The role of Russia in Syria was likewise a primary source of unease for the U.S., which was wary of engaging in a proxy war in Syria against Russian interests. This placed the Obama Administration in a difficult dilemma, particularly as the civilian death toll in Syria rose higher and higher.

Russia: Staunch Support for Assad

Indeed, among the major powers and veto holders on the UN Security Council, Russia was the chief proponent of non-intervention in Syria (Manor 2014). President Putin and Foreign Minister Lavrov were determined not to let the Assad regime fall, fearing that their key ally in the Middle East, perhaps the only major one in this important part of the world, would fall into U.S.-backed Sunni hands. That outcome would have considerably weakened Russia's position in the region—something Putin would not allow. Russia also had a significant economic investment in the Syrian regime, as Syria has constituted a major weapons client for the Russians. Some analysts have estimated the value of Russian arms sales to Syria to be at least $4 billion, with other Russian business investments amounting to nearly $20 billion (CNN Wire Staff 2012). Finally, the Russians remained wary of setting a precedent of international intervention in states' internal conflicts, given their own often heavy-handed approach to Chechen rebels.

Statements made by Russia's UN Ambassador, Vitaly Churkin, echoed these concerns: "The council cannot impose the parameters for an internal political settlement ... We are convinced that at a time of intense internal political crisis, the role of the international community should not be one of exacerbating conflict, nor meddling by use of economic sanctions or military force" (CNN Wire Staff 2012; Manor 2014). Moreover, Russia backed up its opposition to intervention with the shipment of military equipment to Syria and the visit of Russian warships to the Syrian naval port of Latakia (CBS/AP 2012). Following the liberal interpretation by NATO of the UN Security Council resolution to establish a no-fly zone over Libya, these Russian concerns were exacerbated and cited as a primary reason for Russia's reluctance to include any threat-of-force language in subsequent resolutions.

President Obama understood rather early in the process that it was risky to mess with the Russians in Syria.[10] He realized that the Assad regime was important for the Russians, and that, even during the conflict, Russia had sent naval warships to Syria and continued to arm the regime. In contrast to most of his military advisors, President Obama decided to refrain from military intervention in Syria, even in the face of very tragic circumstances. At the time of this writing, Russia had vetoed three UN Security Council resolutions on Syria in three years. As of the summer of 2013, the U.S. had essentially been deterred by Putin's early moves in Syria, even after Assad crossed President Obama's "red line" and used chemical weapons against his citizens.[11]

France: Support for Military Intervention against Assad

Of the UN Security Council permanent members, France has, in contrast, consistently held the most hawkish perspective with regard to the Syrian leadership (BBC News 2014; Manor 2014). It was France that spearheaded the proposal of the July 19, 2012, UN Security Council resolution that, operating under Chapter VII of the UN charter (the chapter that enables sanctions and possible military force against countries in violation of UNSC resolutions), proclaimed that if Syria failed to comply with international demands to end violence, the UNSC "shall impose immediately measures under Article 41 of the UN Charter"— essentially opening the door to possible foreign military intervention in Syria. Analysts have speculated that France's hawkish stance stemmed from a historic sense of responsibility toward Syria because of its past involvement in the region. Illustrating this, Denis Bauchard, an analyst at the French Institute of International Relations, said, "Since the very beginning of the crackdown by Bashar Assad following the uprising in Deraa in March 2011, France has kept the same stance: At the time, the foreign minister Alain Juppe condemned the crackdown as an 'act of barbarism' and a 'crime against humanity' . . . When Hollande took office in 2012, he continued in the same direction" (quoted in Barzegar 2013).[12]

The United Kingdom:
Arm the Rebels, No Foreign Military Operation

The United Kingdom has largely stood alongside France in pressing for more urgent action as a Syrian humanitarian crisis loomed (Manor 2014). However, its war-weary public has kept the UK and France from fully embracing the potential for military action.[14] On August 10, 2012, following the Russia/China veto of the UNSC resolution, the UK announced that it would begin to formally support opposition groups, "expanding support to the Syrian people and the Syrian political opposition, with an extra £5 million in non-lethal practical assistance." The UK has been one of the U.S. staunchest allies in the international arena. By usually acting in tandem with Washington, "Britain has been able to wield a greater influence in global politics than it would on its own" (New York Times Editorial Board 2013). However, on the issue of Syria, divergent public opinions in the two countries may yet mean that Syria could become one of the rare instances where "one nation acted with military force without the other" (New York Times Editorial Board 2013).

China: The Principle of Non-intervention

China has also supported non-intervention in Syria (Manor 2014). China aimed at primarily limiting U.S. hegemony in the Middle East, partly because of its own economic interests there, and partly because of its desire to prevent Western intervention in domestic affairs. In May 2011, Chinese Foreign Ministry spokesperson Jiang Yu was quoted as saying:

> China believes that when it comes to properly handling the current Syrian situation, it is the correct direction and major approach to resolve the internal differences through political dialogue and maintain its national stability as well as the overall stability and security of the Middle East. The future of Syria should be independently decided by the Syrian people themselves free from external interference. We hope the international community continues to play a constructive role in this regard.[14]

This stance has caused China to repeatedly veto UN Security Council resolutions against the Syrian regime. In June 2012, China released a joint statement with Russia emphasizing that "both sides firmly oppose any attempt to resolve the Syrian crisis through foreign military intervention as well as promoting forced 'regime change' at the U.N. Security Council and other venues" (as quoted by FlorCruz 2012). Indeed, both nations have done all they could to prevent the U.S. and its Western allies from intervening in Syria (Manor 2014).

Deadlock in the Security Council

Thus, the 2012 UN Security Council deliberations on the July 19 sanctions resolution were wracked by Polythink at the international level. This Polythink process was essentially characterized by several UN veto-holding permanent members advocating non-intervention (China and Russia) as opposed to the

U.S. and its allies (France and the UK), who sought more forceful measures. However, even these countries were extremely war-weary, wanting to put an end to the tragedy but unwilling to enter another war alone, following the involvement of the U.S. and some of its Western allies in Afghanistan and Iraq. The rise of ISIS and other extremist factions fighting in Syria and Iraq in 2013 and 2014 has challenged the decisions by world powers not to act early on to address the growing chaos in Syria.

The Kerry Israeli-Palestinian Peace Initiative of 2013–14

At the end of 2013, U.S. Secretary of State John Kerry was able to bring both the Israelis and the Palestinians to the negotiation table, breaking, temporarily, the long-term stalemate between the two parties. Kerry also designated a nine-month time frame for setting the framework for negotiating peace in the Middle East. Bringing the two sides to the table was in and of itself particularly challenging and clearly an accomplishment. To achieve the renewal of negotiations, "Kerry combined his own relentless and willfulness (six trips to the region in four months) with something else: Neither Abbas nor Netanyahu want[ed] to say no to America's top diplomat and take the blame for the collapse of the process" (Miller 2013).

To break the deadlock that prevented both the Israelis and the Palestinians from discussing peace in the Middle East for several years, Secretary Kerry used some imaginative, out-of-the-box tactics. Specifically, he did not a priori demand from the Israelis and Palestinians concessions on key items that were essentially non-negotiable for each of them (such as a settlement freeze for Israel and concessions on the right of return for Palestinians). Instead, Kerry attempted to reinvigorate the negotiation process by introducing a new dimension/idea into the negotiation: the release of Palestinian terrorists from Israeli jails. This move did not present a non-compensatory political problem (i.e., did not constitute a non-negotiable issue) for any partner in the Israeli coalition and was also a highly beneficial move domestically for Palestinian President Mahmoud Abbas (Abu-Mazen).

However, as the negotiations proceeded, Polythink among members of the Israeli governmental coalition partners and among the Palestinian factions was evident and contributed to the collapse of the talks. On the Israeli side, Cabinet members representing different political parties expressed competing, even opposing views. For example, the Bait Ha'Yehudi (Jewish Home)

Party (Cabinet members Naftali Bennett and Uri Ariel) opposed any concessions to the Palestinians: they publicly lobbied against a Palestinian state, an
Israeli withdrawal from the West Bank, a freeze on Israeli settlement construction in the Territories and East Jerusalem, or any release of Israel-Arab terrorists. Most members of the Likud-Beitenu Party also opposed the release of
Israeli-Arab terrorists and a freeze on settlement construction. In contrast, the
centrist party Yesh Atid, led by Finance Minister Yair Lapid and the more center-left Hatnua Party led by Justice Minister Tzipi Livni, supported the peace
process and the two-state solution to the conflict. Reflecting these divergent
policy preferences and the Polythink dynamic within the Israeli government,
declarations of new housing projects and settlements in East Jerusalem and
the West Bank were frequently made by Housing Secretary Ariel, but then
condemned by Minister Livni—both serving in the coalition of Prime Minister Netanyahu.

   Similarly, on the Palestinian side, the announcement of reconciliation between Hamas and Fatah just days before the end of the negotiation process on
April 29, 2014 (plus the Palestinian turning to the UN for recognition) essentially ended the 2013–14 round of Israeli-Palestinian negotiations that Kerry had
initiated.[15] Typical of Polythink, it created a situation whereby the Palestinian
negotiating partner spoke in two voices about the future of the negotiations,
with Fatah essentially calling for a two-state solution and Hamas continuing its
hawkish campaign claiming it will never recognize the Jewish state and calling
for its destruction.

   Polythink, on both sides, with spoilers of peace interfering in the negotiations, was the main reason for the collapse of the Kerry-brokered talks. The
stalemate in the negotiations between the Israelis and the Palestinians over the
conditions for peace in the Middle East has been partially the result of both
sides exhibiting signs of this dynamic. On the Palestinian side, it is a natural
by-product of the differences in views and policies between Hamas and Fatah.
On the Israeli side, given the nature and structure of the Israeli governmental
coalition of 2013–14, in which the Right, Center, and Center-Left parties were
all represented in the Netanyahu coalition, there is certainly evidence of Polythink affecting the peace process as well.

   Interestingly, the Polythink dynamic has also continued to characterize
both the Israeli security cabinet and political decision making on the Palestinian side. A prime example of Polythink was the Israeli security cabinet's
decision-making process during the summer 2014 military campaign vis-à-

vis Hamas in Gaza, known as Protective Edge. Throughout this campaign, members of the decision unit (i.e. the Israeli security cabinet) not only disagreed on the goals of the military campaign and specific tactics, but also often turned to the media to leak their competing views on what should be done at the tactical level. Accusations of deliberate leaks of cabinet members' positions, and framing and counter-framing of such views were also noticeable. Similarly, on the Palestinian side, the Palestinian Authority, led by Abu Mazen, repeatedly called for a cease-fire in Gaza during the summer 2014 campaign, whereas the Hamas leadership, Khaled Meshal and Ismail Haniyeh, refused to accept these calls and ordered the continued launching of rockets at Israeli cities.

The Fall 2014 Decision to Attack the Islamic State (ISIS)

In late summer 2014, the U.S. found itself facing a new crisis as a radical terror organization calling itself "the Islamic State"[16] began to take over large swaths of Iraqi territory. The U.S. had to decide whether and how to stop ISIS.

Officially created in 2006 as an offshoot of al-Qaeda in Iraq, ISIS capitalized on the power vacuum created by the Syrian and Iraqi wars, merging with extremist Sunni rebel groups in Syria in late 2013. By the summer of 2014, ISIS had captured key cities across Iraq—Mosul and Tikrit. They had also made inroads into Syrian coastal cities such as Al-Qaim and key Syrian oil fields such as al-Omar (which produces almost 75,000 barrels of oil daily). Moreover, as ISIS expanded its control to large areas of Iraqi Kurdistan, Iraq's Christian and Yazidi populations were facing imminent genocide.

After months of ISIS advances, the U.S. carried out air strikes against ISIS battalions in that region on August 8, 2014, ostensibly to prevent potential genocide of the non-Muslim populations there. Weeks later, ISIS publicly executed two U.S. journalists, James Foley and Steven Sotloff, who had been captured while they were covering the Syrian War, and a British aid worker, David Haines. The U.S. was now faced with a critical policy decision: should it further its military intervention in Iraq (and even in Syria) to try and halt ISIS' relentless march across the region less than three years after the U.S. had finally succeeded in withdrawing troops from that same country? An analysis of the decision-making process, including intragroup dynamics at the highest level, behind the U.S. policy choice to once again engage in military action in a region it had so recently extricated itself from, is critical to understanding this 180-degree policy turn.

Strategy vs. Tactics

With the rise of ISIS, the U.S. Administration once again confronted a dilemma on how to respond to events in a turbulent and volatile Middle East. The Administration was caught by surprise by the swift rise—and spread—of the ISIS organization. In a September 28, 2014 interview on *60 Minutes*, President Obama stated that "intelligence agencies had underestimated the peril posed by the Islamic State," quoting James R. Clapper, Jr., the Director of National Intelligence, and claiming that analysts "did not foresee the stunning success of Islamic State forces or the catastrophic collapse of the Iraqi Army" (Baker and Schmitt 2014).[17] Did the decision follow the pattern of Groupthink, Polythink, or Con-Div? Interestingly, in the U.S. decision on ISIS, as in many decisions on the use of force, we need to distinguish between the strategic decision and tactical decisions.

On August 28, 2014, just days before the public announcement of increased U.S. military engagement against ISIS, President Obama, in what many consider an unfortunate verbal gaffe, stated, "We don't have a strategy yet" on dealing with ISIS (Ackerman 2014). However, the Administration's strategy was exactly what many in Washington (and the American people) wanted to know—"and not just regarding ISIS in Syria, but so many of the other troubled countries in the region where Western intervention has such a chequered history" (Roberts 2014). CNN military analyst Colonel Rick Francona believed that the Administration was "looking at [ISIS strikes] very tactically and I don't know if they have a strategic vision here" (Diamond 2014). Republican critics of the Obama Administration such as Senator John McCain and House Speaker John Boehner were also quick to blame Obama's "policy of half measures" and "ongoing absence of strategy," respectively (Diamond 2014). Others—such as former Secretary of Defense Leon Panetta—have pointed to the growth of ISIS as a direct result of Obama's withdrawal from Iraq and non-interventionist stance on Syria, claiming that the power vacuum in both of these countries enabled ISIS to capitalize on disorder and grow in strength (Panetta, 2014b).

By September 10, President Obama authorized "a major expansion of the military campaign against rampaging Sunni militants in the Middle East, including American airstrikes in Syria and the deployment of 475 more military advisers to Iraq" (Landler 2014a). This strategy aimed to degrade and ultimately destroy ISIS through an American-led international coalition that would use military air power to attack ISIS positions. In addition, the U.S. would advise and train Iraqi military troops in their efforts to attack ISIS on the ground and work with the Iraqi government to attempt to stabilize it, bringing discontented Iraqi Sunnis back into the fold and away from ISIS influence. In Syria, "opposition forces to be recruited by the U.S. military and its coalition partners will be trained to defend territory, rather than to seize it back from the Islamic State" (Chandrasekaran 2014). This is because "officials did not believe the newly assembled units would be capable of capturing key towns from militants without the help of forward-deployed U.S. combat teams, which President Obama has so far ruled out" (Chandrasekaran 2014).

At the overall strategic level, there was near unanimous support in the U.S. government for the idea of eliminating ISIS—a key symptom of Groupthink. Moreover, outside the decision unit, Congressional and public support for this decision was high. "In Washington, Republican and Democratic leaders in Congress offered bipartisan support, broadly reflecting the changed mood of their constituents" since ISIS' march across the Levant (*The Economist* 2014). Indeed, even the House of Representatives—generally no ally of President Obama— agreed on September 11, a day after the President's announcement of his intention to "degrade and ultimately destroy ISIS," to summon its members back to the Capitol in order to pass legislation that would authorize the American military to train Syrian rebels to fight ISIS militants (Weisman 2014). This strong support in the House for the President's plan may have been buffeted by the public support for military action against ISIS: In a Pew poll conducted in the days following Obama's televised address, 64 percent of Republicans and 60 percent of Democrats approved of the President's overall plan (Pew Research Center 2014). The strategic discussions in both the Administration and Congress concerning the need to combat ISIS thus represented more of a Groupthink dynamic.

Interestingly, however, there was widespread debate in the Administration about how best to accomplish this task, which tactics were feasible, and which should be "off the table"—essentially reflecting a *Polythink* dynamic at the tactical decision-making level. Indeed, part of the reason for this may be that Polythink is more likely at the implementation phase of policy because of the many micro-decisions that must then be made. Even after the formal announcement of U.S. air strikes on September 10, 2014, the extent of U.S. military activity was unclear. President Obama and his close advisors stated that there would be no boots on the ground in Iraq and Syria. However, the Pentagon and the U.S. Armed Forces were less inclined to reject this policy option outright. The heated debate within Obama's national security team in the summer of 2014 likewise "failed to produce a consensus battle plan" (Rogin and Lake 2014). Moreover, there was also confusion over the scope of American goals and tactics in the campaign against ISIS—"whether military might [was] being deployed to bring greater stability to the Middle East or whether the mission [was] much narrower: a counter-terrorist operation to neutralize threats at a distance, and thus protect Americans at home" (*The Economist* 2014).

The tension between two competing U.S. goals made it difficult to formulate a clear tactical vision—"On the one hand, Obama really did have long term ambitions to destroy ISIS . . . On the other hand, he recognized that this is impossible in the near term, and that the best the U.S. could do was lay the groundwork for ISIS' eventual collapse" (Beauchamp 2014). Indeed, the extent to which different members of Obama's advisory team agreed with the idea that (1) an America-centric, military engagement could be effective against ISIS, or (2) U.S. "political pressure on Baghdad, and support for some kind of political resolution in Syria" were needed "for Iraqis and Syrians to do what's ultimately necessary to [militarily] root out ISIS on their own" (Beauchamp 2014) fundamentally framed the tactical debate within the Obama Administration.

For example, on September 10, 2014, in the official announcement of an expanded military operation against ISIS, Obama "likened this campaign to the selective airstrikes that the United States has carried out for years against suspected terrorists in Yemen and Somalia, few of which have been made public" (Landler 2014a). This characterization implied that the scope and goals of the U.S. operation would be relatively limited, in terms of both military force and time commitment. In other words, military action against ISIS was not a war (and, importantly, as such, did not require Congressional approval). Instead, the main emphasis would be on strengthening the capacity of the Iraqis (and, ideally, the pro-Western Syrian rebels) to tackle ISIS themselves. Two weeks later, in a *60 Minutes* interview, Obama frankly stated, "We cannot do this for them," emphasizing instead the importance of long-term political solutions (Kroft 2014). The President explained, "If we make the mistake of simply sending U.S. troops back in, we can maintain peace for a while, but unless there is a change in how not just Iraq, but countries like Syria and some of the other countries in the region think about what political accommodation means, think about what tolerance means," the peace will not last (Kroft 2014).

Less than a week after Obama's formal announcement of air strikes, however, the Chairman of the Joint Chiefs of Staff, General Martin Dempsey, testified before the Senate Armed Services Committee, stating: "If we reach the point where I believe our advisers should accompany Iraqi troops on attacks against specific ISIL targets, I'll recommend that to the president," signaling a departure from the President's position on no ground troops and his emphasis on the importance of Iraqi ownership of the military campaign. Thus, public disagreements regarding the scope of the military operation and its tactics had become evident shortly after the decision to attack ISIS has been made. This "off-message" comment may also have been caused by the fact that the White House failed to confer with the military before the public announcement of the ISIS policy on September 10. As documented by *Politico*:

> The White House failed to consult with the Pentagon . . . on the timing or de-tails of the announcement . . . the Pentagon was surprised by the president's timing, according to a senior defense official. "We didn't know it was going to be in the speech," he said, referring to Obama's Sept. 10 address to the nation. [Moreover] the White House neglected to give Pentagon lawyers a chance to revise and approve the proposed legislative language before it went to the Hill, which is considered standard practice. (Hirsh 2014)

But this was not the end of the confusion and dissent between the White House and the military and defense leadership. On October 30, 2014, it emerged that Secretary of Defense Chuck Hagel had written a sharply criti-cal memo to National Security Advisor Susan Rice, challenging the U.S. Syria policy, related to the lack of a concrete plan concerning the Assad regime and the fact that "US airstrikes in Syria against ISIS can benefit the Assad regime which also opposes ISIS" (Starr 2014a). Indeed, less than one month after this memo, Secretary of Defense Chuck Hagel resigned in what was widely seen as a sign of the rift between Hagel and Obama's other advisors at the National Security Council on how best to combat ISIS and other new threats in the region (Starr 2014b).

This dissent by the defense establishment—a common occurrence dur-ing the Obama Presidency—meant that "even as the administration received congressional backing for its strategy . . . a series of military leaders criticized the president's approach against the Islamic State militant group" (Whitlock 2014b). For example, retired Marine General James Mattis (who served under Obama until 2013) argued before the House Intelligence Committee that Obama was tying the hands of the military, that "half-hearted or tentative ef-forts, or airstrikes alone, can backfire on us and actually strengthen our foes' credibility," and that "we may not wish to reassure our enemies in advance that they will not see American boots on the ground" (Whitlock 2014b). The White

House and the Pentagon were largely in agreement on the basic outlines of a strategy to fight ISIS, "one that center[ed] on arming and training proxy forces, including Syrian rebels, Kurdish fighters and the Iraqi army, backed by U.S. and allied air power" (Whitlock 2014b). However, the Pentagon preferred to leave the option of ground troops open. Obama, who considered ending the War in Iraq one of his crowning achievements, was loath to put boots back on the ground there (Whitlock 2014b).

In many ways, thinking strategically instead of tactically is "one of the biggest problems in Washington"—according to retired General James Jones, "You'd wake up and there would be a new crisis and you'd be scrambling to deal with them" (Rohde and Strobel 2014). However, some cite Obama's reliance on cautious close aides as opposed to more hawkish cabinet members as another key reason for his lack of a strategic plan as the ISIS crisis grew larger over the summer of 2014:

> Both [McDonough and Rice] were skeptical about being drawn into the civil war in Syria . . . Their caution, one official said, tends to reinforce Mr. Obama's own instincts. That may have been a factor in the slow American response to the threat of the Islamic State. [Subsequently] Mr. McDonough . . . [has] acknowledged that the administration misjudged the robustness of the Iraqi Army. (Landler 2014b)

This reluctance to involve the U.S. in the region once more meant that the Obama Administration found itself playing catch-up in August 2014, as it struggled to formulate a coherent strategy to address the growing threat posed by the Islamic State. Recognizing rising discontent with his middle-ground approach, President Obama ordered a review of U.S. strategy on ISIS and Syria in mid-November 2014. This review has been interpreted by some as "a tacit admission that the initial strategy of trying to confront ISIS first in Iraq and then take the group's fighters on in Syria, without also focusing on the removal of al-Assad, was a miscalculation" (Labott, Acosta, and Bentz 2014).

As we have shown, the ISIS decision featured an interesting group decision-unit dynamic in which there was widespread agreement on one component of the decision—to degrade and destroy ISIS—but extensive disagreement on another component—the question of *how* to achieve that objective tactically. With regard to the differences in tactics, they reflected an ad-hoc policy as there was no solicitation of input by the Administration from various organizations and no balanced evaluation of alternatives, which would have characterized

Con-Div. This demonstrates a pattern we have seen in many U.S. decisions on military intervention whereby the overall goal or *strategy* is initially agreed upon, but the *tactics* to achieve these goals are widely debated—representing a more Polythink-oriented syndrome. This pattern also characterized some key U.S. decisions on exiting wars (Afghanistan, Iraq).

Conclusion

The three cases analyzed in this chapter further illustrate the broad applicability of Polythink and its relevance to U.S. and UN decisions (i.e., with multiple players), to negotiation processes (decisions in strategic interaction), and to tactical versus strategic decisions (as in the ISIS decision). Furthermore, the multiple cases analyzed in the book as a whole show the prevailing presence of Groupthink and Polythink in U.S. governmental decision-making circles.

8 The Global Nature of Polythink
and Its Productive Potential

In previous chapters we showed that Polythink is applicable to group decision-making dynamics on national security and foreign policy of the U.S. government, the United Nations Security Council, and other governments and organizations. Analysis of key policy decisions has demonstrated that the Polythink dynamic can lead to sub-optimal decisions or even to decision paralysis. However, Polythink, Con-Div, and Groupthink are also applicable to myriad other realms where groups are involved: business decisions, research and development (R&D) decisions, marketing and sales decisions, production chain decisions, finance and budgeting decisions, domestic policymaking, voluntary and not-for-profit decisions, and small-group decisions in individuals' daily lives.

Polythink in Business and Industry
Polythink exists widely in business and the corporate world. For example, many sales teams exhibit some of the symptoms of Polythink, such as internal disagreements, intragroup competition, and inability to speak with one voice. These symptoms can negatively affect performance of such teams and the bottom line of corporations. Marketing teams can benefit from plurality of opinions in groups, if managed correctly, although marketing groups that exhibit destructive Polythink and cannot think out of the box are likely to end with poor results.

Tactics to transform Destructive Polythink into Productive Polythink may lead to better outcomes, but such success often depends on the leader's style, charisma, vision, and the special circumstances of the group. Consider, for example, the effects of Polythink, Groupthink, and Con-Div on budgetary decisions in business and industry, nonprofit organizations, and at the local, state, or federal level. It is clear that in government, such small-group dynamics affect the ultimate choice and allocation and distribution of resources, for example, to national security versus social welfare programs—what is known as the "guns" versus "butter" dilemma. As group processes, Polythink, Con-Div, and Groupthink naturally affect virtually every decision that involve more than a single decision maker. These group dynamics have broad applicability worldwide, far beyond the U.S.

Future Applications of Polythink

Polythink may be applied to any international situation involving groups, including environmental decisions; foreign economic, trade, and financial decisions; e-commerce and stock purchase decisions; armament and disarmament decisions; and decisions on crisis management, conflict resolution, and negotiations. In some situations, Polythink may even help predict the outcome of decisions. Essentially, all governmental decisions in democracies and in some authoritarian regimes are influenced by the structure of the group making the decision and the Polythink-Groupthink-Con-Div dynamic, among other factors. Moreover, in hierarchical organizations such as the Armed Forces, we are less likely to encounter Polythink than in less-hierarchical units. In intelligence units and organizations, it is important to "engineer" Productive Polythink, including using the strategy of devil's advocate and challenges to the dominant view and position. In other fields, such as medicine, group decision making is also likely to be affected by group dynamics such as Groupthink, Con-Div, or Polythink. Future applications of Polythink can be in the fields of robotics, artificial intelligence, and space and cyber technology decisions. Group dynamics can even be automated (computerized), mapped and programmed as a multi-player dynamic, containing disagreement within the decision unit.

Productive Polythink:
How Can Leaders Benefit from a Plurality of Opinions?

"It is a Washington truism that every White House likes Cabinet consensus and hates dissent" (Ignatius 2013b). Despite this, dissent in any group, and especially in Washington, is common. Can Polythink lead to high-quality decisions?

Can a "clever" choice architecture that is built around Polythink lead to good decisions? How can an executive or leader turn Polythink into an asset rather than a liability? How do Polythink, Con-Div, and Groupthink affect the quality of decision making? Under what conditions of Polythink can the quality of decision making actually improve?

As we demonstrated in this book, some of the potential consequences of Polythink are paralysis in decision making, sub-optimal decisions, and inaction. Important public policy plans and promising projects may be blocked and not implemented due to Polythink. Consequently, it is counterintuitive to expect high-quality choices from groups characterized by the Polythink syndrome. Can Polythink ever be beneficial to decision makers? If yes, how?

The existence of Polythink symptoms in groups typically means conflict, confusion, leaks, biased information processing, framing and counter-framing, and sub-optimal, lowest-common-denominator decisions. Turning Polythink into an asset in decision making is, therefore, challenging, as one needs to overcome its negative symptoms and consequences.

The Good News

In Chapter 2 we showed that Polythink actually reduces information processing biases, and other motivated and unmotivated biases in group decision making. For example, Polythink reduces the likelihood (although not completely eliminating it) of a group leader being susceptible to a wishful-thinking bias, to the plunging-in bias, the lock-in bias, the ignoring-critical-information bias, and even the poliheuristic bias. Polythink may lead to broader vision as a result of the plurality of group members' opinions. Polythink is thus less likely to lead to the "narrowing of vision" syndrome that often characterizes Groupthink. A diversity of opinions in a group is likely to prevent, or at least weaken, such biases and errors in decision making. This can be effective, however, only if the leader of the group is attentive to the plurality of members' opinions, refrains from blocking off conflicting information, and turns Polythink into an asset rather than a liability. Otherwise, the group and its leader are likely to be trapped or become susceptible to biases that too often lead to sub-optimal decisions.

Quality decisions can be reached even when Polythink exists among group members, but such an outcome typically needs to be "engineered." This is because Polythink is inherently tied to the composition, structure, and dynamic of the decision-making unit, as we have shown in our analysis of decisions on

9/11, Afghanistan, Iraq, Iran, Syria, and ISIS. Furthermore, the group dynamic also typically influences the decision outcome.

We suggest five ways that a leader can turn a Polythink process into a quality decision, and provide some examples to illustrate how this was accomplished in the past by U.S. presidents.

Remedies to Polythink

Leaders of groups characterized by Polythink can leverage a plurality of opinions in order to achieve high-quality decisions in several different ways:

1. design a balanced decision unit

2. leverage Polythink for brainstorming

3. use Polythink as a divide-and-conquer tactic

4. use Polythink to subdivide major policy issues into smaller, more-manageable decision problems

5. use decision support systems and other analytic techniques for objective, Polythink-free decision making.

Design a Balanced Decision Unit

The key to overcoming Polythink and Groupthink lies in the concept of Decision Unit Architecture (or "Engineering"). Decisions are shaped and influenced by the composition of the Decision Unit (DU) (Russett, Starr, and Kinsella 2006). Therefore, executives in business, politics, domestic policymaking, foreign policy, national security and other domains need to carefully compose the decision unit in advisory groups, to ensure optimal decisions. Other things being equal, a quality process is likely to lead to better decisions than a non-systematic, intuitive, unstructured process.

Plenty of historical evidence exists that shows that poor decision-making processes lead to poor decisions. However, there are also numerous historical and contemporary examples and case studies that show that this is not always the case and that a more organized decision-making process does not always lead to a "better" decision.

The classic example that "good," systematic processes do not necessarily lead to good decisions is, of course, the series of decisions made by former Secretary of Defense Robert McNamara and the Pentagon during the Vietnam War. Many have claimed that McNamara's decisions before, during, and toward the end of the war were made carefully and systematically. Yet those decisions led to a foreign policy fiasco: American and Vietnamese casualties were heavy and the end result, the Vietnam syndrome, was a failure, from the point of view of the U.S. Administration, the public, and the key U.S. ally in the conflict—the South Vietnamese government.

The first recommendation we offer for Productive Polythink, to enhance the likelihood of successful group decisions, is to focus on the Decision Unit Architecture when initially forming advisory units. Policymakers should try to think of the policies and solutions they want to achieve and implement down the road, and design their decision making group to meet these goals. This should be done preferably in a Con-Div, balanced decision mode, where there can be "healthy" divergent perspectives among group members but a general consensus on policy goals and the overall direction of the group. Indeed, functional decision units are often governed by group decision rules (Hermann 2001). If such groups do not use rules such as deciding by majority, or by unanimity, or simply by following the leader, or using another decision rule, chaos can ensue. The more established these rules are, the more stable the decision-making process is.

One intriguing example of Decision Unit Engineering can be found in the deliberate construction of President Obama's second-term team. One of the characteristics of this advisory group is that its worldview, including group members' conception and view of the limitations of American military power, is more unified than that of the more diverse "team of rivals" group of Obama's first term. Many analysts viewed this as a deliberate move by the President, a result of the discord he faced in his first term in office among his cabinet members. It was predicted early on in his second term that the new team would have a top-down consensus (Ignatius 2013). And indeed, in the second term, the Obama Administration has often been critiqued as veering further and further into the realm of Groupthink, as Obama loyalists gained influence in the decision-making unit. Obviously, the composition and dynamic of advisory groups to the President are likely to have implications for U.S. foreign policy and national security decisions.[1]

Leverage Polythink for Brainstorming
Polythink can be very beneficial to decision makers in brainstorming. One of the key principles of brainstorming is taking advantage of diverse viewpoints to consider a wide array of options before arriving at a good choice. A wide

variety of opinions gives the decision maker the ability to deliberate the pros and cons of various policy options. Thus, Polythink can prove useful and constructive in brainstorming. For example, leaders of a group and other key decision makers can ask group members for their advice and input, and use this information to brainstorm about potential consequences and optimal courses of action, plans, and solutions. More analytic and technology-savvy leaders can even ask advisors to construct decision matrices (with or without the use of the Decision Board software), and then compare these individual matrices to identify similarities and differences, with the ultimate goal of creating a comprehensive decision matrix that represents such diverse views. When Polythink is evident, the group leader can also subdivide the group into small groups that can each present its own view. These will be discussed by various subgroups and elevated to the next level of discussion. The subgroups' recommendations and conclusions can then be consolidated into a group decision. In practice, establishing joint policy *desks* for sharing and analyzing information originating from a variety of sources (e.g., various intelligence agencies) provides another way to reduce Polythink in a group.

Use Polythink as a Divide-and-Conquer Tactic[2]

In some situations when Polythink is evident in a group, leaders can actually exploit the Polythink dynamic for their benefit. For instance, it might be useful for leaders if the opinions of group members in an advisory group are diverse, as the leader might have more flexibility of choice among those opinions. This is because there are supporters in the group for the various different policies they propose (Janice Stein, personal communication 2012). In other words, Polythink divisions among group members can paradoxically provide leaders with more flexibility than the homogeneous Groupthink view—for example, if the group promotes an opinion that contradicts the view of its leader. In the effort to rescue the U.S. hostages from Iran, for example, President Carter made the decision to pursue the military option while keeping Secretary of State Cyrus Vance, who opposed the mission, out of the loop. The President relied on the advice of others in the advisory unit.

In the early stages of the Geneva negotiations of the P5+1 with Iran in November 2014 regarding its nuclear program, plurality of opinions and disagreement were apparent. This kind of dissent can paradoxically legitimize the ultimate decision, as the public sees that even conflicting and challenging opinions were taken into account in making the decision.

Use Polythink to Subdivide Major Policy Issues into Smaller, More-Manageable Decision Problems

Group leaders can leverage the expertise and knowledge of group members in different policy areas and domains to help shape their own decisions. For example, President Bush leveraged the expertise of various think tanks in Washington, D.C., and experts in Congress in his decision on the Surge in Iraq. While the President did not end up taking the advice of all groups and think tanks, he benefited from their diverse viewpoints. There are at least two reasons it is important for the chief executive to listen to diverse opinions: (a) the leader/politician can claim credit for instituting and embracing a bipartisan approach, which is rare in Washington; and (b) by consulting groups that do not even agree with the policy, the chief executive can often not only co-opt opponents but also provide political and institutional cover, spread the responsibility, and reduce the amount of criticism if things do not go well or as planned. This was apparently the case with Truman's decision to execute the nuclear attacks on Japan during World War II (Pinter 2013).

In the summer of 2013, President Obama turned to Congress to seek authorization for the use of force against the Assad regime in Syria. Since the public and Congress did not support such an act, the President decided to reach an agreement with Russia's Putin on the removal of chemical weapons from Syria. Polythink thus played a role.

The concept of "honest broker" is relevant here as well. The role of the honest broker has often been described as "a contributor to effective presidential decision making" (Burke 2005, 554). One key illustration of this idea is the role of Condoleezza Rice during the presidency of George W. Bush. As a National Security Advisor, Rice assumed the role of a broker during three crucial decision-making processes in George W. Bush's first term: (1) discussions during the aftermath of the September 11 attacks that ultimately led to the decision to go to war in Afghanistan; (2) talks that led up to the war in Iraq; and (3) deliberations concerning the stabilization and reconstruction of postwar Iraq (Burke 2005). According to Burke (2005, based on Sciolino 2000), the broker role "was in George W. Bush's mind when he picked Rice for the post in December 2000." She was, in his words, "both a good manager and an honest broker of ideas" (Burke 2005). In a Polythink environment, an honest broker can coordinate a plurality of views and oversee the fairness, accuracy, and completion of the decision-making process. Of course, the impact of the broker on how information is presented to the chief executive as well as what information is presented and not presented and the sequence of presentation can have an enormous effect on the ultimate choice.

Polythink can also be turned into multiple advocacy. For example, the group leader can transform opposing viewpoints into strategic, beneficial input. Multiple advocacy and the so-called "competitive advisory system" are typically planned in advance by the decision maker to generate multiple opinions, even devil's advocacy. Productive Polythink reflects the ability of the group leader to incorporate opposing viewpoints into a "good" decision, without a priori planning or soliciting such advice. In other words, it is making the best out of a potentially detrimental situation.

Use Decision Support Systems and Other Analytic Techniques for Objective, Polythink-Free Decision Making

Another method of countering unbalanced, pluralistic decision-making views is through the use of analytic tools such as a decision support system (DSS). The use of an objective, computerized system may be one way of assisting chief executives in avoiding Polythink and Groupthink in their decision units. One such system is the Decision Board computerized platform developed by Mintz et al. (1997). The benefits of using a decision support system in group decision making are:

1. The DSS can display a wide range of policy alternatives, including those that the president/executive may not typically use and those that can be viewed as representing "outside the box" ideas.

2. A DSS can take into account a large set of criteria for selecting the optimal policy for the President. The human mind cannot comprehend and calculate so many dimensions of a decision without a computerized system that aids the policymaker in formulating a decision. This is another advantage of using such systems.

3. A DSS enables the President and his advisors (and other group leaders) to conduct "if-then" analysis, based on various dynamic and static assumptions and scenarios to determine an optimal outcome. One cannot expect the President to actually use a DSS, but the executive's advisors can and probably should carefully examine the consequences of a wide range of policy alternatives to determinate optimal outcomes.

4. A DSS can lead to a careful evaluation of alternatives and dimensions in a comprehensive way, thus overcoming many of the problems associated with

the Polythink syndrome, biases in information processing, biases in group dynamics and in individual decision making. It can also assist in organizing alternatives in a clearer, more controlled manner. In addition, it has the benefit of displaying all the information in a systematic way for key decision makers.

For example, the use of a decision support system by advisors to President Obama during deliberations on the Iran nuclear issue could have aided the President in determining and deciding on the "best" policy options to pursue, in a relatively objective, systematic way. It would also potentially help neutralize information-processing biases and other cognitive biases, even in the chaotic and ever-changing environment of the Middle East. This may help the chief executive avoid the Polythink and Groupthink syndromes. We now turn to discuss some key insights from our analysis.

Key Insight 1: Polythink and Groupthink in War Entry Decisions versus War Exit Decisions

In this book, we showed that the Polythink, Con-Div, and Groupthink processes have wide-ranging implications for war-initiation decisions, escalation and de-escalation decisions, and conflict-termination decisions. Interestingly, we show that most key U.S. decisions on war *entry* following 9/11 tended to possess many symptoms and characteristics of a Groupthink dynamic. In contrast, in U.S. decisions to *exit* wars in the Middle East in the post-9/11 era, the Polythink dynamic appears more dominant. Specifically, U.S. decisions to enter wars in Iraq and Afghanistan and to conduct air strikes against ISIS were based on a more homogeneous and cohesive decision unit, whereas decisions to withdraw from Iraq and Afghanistan were taken with much less consensus and had more symptoms of Polythink. Moreover, *negative* decisions on war entry, when military action was considered and *not* chosen, were also characterized typically by Polythink (the U.S. decision on Syria, the Israeli decision on Iran).[3]

One key reason for the apparent difference in the group dynamic in entering and exiting wars in which the U.S. has been involved is most likely the necessity, in democracies, to obtain strong consensus before committing to new military engagements, and especially to full-scale wars. However, once the U.S. is at war, there are typically some voices in the Administration who advocate withdrawal while other voices defend the "stay the course" option. Moreover, the dissent caused by the frequent setbacks and problems that democracies face in many asymmetric conflicts can trigger Polythink as some policymakers try to recoup losses with even more force (sensitivity to sunk costs), while others, discouraged by setbacks, advocate withdrawal. The high audience costs that democratic leaders face for "losing" a war may also play a role as leaders attempt to avoid the "regret" of a withdrawal decision.[4] These disagreements can become particularly pronounced in complex counterinsurgency-style warfare, which is often characterized by small victories followed by multiple setbacks and slow overall progress.

Thus, critical decisions of war and peace in the post-9/11 era tended to fall at the extremes of the decision-making continuum—either the cohesiveness of Groupthink or the divisiveness of Polythink. Interestingly, we hardly observe the Con-Div dynamic at play in these important decisions. Why do Con-Div processes so often fail to take hold in these contexts? Why is the more optimal process (of Con-Div) least likely to be adopted in war entry and war exit decisions? One reason might be that in hierarchical systems, once the President expresses a preferred opinion on such key policy decisions as entering or not entering war, many Cabinet members follow suit (but see Colin Powell on Iraq), whereas in war-exit decisions few want to be blamed for the withdrawal, especially if the mission has not been accomplished or is perceived as a "loss." We leave this important question for future research as well as the application of Con-Div dynamic to many other small-group decisions. Additional analysis should also be undertaken to address these questions empirically with a larger number of cases examined. Our conclusions about the probability of Groupthink and Polythink in different war and peace contexts are important insights rather than confirmed results.

Key Insight 2: Polythink versus Groupthink at the Strategic and Tactical Levels

Another important insight that we offer on the basis of our analysis of group dynamics characterizing U.S. decisions to engage in and exit from wars in the Middle East in the post-9/11 period is the tendency of Groupthink to most often characterize strategic decisions, whereas Polythink tends to be more evident in decisions at the tactical level, at least in the case studies we have analyzed.[5] In other words, there typically is broad agreement concerning overarching foreign policy goals, but then little agreement about how to reach and implement those goals.

A key reason for this finding is that in the U.S., once a decision on war entry is made by the Commander in Chief, it is backed in most cases by his top advisors. In contrast, tactical decisions are typically made by the Joint Chiefs of the armed forces, with various branches of the military advocating different courses of action, a sign of Polythink at the tactical level. At the strategic level, there is input from the various organizations involved in formulating national security policy, Congress, public opinion, and other groups, including interest groups, and politicians. Yet, ultimately the chief executive makes the decision and his advisors usually "fall in line" behind. However, at the tactical level, traditional rivalries among branches of the military as to the preferred course of action, budgets, procurement, and operation may contribute to Polythink regarding potential tactics, as each branch pushes policies in its own direction. Specifically, the decision to attack ISIS is an example of this phenomenon, as explained in Chapter 7, as are U.S. decisions of when to withdraw from a war.

Implications

Polythink is widespread in national security and foreign policy decisions. Thus, group dynamics should not be neglected in the study of such decisions. One can expect that when applied to war-and-peace decisions, Polythink, Groupthink, and the Con-Div processes will affect conflict initiation decisions, conflict escalation and de-escalation decisions, and conflict termination decisions in different ways. Furthermore, the divisiveness triggered by Polythink and the extremely cohesive decision dynamics caused by Groupthink can be incredibly costly. Paradoxically, both can also prevent the governmental responsiveness required to stave off or appropriately prepare for impending crises. For example, there has been a lot of media discussion and coverage of the neocon group that dominated the Bush Administration in the lead-up to the war in Iraq (Woodward 2010). There is little doubt that this group made decisions that differ greatly from decisions that a more ideologically diverse, Polythink group would have made. The challenge for the policymaker is to build a decision unit that represents and reflects the various opinions of group members but in a balanced, constructive, and productive way.

When Polythink is evident in an advisory group, the group leader or policymaker should strive to leverage the plurality of inputs into successful and balanced decisions whether in government, business, or industry. Leaders' experience, management style, beliefs, and authority are some of the key factors that can lead to productive or destructive Polythink.

Our book has several specific policy implications for national security, foreign policy, conflict management, and conflict resolution decisions:

1. The composition of the group making the decision and the dynamics within such groups affect the ultimate choices that executives and other group leaders make.

2. Decision units exhibit Groupthink, Polythink, or various Con-Div configurations.

3. Whereas sunk costs affect most policy decisions, leaders should avoid falling into a path-dependent trap that is likely to lead them to irreversible decisions. Many conflicts result from such path-dependent processes.

4. Polythink can be beneficial if group leaders successfully manage and leverage the plurality of opinions in the group to be an important input for decision making. Polythink can even result in the unfreezing of closed-mindedness of some group members who are exposed to a diverse set of opinions.

5. Polythink can have a negative effect on long-term planning in both government and business, as conflicting opinions and disagreements within the decision unit and the advisory group lead to some satisficing, incremental, mediocre decisions rather than to carefully planned, long-term decisions. This can impede policy design, planning, and implementation.

The Bottom Line

Polythink, Con-Div, and Groupthink are generic group concepts that are applicable to myriad realms. Consequently, these concepts can be applied to a wide variety of arenas and domains, in domestic, foreign, and national security policymaking, corporate and business decisions, international and domestic organizational decisions, and even personal decisions. Polythink is essentially a global phenomenon, not confined to one country or one society or a specific governmental system. The three models of group decision making discussed in this book, characterize most group decisions. Transforming Destructive Polythink to Productive Polythink is key to what we discuss in this book. Engineering the decision unit to follow a Con-Div structure can steer the decision-making process away from the "defective" Groupthink and Polythink dynamics and ensure a more balanced evaluation of policy alternatives en route to "good" decisions.

The composition of the decision unit, the group dynamics within this unit, and between the decision unit and other groups affect the choices the decision unit makes. Understanding these dynamics is crucial to explaining, predicting, and improving national security and foreign policy decisions, business and corporate decisions, and individual decisions. Indeed, appreciating the dynamics of the group making the decision leads to policy predictions that cannot otherwise be reached.

Notes

Chapter 1

1. The famed line from President Franklin Delano Roosevelt's Declaration of a State of War with Japan, Germany, and Italy to the U.S. Senate (Senate Document No. 148, 1941).

2. Empirically testing these insights with a large pool of cases/observations is an important direction for future research on the Polythink dynamic.

3. Memoirs used include those of former President George W. Bush; former Chairman of the Joint Chiefs of Staff General Hugh Shelton; former NSA and Secretary of State Condoleezza Rice; former FBI Director Louis Freeh; former Secretary of Defense Donald Rumsfeld; former Vice President Dick Cheney; former National Coordinator for Security, Infrastructure Protection, and Counter-terrorism Richard Clarke; former ISAF Commander General Stanley McChrystal; former Secretary of Defense Leon Panetta; former Secretary of State Hillary Clinton; former Secretary of Defense Robert Gates; former Director of the CIA George Tenet.

Chapter 2

1. This focus on small-group dynamics differs from many other important characterizations and studies of national security and foreign policy decision making, which focus on a unitary actor (see, for example, Brams 2003, 2011; Bueno de Mesquita 1981, 1992).

2. This conception of framing is in line with the well-known discussion of framing effects in Kahneman and Tversky's (1979) *Prospect Theory*. While Kahneman and Tversky point to a "loss" or "gain" frame, our use of the term here implies other potential frames as well. For example, the same issue can be framed as a "security problem" or as a "diplomatic problem" with all the requisite differences in approach that those competing frames imply.

3. This section is taken from Mintz, Mishal, and Morag 2005.

4. In the business world, various issue positions can be advanced by marketing and sales representatives, financial managers, and R&D managers. Such diversity is common and reflects Polythink in many corporate and business structures.

5. As described in Janis (1972, 1982), groups characterized by Groupthink will contain seven major defects that will negatively impact the decision-making process: (1) The group's discussion will be limited to only a few potential courses of action and will therefore lack a review of the full range of alternatives. (2) The group will not adequately answer the questions "What are the key objectives?" and "What values are implicated by the chosen strategy?" (3) The group will consistently fail to reexamine the course of action that was initially preferred by the majority of members in order to look for non-obvious risks and drawbacks that may not have been considered when it was originally evaluated. (4) The members of the group will also neglect courses of action that were initially evaluated as unsatisfactory by the majority of the group, failing to see non-obvious benefits of these actions. (5) Members of the group will make little or no attempt to obtain information from external experts who can supply important estimates or projections of the potential gains and losses of a particular strategy. (6) The group will exhibit selective bias in its reaction to factual information and relevant judgments from experts, the mass media, and outside critics, processing information that confirms its preexisting beliefs and ignoring information that challenges those beliefs. (7) Finally, the group members will spend very little time deliberating about how "the best-laid plans" could be derailed (Janis 1972). Consequently, they fail to develop contingency plans to cope with potentially foreseeable setbacks, thereby endangering the overall success of the chosen course of action.

6. We would like to thank Ehud Eiran for suggesting the importance of such interlinking subgroups.

7. There are some exceptions to this; for example, groups that operate in secret (e.g., intelligence units) forbid leaks, yet are often still characterized by Polythink.

8. The Con-Div dynamic is illustrated in the U.S. decision on the Surge in Iraq (see Chapter 5). However, since the book is about Polythink in U.S. decisions on entry to and exit from wars, explicit testing of the Con-Div hypotheses is beyond the scope of this study and is an avenue for future research.

9. In many ways, the Con-Div group dynamic and process can be thought of as a type of group-based integrative complexity that results in a more nuanced understanding of policy issues and can therefore promote balanced and successful policymaking. Thus, while the integrative complexity literature focuses on the degree of integration of multiple perspectives and possibilities at the individual level, integrative complexity may also function at the group level. Indeed, there has been much research on the important role of higher levels of integrative complexity (an iterative process of divergent and convergent thinking) on constructive decision making by political leaders (see Suedfeld, Tetlock, and Ramirez 1977). In the war on terrorism project, Suedfeld and colleagues (see, for example, Suedfeld and Leighton 2002) sought to analyze changes in the integrative complexity of world leaders prior to 9/11 and up until the end of the Iraq

War. Specifically, the authors examined the integrative complexity of world leaders during the war on the Taliban regime in Afghanistan and the war on the Saddam Hussein regime in Iraq and during the broader War on Terrorism.

10. Several researchers have focused on strengthening the Groupthink theory by augmenting and adding to the original theory. For example, in *Beyond Groupthink*, 't Hart, Stern, and Sundelius (1997) identify several functions that small groups serve in policy-making processes. Many of these functions can potentially contribute to the Groupthink phenomenon. For example, policy groups often try to serve as "think tanks," helping make sound policy recommendations, or as a command center designed to streamline the chain of command; yet these tasks are often unfortunately inhibited by the policy groups' more problematic roles, as "smokescreens" simply to give the illusion of deliberation to already decided policies, as an "ideologue" designed to help decision makers merely reinforce their own entrenched ideologies, or as a "sanctuary" for group members to rehabilitate positive in-group self-esteem in the face of outside criticism and stress ('t Hart, Stern, and Sundelius 1997). These myriad competing functions can lead to sub-optimal decision-making processes that exacerbate the effects of Groupthink as enumerated by Janis.

Other researchers have also worked to sharpen and reframe Groupthink's original framework. For example, Baron (2005) proposes a ubiquity model of Groupthink that identifies additional causes of it, including social identification, salient norms, and low self-efficacy. Aldag and Fuller have also suggested a new model for Groupthink that they term the General Group Problem-Solving Model which incorporates "a variety of antecedent conditions, emergent group characteristics, decision-process characteristics and group decision outcomes" (Aldag and Fuller 1993, 533). Others have critiqued the analysis of the specific case studies of Janis (1972). Kramer (1998), for example, argued that in the Bay of Pigs invasion the President had sought advice from experts outside his advisory group and that much of the blame for the attacks could be placed on the President's biased construal of the situation, rather than on that of the group as a whole. These modifications and criticisms to the original formulation of Groupthink notwithstanding, Groupthink remains a powerful and credible theory for analyzing the roots of faulty foreign policy decision-making processes at the highest levels of government.

11. As U.S. decisions on war entry and exit are typically closer in their dynamic to Groupthink or Polythink, and our book focuses on Polythink, we do not analyze Con-Div here, except for the decision of the Bush Administration on the Surge in Iraq, which is analyzed in Chapter 5.

Chapter 3

1. Admiral King was the head of a military commission that conducted one of the inquiries into Pearl Harbor.

2. It is important to note that the design and execution of foreign policy agendas, while strongly influenced by group decision-making processes, is also affected by a host of other practical and political concerns, Thus, while Polythink was indeed a strong contributory factor to the failure to prevent the 9/11 attacks, as we show in this case

study, it was not the sole reason. Many other factors—limited public support for war and military action, the lack of clear terrorist targets to attack, ambiguities in interpreting international law, and more—also contributed to limiting the options available to U.S. policymakers in the months and years leading up to September 11.

3. Rumsfeld's relationship with other key officials was similarly problematic, as he maintained a staunch distrust and fear that others were encroaching on his power and turf. General Shelton of the Joint Chiefs describes his relationship with Rumsfeld as "laborious" and characterized by "a sense of distrust—a sense of his not really wanting to ask my advice for fear that it would be viewed as his not being in charge—viewed as a weakness" (Shelton, Levinson, and McConnell 2010, 408). He goes on to state that "we needlessly wasted a lot of time . . . as he would try to diminish my authority or eliminate members of my staff. It was the worst style of leadership I witnessed in thirty-eight years of service or have witnessed at the highest levels of the corporate world since then" (413). Condoleezza Rice also had a strained relationship with Rumsfeld. She explains, "I am convinced that Don simply resented the role I had to play as national security advisor. . . . Don interpreted [my] actions as a violation of his authority" (Rice 2011, 18).

4. Information sharing was further hampered by woefully inadequate communication systems that prevented the parts of the large and unwieldy federal bureaucracy from effectively communicating with one another. For example, President Bush (2010) recounts, "One of [my] greatest frustrations on September 11 was the woeful communications technology on Air Force One. The plane had no satellite television. We were dependent on whatever local feeds we could pick up. After a few minutes on a given station, the screen would dissolve into static" (130). Louis Freeh (2005), former Director of the FBI, also lamented the outdated communications technology of the FBI, noting that he was "embarrassed that on the afternoon and evening of September 11, 2001, FBI agents had to send photos of the suspected terrorists via express mail service because they still lacked the computing power to scan and send images" (289).

5. Richard Clarke makes this point forcefully in his 2004 memoir, arguing that after 9/11 "we would finally bomb the camps, probably invade Afghanistan. Of course, now bin Laden and his deputies would not be at the camps. Indeed, by now the camps were probably as empty as the White House" (17). The same claims were voiced by others as well.

6. In hindsight, however, it seems that the hesitancy of the U.S. to respond militarily to these many attacks most likely encouraged al-Qaeda in its endeavors, as they learned not to expect or fear major retaliatory measures for their assaults.

7. Though four countries have been designated as "State Sponsors of Terrorism" in the past: Cuba (1982), Iran (1984), Sudan (1993), and Syria (1979).

8. Louis Freeh (2005) seconds this notion, saying the FBI was "in the dark ages" in terms of its communication technologies.

9. For example, Chairman of the Joint Chiefs General Hugh Shelton also had a strained relationship with new Bush Administration appointees, explaining that "like Secretary Rumsfeld, Secretary Cohen [Secretary of Defense under Clinton] was a Republican. Unlike Rumsfeld, Secretary Cohen was brought in by President Clinton as a Republican in a Democratic administration, an attempt to reach out and cross party

lines. Such attempts at bipartisanship were not in the game plan of the George W. Bush administration" (Shelton, Levinson, and McConnell 2010, 418).

10. Paradoxically, in the years since 9/11, these roles seem to have flipped, with the military now consistently offering more hawkish advice than civilian advisors do.

11. Hermann (1980) explains further: "One head of state may focus foreign policy-making within his own office, while his predecessor may have been willing to let the bureaucracy handle all but problems of crisis proportions. One head of state may be given to rhetoric in the foreign policy arena; his predecessor may have wanted action. Moreover, the bureaucracy tends to adjust to changes in style from one chief executive to the next hoping to minimize differences between itself and the chief executive. The result may be to accentuate the stylistic predilections of high level decision makers. In turn, the policy begins to reflect the stylistic preferences of these high level policy makers." (11)

Chapter 4

1. Bush himself explains, "I did not try to manage the logistics or the tactical decisions. My instinct was to trust the judgment of the military leadership. They were the trained professionals; I was a new commander in chief" (Bush 2010, 195).

2. Rajiv Chandrasekaran (2012b), senior correspondent and associate editor of the *Washington Post*, echoes this sentiment, stating, "Instead of capitalizing on Holbrooke's experience and supporting his push for reconciliation with the Taliban, White House officials dwelled on his shortcomings . . . At every turn, they sought to marginalize him and diminish his influence. The infighting exacted a staggering cost: The Obama White House failed to aggressively explore negotiations to end the war when it had the most boots on the battlefield" (*Little America* excerpt published in the *Washington Post*, June 2012).

3. Often, Vice President Biden would hold a series of off-line meetings with other Surge skeptics such as Tom Donilon, Douglas Lute, Tony Blinken, Denis McDonough, and John Brennan, to discuss other options. This group was "close to Obama in different ways" and served as "a balance to the united [pro-Surge] front put up by Gates, Mullen, Petraeus, McChrystal and Clinton" (Woodward 2010, 254–255).

4. Though, notably, not Secretary of State Hillary Clinton.

5. This phenomenon is distinct from Janis' "mindguards" in that gatekeepers are not seeking to protect one dominant view, but in fact themselves disagree about what the correct view should be.

6. General McChrystal (2013) sums up these differing institutional considerations: "I understood that for an administration that needed to factor domestic support into its strategic calculus, it could seem like taking unnecessary political pain to announce, in the spring of 2009, the deployment of troops who could not physically deploy to Afghanistan before the election that August. I also understood the appeal of not deploying additional forces until the first tranche of troops arrived and their impact could be assessed. The view from the Pentagon, which I shared, was different. Forces are shaped and deployed in packages to ensure they have every capability required. Also, military leaders, many of whom were students of counterinsurgency, recognized the dangers of incremental escalation, and the historical lesson that 'trailing' an insurgency typically condemned counterinsurgents to failure" (286).

Chapter 5

1. An earlier version of this chapter appeared as Alex Mintz and Carly Wayne, "Group Decision Making in Conflict: From Groupthink to Polythink in the War in Iraq," in *The Handbook of Conflict Resolution: Theory and Practice*, eds. Peter Coleman and Morton Deutsch, 331–352 (San Francisco: Jossey-Bass, 2013). The chapter that appears here has been substantially revised and expanded from that version.

2. The rise of ISIS in the region has spurred renewed debate over the role of the U.S. military in Iraq and elsewhere, and has, as of this writing, led to new U.S. air strikes against ISIS targets there (see Chapter 7).

3. The growth of the terrorist group ISIS in the power vacuum left by the U.S. across large swaths of Iraq is a primary example of the consequences of some of the less-well-managed aspects of this Polythink decision.

4. This group conflict is perhaps best represented in the high turnover of staff in the Obama Administration. By the end of Obama's third year in office, only one of the top eight officials in the government's foreign policy apparatus was in the same job as at the start of the Administration: Hillary Clinton (Mann 2012).

5. Odierno had replaced General David Petraeus in 2008, when Petraeus was assigned to head CENTCOM (U.S. Central Command).

6. This conclusion was reassessed and to some extent reversed with the emergence of the ISIS threat in 2014.

7. The relationship between Gates and Obama was, however, strained throughout Gates's term, as Gates made clear in his memoir *Duty: Memoirs of a Secretary at War*. In the book, Gates claims that he had serious doubts about Obama's support for the mission of the Afghanistan and Iraq Wars. Gates's accusations are all the more serious given the rarity with which "a former Cabinet member, let alone a defense secretary occupying a central position in the chain of command, [would] publish such an antagonistic portrait of a sitting president" (Woodward, *Washington Post*, January 7, 2012).

Chapter 6

1. The U.S. and its international counterparts were faced with several potential options with regard to Iran's nuclear program. At one extreme, the international community could accept the program. However, given that most actors were unified in their opposition to further nuclear proliferation, they could also attempt to stop or delay the program through (1) diplomatic overtures (the "carrot" approach), (2) economic sanctions (a more "stick-based" tactic), or (3) by taking an even harder line, threatening or engaging in covert or overt military action against the program.

2. Subsequently, the Obama Administration was, however, able to engage in diplomatic negotiations with Iran with the signing of the Geneva Interim Agreement in November 2013. This outcome was in many ways the result of Obama's restructuring of his national security team into a more cohesive, like-minded decision unit that could pursue a unified Iran policy. Changes were also made within the Iranian bureaucratic structure with the election of Hassan Rouhani. International sanctions on the Iranian economy have also contributed significantly to the softening of Iran's policy.

3. This reluctance of the U.S. to negotiate reverberated at the international level and in fact deeply "undermined the diplomatic process led by the European Union. Talks with Iran should be held initially without the precondition that Iran suspend its uranium enrichment program" (Albright and Shire 2009, 4). Finally, within Iran, the diplomacy option also caused deep internal divisions. Iran has several main power centers and "diplomacy had to be conducted with all [of these] major Iranian power centers . . . Just as [the Brazilians and the Turks] engaged with the White House, State Department, Pentagon, and Congress on the U.S. side, they recognized that no major decision was likely to be made in Iran unless a range of key stakeholders was brought into the discussion" (Parsi 2012, 221).

4. Importantly, at the international level, gaining consensus for enhanced sanctions against the Iranians in 2009 was fraught with divergent preferences and interests and was essentially a Polythink dynamic. The Obama Administration's success in assembling "a broad [international] coalition committed to real penalties against Tehran—including a global ban on conventional weapons sales, a European withdrawal from investing in Iran's energy sector, and wide-reaching restrictions on dealing with Iranian banks, among other measures" was truly an achievement, demonstrating Obama's ability to, at times, effectively manage a Polythink dynamic and achieve at least moderate consensus (Maloney 2011). However, even this consensus was incomplete, as Brazil and Turkey voted against sanctions, signaling "a serious divide between the haves and have-nots of nuclear technology" (El-Khawas 2011, 107).

5. Perhaps because of their previous lack of success, support for sanctions at the *international* level fluctuated. In other words, the international dynamic among the P5+1 countries was, at times, characterized by Polythink on this issue. For example, political scientist Efraim Inbar explained as early as 2006, "While the Europeans may join the United States in mandating and applying sanctions, China and Russia, which have veto power in the UNSC, are less likely to cooperate in engineering an American-sponsored campaign against Iran . . . They have their own economic interests in Iran and want to play a role in the region rather than defer to American leadership" (Inbar 2006, 94). However, ultimately the U.S. was able to gain the approval of the UN Security Council for Resolution 1929 in June 2010. This was one of the main reasons the diplomacy track spearheaded by Brazil and Turkey was abandoned. Indeed, for the Turks and the Brazilians, "the fight for diplomacy was a race against sanctions" (Parsi 2012, 182).

6. This confusion and lack of clarity regarding U.S. policy preferences continued internationally and deeply affected the efficacy of the Turkish-Brazilian-led diplomacy efforts. U.S. officials admitted to sending "mixed messages" to Turkey and Brazil and acknowledged "that it was a mistake" to inadvertently "keep the October swap deal on the table (a week prior to Lula's visit to Tehran, a White House official reiterated that the deal was still valid) . . . The letter should have been withdrawn in January when, in Washington's view, it expired" (Parsi 2012, 203). This lack of communication with key international allies on the nuclear issue fundamentally contributed to the failure of the diplomatic process in 2009 and led the U.S. deeper down the sanctions path.

7. The 2013 Geneva Interim Agreement between the U.S.(and P5+1) and Iran represented a departure from this trend, and in many ways was a result of the change in administration structure in both the U.S. and especially Iran that enabled both sides to develop and execute cohesive negotiation policies.

8. This type of intelligence assessment famously occurred in the Bush Administration as well. In 2007, the Department of Defense issued a National Intelligence Estimate in which the main claim was that "we judge with high confidence that in fall 2003, Tehran halted its nuclear weapons program." In a footnote, however, a clarification appears: "For the purposes of this Estimate, by 'nuclear weapons program' we mean Iran's nuclear weapon design and weaponization work and covert uranium conversion-related and uranium enrichment-related work; we do not mean Iran's declared civil work related to uranium conversion and enrichment." By framing Iran's program in this way—as essentially halted, with a small footnote to explain that this referred only to *a portion* of the program—the authors of the report were able to reduce pressure on the President to take decisive action against Iran.

9. Notably, the Obama Administration also expanded the Bush Administration's policy of cyber-attacks on Iran's nuclear facilities. Indeed, beginning with his first months in office, "President Obama secretly ordered increasingly sophisticated attacks on the computer systems that run Iran's main nuclear enrichment facilities, significantly expanding America's first sustained use of cyber-weapons" (Sanger 2012).

10. By 2012, when the structure of Obama's Cabinet was much more cohesive (deliberately so), with much less dissent, a diplomatic policy toward Iran could be more easily formulated. This approach was partially responsible for the breakthrough Geneva Interim Agreement in November 2013.

11. This also makes an attack on Iranian nuclear facilities less desirable to the West, as China and Russia have not committed *not* to resupply Iran with nuclear material and facilities after such an attack.

12. Translation of the original Hebrew.

13. Attack proponents now also claim that the effective performance of the Iron Dome system that Israel has developed (largely with U.S. funds) has significant implications for the (reducing of the) likelihood of a successful retaliation by Iran and its proxies to a potential Israeli attack on Iran. In contrast to the Second Lebanon War, in 2006, the performance of Iron Dome showed that Israel has defensive capabilities, at least for stopping short-range rockets. This performance has strong implications for the perception of effectiveness of other Iron Dome–type systems, such as Sharvit Ksamim ("David's Sling"), for intercepting medium-range missile attacks, and the Arrow system.

Chapter 7

1. Rothkopf is far from alone in expressing this sentiment. Other analysts have also remarked how, by 2012, Obama began "leaning more than ever on his small circle of White House aides, who forged their relationships with him during his 2008 campaign and loom even larger in an administration without weighty voices like those of Rob-

ert M. Gates, the former defense secretary, or Hillary Rodham Clinton, the former secretary of state" (Landler 2014b).

2. Other key posts outside the White House had also been populated by staffers
more loyal to the President—Samantha Power at the United Nations and John Brennan
at the CIA, among others.

3. In one scathing editorial in the *Washington Post*, the editorial board states: "An
unlikely consensus is emerging across the ideological spectrum about the war against
the Islamic State: President Obama's strategy to 'degrade and eventually destroy' the
terrorist entity is unworkable. The military means the president has authorized cannot
accomplish his announced aims" (Washington Post Editorial Board, 2014).

4. Although the emergence of the ISIS threat and the violence in Syria have nothing
to do with the Israeli-Palestinian issue, the Israeli-Palestinian negotiations are nonetheless included in this chapter as they present a separate ongoing foreign policy challenge
to the U.S. in the region.

5. By 2014, this number had increased tenfold, with close to 200,000 casualties
(Cumming-Bruce, *New York Times* 2014).

6. One year later, the U.S. would be faced with a subsequent critical Syria decision—whether to launch air strikes against Assad after he had crossed Obama's defined
"red line" and used chemical weapons against his own citizens.

7. As Director of the CIA, Petraeus was not technically Cabinet level, since this position had been downgraded from Cabinet status in 2001 (back when Tenet was CIA
Director).

8. In 2014, the importance of this decision became clear, as many critics of President
Obama pointed to ISIS as a result of the power vacuum he had allowed to continue in
Syria (and in Iraq). Leon Panetta in his 2014 memoir and a 2014 *60 Minutes* interview
claimed that the U.S. was now "paying the price for not [arming the rebels] in what we
see happening in Syria" (Panetta 2014a).

9. Valerie Jarrett, Obama's White House advisor and his close personal friend,
played a strong role in the internal deliberations on Syria as well as on other key decisions, and was central to informing Obama's ultimate non-interventionist stance.

10. Obama changed his position of non-intervention in Syria later when deciding
to launch air strikes against ISIS, but this did not threaten Assad. Indeed, ISIS constituted one of Assad's most dangerous enemies.

11. By 2014, the U.S. and its allies did begin military intervention in Syria, not to
combat the Russian-backed Assad but rather to counter a fast-rising ISIS (which, inci-
dentally, fought *against* Assad).

12. France was later the first country to recognize the Syrian rebels as a legitimate
political actor, in November 2012, following the controversial Russian and Chinese ve-
toes in July 2012 (Erlanger and Gladstone 2012).

13. For example, subsequently, in 2013 the UK parliament failed to pass a resolution in support of potential military action against Syria after the government's use of
chemical weapons against its citizens.

14. This statement essentially reiterates the Russian line of thinking—concern for

setting a precedent of international intervention in situations of domestic political violence.

15. Secretary Kerry's focus on the sudden crisis in Ukraine might have shifted his primary attention from the Israeli-Palestinian negotiations at a critical time—leaving the two sides to advance policies and agendas that contributed to the collapse of the talks.

16. Sometimes followed by "in Iraq and Syria" and called ISIS or by "in Iraq and the Levant" and called ISIL.

17. This statement triggered a strong backlash among those in the intelligence community who felt that Obama was scapegoating them without mentioning his own misjudgments in trying to avoid responsibility (Baker and Schmitt 2014).

Chapter 8

1. Thus, for example, during Jimmy Carter's term as President, his Secretary of State, Cyrus Vance, and National Security Advisor Zbigniew Brzezinski had very different views and philosophy on how U.S. foreign policy and national security should be conducted. And during the Nixon presidency, the National Security Advisor, Henry Kissinger, and the Secretary of State, William P. Rogers, often clashed on policy direction, issues, and influence.

2. We thank Janice Stein of the University of Toronto for suggesting this strategy.

3. Although the period following 9/11 presents only a few cases, this is an important insight that needs to be explored further empirically, with a larger number of events and decisions.

4. Interestingly, as pointed out above, situations in which the U.S. ultimately decided not to engage in military conflict in the post-9/11 era were also marked by Polythink (e.g., the 2012 Syria decision and the 2009 Iran nuclear negotiation decision). Dissent regarding the best policy choice essentially prevented the President from pursuing military options, as did the lack of public and Congressional support to attack Syria in the summer of 2012.

5. This hypothesis needs to be rigorously tested on a larger number of cases in order to be empirically substantiated and validated.

References

9–11 Commission. 2004. *The 9/11 Commission Report: Final Report of the National Commission on Terrorist Attacks upon the United States.* New York: W. W. Norton.

Ackerman, Spencer. 2014. "Obama: 'We Don't Have a Strategy Yet' to Combat ISIS Militants." *The Guardian*, August 28.

Adamsky, Dima. 2011. "The War over Containing Iran: Can a Nuclear Iran Be Stopped?" *Foreign Affairs* 90, no. 2: 155–168.

Address by the President of the United States. December 8, 1941. In *Declarations of a State of War with Japan, Germany, and Italy.* Senate Document No. 148 (77th Cong., 1st Sess.), at p. 7.

Albright, David, and Jaqueline Shire. 2009. "Nuclear Iran: Not Inevitable." Institute for Science and International Security, January 21.

Aldag, Ramon J., and Sally R. Fuller. 1993. "Beyond Fiasco: A Reappraisal of the Groupthink Phenomenon and a New Model of Group Decision Processes." *Psychological Bulletin* 113, no. 3: 533–552.

Allison, Graham T. 1971. *Essence of Decision: Explaining the Cuban Missile Crisis.* Boston: Little, Brown.

Allison, Graham T., and Shai Feldman. 2012. "Why Netanyahu Backed Down." *New York Times*, October 12.

Alter, Jonathan. 2010. *The Promise: President Obama, Year One.* New York: Simon and Schuster.

Arens, Moshe. 2013. "As North Korea Blusters, the Iranian Nuclear Clock Ticks Away." *Haaretz*, April 21.

Badie, Dina. 2010. "Groupthink, Iraq, and the War on Terror: Explaining US Policy Shift toward Iraq." *Foreign Policy Analysis* 6:277–296.

Baker, James A., and Lee Hamilton. 2006. *The Iraq Study Group Report.* United States Institute of Peace.

Baker, Peter. 2009. "How Obama Came to Plan for 'Surge' in Afghanistan." *New York Times*, December 5.

———. 2010. "Woodward Book Says Afghanistan Divided White House." *New York Times*, September 21.

———. 2014. "New Military Campaign Extends a Legacy of War." *New York Times*, September 10.

Baker, Peter, and Eric Schmitt. 2014. "Many Missteps in Assessment of ISIS Threat." *New York Times*, September 29.

Baron, Robert S. 2005. "So Right It's Wrong: Groupthink and the Ubiquitous Nature of Polarized Group Decision Making." *Advances in Experimental Social Psychology* 37:219–253.

Barzegar, Karine G. 2013. "Analysis: France's Hawkish Stand on Syria a Pattern." *USA Today*, September 8.

BBC News. 2011. "China and Russia Veto U.N. Resolution Condemning Syria." October 5.

———. 2014. "Syria Crisis: Where Key Countries Stand." February 18.

Beauchamp, Zack. 2014. "Obama's Rhetoric on ISIS Is Confused Because His Policy Is Confused." VOX.com, September 3.

Behar, Richard. 2002. "FBI's Phoenix Memo Unmasked." Forbes.com, May 22.

Bender, Eric. 2012. [Hebrew] "The Prime Minister's Crackdown on Peres Is Crude and Aggressive." *Maariv*, August 16.

Benn, Aluf. 2012. "How Iran Strengthened Israeli Democracy." *Haaretz*, August 20.

Blunt, Roy. 2006. "Blunt Speech on GOP Future." Project Vote Smart, November 9.

Boot, Max, and Steven Simon. 2008. "Has the Surge Put Iraq on the Path to Success?" Council on Foreign Relations, online debate, May 8.

Bowen, Wyn Q., and Joanna Kidd. 2004. "The Iranian Nuclear Challenge." *International Affairs* 80, no. 2: 257–276.

Brams, Steven J. 2003. *Negotiation Games: Applying Game Theory to Bargaining and Arbitration*. Routledge Advances in Game Theory, Vol. 2. Rev. ed. London and New York: Routledge.

———. 2011. *Game Theory and Politics*. Mineola, NY: Dover Publications.

Broad, William J., and David E. Sanger. 2009. "Report Says Iran Has Data to Make a Nuclear Bomb." *New York Times*, October 3.

Brown, M. Helen, and Diane M. Hosking. 1986. "Distributed Leadership and Skilled Performance as Successful Organization in Social Movements." *Human Relations* 39, no. 1: 65–79.

Bruno, Greg. 2009. "A Costly Exit from Iraq." Council on Foreign Relations, March 6.

Bueno de Mesquita, Bruce. 1981. *The War Trap*. New Haven, CT: Yale University Press.

Bueno de Mesquita, Bruce, and David Lalman. 1992. *War and Reason: Domestic and International Imperatives*. New Haven, CT: Yale University Press.

Burke, John P. 2005. "The Contemporary Presidency: Condoleezza Rice as NSC Advisor: A Case Study of the Honest Broker Role." *Presidential Studies Quarterly* 35, no. 3: 554–575.

Bush, George W. 2010. *Decision Points.* New York: Random House Digital.

Caldwell, Dan. 2011. *Vortex of Conflict: U.S. Policy toward Afghanistan, Pakistan, and Iraq.* Stanford, CA: Stanford University Press.

Campbell, Kurt M., and James B. Steinberg. 2008. "Managing Foreign Policy and National Security Challenges in Presidential Transitions." *Washington Quarterly* 31, no. 4: 7–20.

Cannon-Bowers, Janis A., Eduardo Salas, and Sharolyn Converse. 1993. "Shared Mental Models in Expert Team Decision Making." In *Current Issues in Individual and Group Decision Making,* edited by N. John Castellan, Jr., 221–246. Hillsdale, NJ: Erlbaum. ?

CBS/AP. 2012. "U.S.: Russian Military Ship en Route to Syria." CBS, June 15.

Chandrasekaran, Rajiv. 2012a. *Little America: The War within the War for Afghanistan.* New York: Random House Digital.

———. 2012b. "Obama's Troops Increase for Afghan War Was Misdirected." Excerpt from *Little America. Washington Post,* June 22.

———. 2012c. "Infighting on Obama Team Squandered Chance for Peace in Afghanistan." Excerpt from *Little America. Washington Post,* June 22.

———. 2014. "Syrians to Be Trained to Defend Territory, Not Take Ground from Jihadist, Officials Say." *Washington Post,* October 22.

Cheney, Dick. 2011. *In My Time: A Personal and Political Memoir.* New York: Threshold Editions.

Chubin, Shahram. 2011. "A Grand Bargain with Iran." *Foreign Affairs* 90, no. 2: 163–166.

Clarke, Richard A. 2004. *Against All Enemies: Inside America's War on Terror.* New York: Free Press.

CNN. 2011. "U.S. Troops in Afghanistan." Afghanistan.blogs.CNN.com, June 22.

———. 2014. "ISIS Fast Facts." CNN.com, October 9.

CNN Wire Staff. 2012. "U.N. Security Council Debates Syria as Violence Rages." CNN, September 26.

Cooper, Helene. 2009. "Afghan War Is New Topic of Dispute with Cheney." *New York Times,* October 22.

CostOfWar.com. 2013. "Cost of War to the United States."

Costs of War. 2013. "Afghanistan: 16,725–19,013 Civilians Killed."

Cumming-Bruce, Nick. 2014. "Death Toll in Syria Estimated at 191,000." *New York Times,* August 22.

Daalder, Ivo H., and James M. Lindsay. 2003. *America Unbound: The Bush Revolution in Foreign Policy.* Washington, D.C.: Brookings Institution.

Debs, Alexandre, and Nuno P. Monteiro. 2012. "The Flawed Logic of Striking Iran." *Foreign Affairs,* January 17.

Diamond, Jeremy. 2014. "Why Obama Decided to Strike ISIS." CNN.com, August 9.

Dobbins, James. 2007. "Who Lost Iraq?" *International Herald Tribune,* April 16.

Donig, Mark, and Michael Sussman. 2011. "A Nuclear Iran and a Defiant China: America's Next Hegemonic Threat." In *Iran: The Day After Simulation: An Assess-*

ment, edited by Alex Mintz, Lesley Terris, and Haim Assa, 42–49. Herzliya, Israel: Interdisciplinary Center.

Downs, Erica, and Suzanne Maloney. 2011. "Getting China to Sanction Iran." *Foreign Affairs* 90, no. 2: 15–21.

The Economist. 2014. "Attacks on Islamist State: Another Long War." September 27.

Edwards, George III. 2003. *On Deaf Ears: The Limits of the Bully Pulpit.* New Haven: Yale University Press.

Eikenberry, Karl. 2009. "Ambassador Eikenberry's Cables on U.S. Strategy in Afghanistan." *New York Times.*

El-Khawas, Mohamed. 2011. "Obama's Engagement Strategy with Iran: Limited Results." *Mediterranean Quarterly* 22, no. 1: 93–113.

Entous, Adam. 2013. "Inside Obama's Syria Debate." *Wall Street Journal,* March 29.

Erlanger, Steven, and Rick Gladstone. 2012. "France Grants Its Recognition to Syrian Rebels." *New York Times,* November 13.

Feldman, M. S. 1990. "Organization Theory and the Study of the Presidency." Paper presented at the Institute for Public Policy Studies, University of Pittsburgh.

Filkins, Dexter. 2008. "Exiting Iraq, Petraeus Says Gains Are Fragile." *New York Times,* August 20.

Fisher, Max. 2014. "Obama Should Blame Himself, Not Chuck Hagel, for Hagel's Failure as Defense Secretary." Vox.com, November 24.

Fiske, Susan T., Donald R. Kinder, and W. Michael Larter. 1983. "The Novice and the Expert: Knowledge-Based Strategies in Political Cognition." *Journal of Experimental Social Psychology* 19, no. 4: 381–400.

FlorCruz, Jaime A. 2012. "Russia, China, and Partners Call for Non-Intervention in Syria, Iran." CNN, June 7.

Forman, Ernest, and Mary Ann Selly. 1996. "Decision by Objectives." McLean, VA: Author.

Fox News. 2014. "Civilian Death Toll in Iraq Highest in Years, Fueling Concern of Al Qaeda 'Resurgence.'" Foxnews.com, January 2.

Francis, David R. 2011. "Iraq War Will Cost More Than World War II." *Christian Science Monitor,* October 25.

Freeh, Louis J. 2005. *My FBI: Bringing Down the Mafia, Investigating Bill Clinton, and Fighting the War on Terror.* With Howard Means. New York: St. Martin's Press.

Fuller, Sally Riggs, and Ramon J. Aldag. 1998. "Organizational Tonypandy: Lessons from a Quarter Century of the Groupthink Phenomenon." *Organizational Behavior and Human Decision Processes* 73, no. 2: 163–184.

Garrison, Jean A. 2001. "Framing Foreign Policy Alternatives in the Inner Circle: President Carter, His Advisors, and the Struggle for the Arms Control Agenda." *Political Psychology* 22, no. 4: 775–807.

Gelb, Leslie H. 2012. "Why Obama Won't Speed U.S. Troop Withdrawal in Afghanistan." *Daily Beast,* March 19.

George, Alexander L. 1972. "The Case for Multiple Advocacy in Making Foreign Policy." *American Political Science Review* 66, no. 3: 751–785.

———. 1980. *Presidential Decisionmaking in Foreign Policy: The Effective Use of Information and Advice.* Boulder, CO: Westview Press.

Geva, Nehemia, and Alex Mintz. 1997. *Decisionmaking on War and Peace: The Cognitive-Rational Debate.* Boulder, CO: Lynne Rienner Publishers.

Gordon, Michael R. 2013a. "Former Advisor Criticizes Obama on Afghan War." *New York Times,* March 3.

———. 2013b. "Q. and A. with Former U.S. Commander in Afghanistan." *New York Times,* January 8.

Gordon, Michael R., and Bernard E. Trainor. 2012. *The Endgame: The Inside Story of the Struggle for Iraq, from George W. Bush to Barack Obama.* New York: Random House.

Greenhalgh, Leonard. 1986. "SMR Forum: Managing Conflict." *Sloan Management Review* 27:45–51.

Greenstein, Fred I. 1993. "The Presidential Leadership Style of Bill Clinton: An Early Appraisal." *Political Science Quarterly* 108, no. 4: 589–601.

———. 2003. "The Leadership Style of George W. Bush." Paper delivered at the 2003 Princeton University conference "The George W. Bush Presidency: An Early Assessment."

Gwertzman, Bernard. 2013. "Stalemate Looms in Afghanistan." Council on Foreign Relations, January 14.

Haass, Richard. 2009. *War of Necessity, War of Choice: A Memoir of Two Iraq Wars.* New York: Simon and Schuster.

Hastings, Michael. 2010. "The Runaway General: The Rolling Stone Profile of Stanley McChrystal That Changed History." *Rolling Stone,* June 22.

Hermann, Margaret G. 1980. "Explaining Foreign Policy Behavior Using the Personal Characteristics of Political Leaders." *International Studies Quarterly* 24, no. 1: 7–46.

———. 2001. "How Decision Units Shape Foreign Policy: A Theoretical Framework." *International Studies Review* 3, no. 2: 47–81.

Hermann, Margaret G., and Charles F. Hermann. 1989. "Who Makes Foreign Policy Decisions and How: An Empirical Inquiry." *International Studies Quarterly* 33:361–387.

Hermann, Margaret G., and Thomas Preston. 1994. "Presidents, Advisers, and Foreign Policy: The Effect of Leadership Style on Executive Arrangements." *Political Psychology* 15, no. 1: 75–96.

Hermann, Margaret G., Thomas Preston, Baghat Korany, and Timothy M. Shaw. 2001. "Who Leads Matters: The Effects of Powerful Individuals." *International Studies Review* 3, no. 2 (2001): 83–131.

Hersh, Seymour M. 2004. *Chain of Command: The Road from 9–11 to Abu Ghraib.* New York: HarperCollins.

Hirokawa, Randy Y., and Marshall Scott Poole. 1996. *Communication and Group Decision Making.* Thousand Oaks, CA: Sage Publications.

Hirsh, Michael. 2014. "Team of Bumblers? Are Susan Rice and Chuck Hagel Equal to Today's New National Security Challenges? *Politico Magazine,* October 26.

Houghton, David. 2008. "Invading and Occupying Iraq: Some Insights from Political Psychology." *Peace and Conflict* 14, no. 2: 169–192.

Hymans, Jacques E. C. 2013. "Iran Is Still Botching the Bomb: It Is Time for Israel and the United States to Stop Overreacting." *Foreign Affairs*, February 18.

iCasualties. 2013a. "Coalition Military Fatalities by Year."

Ignatius, David. 2013a. "Obama Is Criticized for Right Result on Syria." *Washington Post*, September 18.

———. 2013b. "Out: Team of Rivals. In: Obama's Guys." *Washington Post*, February 23.

———. 2014. "New Blood Could Give Obama Lift." Omaha.com, October 10.

Inbar, Efraim. 2006. "The Need to Block a Nuclear Iran." *Middle East Review of International Affairs* 10, no. 1: 85–104.

Isikoff, Michael, and Daniel Klaidman. 2002. "The Hijackers We Let Escape." *Newsweek*, June 9.

Iraq Body Count. 2013.

Janis, Irving L. 1982a. *Victims of Groupthink: A Psychological Study of Foreign-Policy Decisions and Fiascoes.* 2nd ed. Boston: Houghton Mifflin. First published in 1972.

———. 1982b. "Decisionmaking under Stress." In *Handbook of Stress: Theoretical and Clinical Aspects,* edited by Leo Goldberger and Shlomo Breznitz, 69–80. New York: Free Press.

Jervis, Robert. 1976. *Perception and Misperception in International Politics.* Princeton, NJ: Princeton University Press.

Johnson, Richard Tanner. 1974. *Managing the White House: An Intimate Study of the Presidency.* New York: Harper and Row.

Jones, Bryan D. 2001. *Politics and the Architecture of Choice: Bounded Rationality and Governance.* Chicago: University of Chicago Press.

Jones, Jeffrey. 2011. "Three in Four Americans Back Obama on Iraq Withdrawal." Gallup, November 2.

Kahneman, Daniel, and Amos Tversky. 1979. "Prospect Theory: An Analysis of Decision under Risk." *Econometrica: Journal of the Econometric Society* 47, no. 2: 263–291.

Kahneman, Daniel, and Jonathan Renshon. 2009. "Hawkish Biases." In *American Foreign Policy and the Politics of Fear: Threat Inflation since 9–11,* edited by Trevor Thrall and Jane K. Cramer, 79–95. New York: Routledge.

Karl, David J. 2012. "How Well Has Mr. Obama Waged His 'War of Necessity'?" Foreign Policy Association blog, October 13.

Kaufmann, Chaim. 2004. "Threat Inflation and the Failure of the Marketplace of Ideas: The Selling of the Iraq War." *International Security* 29, no. 1: 5–48.

Kingsbury, Alex. 2014. "Why the 2007 Surge in Iraq Actually Failed, and What That Means Today." BostonGlobe.com. *Boston Globe*, 17 November.

Kinne, Brandon J. 2005. "Decision Making in Autocratic Regimes: A Poliheuristic Perspective." *International Studies Perspectives* 6, no. 1: 114–128.

Kissinger, Henry A. 1969. *Nuclear Weapons and Foreign Policy.* New York: W. W. Norton.

Klandermans, Bert. 1988. "The Formation and Mobilization of Consensus." *International Social Movement Research* 1: 173–196.

Knights, Michael. 2012. "A Violent New Year in Iraq." Washington Institute for Near East Policy, February 16.

Kramer, Roderick M. 1998. "Revisiting the Bay of Pigs and Vietnam Decisions 25 Years Later: How Well Has the Groupthink Hypothesis Stood the Test of Time?" *Organizational Behavior and Human Decision Processes* 73, no. 2/3: 238.

Kroenig, Matthew. 2012. "Time to Attack Iran: Why a Strike Is the Least Bad Option." *Foreign Affairs* 91, no. 1: 76–86.

Kroft, Steve. 2014. "President Obama: What Makes Us America." CBSnews.com, September 28.

Krugman, Paul. 2014. "In Defense of Obama." *Rolling Stone*, October 8, 2014.

Kupchan, Charles. 1994. *The Vulnerability of an Empire*. Ithaca, NY: Cornell University Press.

Labott, Elise, Jim Acosta, and Leslie Bentz. 2014. "Sources: Obama Seeks New Syria Strategy Review to Deal with ISIS, Al-Assad." CNN. Cable News Network, November 13.

LaFraniere, Sharon. 2013. "Math behind Leak Crackdown: 153 cases, 4 years, 0 indictments." *New York Times*, July 20.

Landler, Mark. 2014a. "Obama, in Speech on ISIS, Promises Sustained Effort to Rout Militants." *New York Times*, September 10.

———. 2014b. "Obama Could Replace Aides Bruised by a Cascade of Crises." *New York Times*, October 29.

Lindsay, James M. 2011. "George W. Bush, Barack Obama, and the Future of US Global Leadership." *International Affairs* 87, no. 4: 765–779.

Logiurato, Brett. 2014. "Obama Is Getting Slammed for His 'Goldilocks Approach' to ISIS and Syria." *Business Insider*, October 28.

Lubold, Gordon. 2013. "Vali Nasr: How Obama Let Diplomacy Fail in Afghanistan; Johnson on DOMA; The Bumper Sticker for the Hagel Era; Why an Air Force General's Decision Could Animate Reformers on Sexual Assault." ForeignPolicy. com, March 4.

Maloney, Suzanne. 2008. "U.S. Policy toward Iran: Missed Opportunities and Paths Forward." *Fletcher Forum of World Affairs* 32, no. 2: 25–44.

———. 2011. "Progress of the Obama Administration's Policy toward Iran." Brookings Institution, November 15.

Mann, James. 2012. *The Obamians: The Struggle inside the White House to Redefine American Power*. London: Penguin Books.

Manor, Shani. 2014. "Polythink in the UN Security Council's Permanent Five on Military Interventions under Chapter VII." Master's thesis, Lauder School of Government, IDC Herzliya.

Maoz, Zeev. 1990. "Framing the National Interest: The Manipulation of Foreign Policy Decisions in Group Settings." *World Politics* 43, no. 1: 77–110.

Marsh, Kevin. 2013. "Obama's Surge: A Bureaucratic Politics Analysis of the Decision to Order a Troop Surge in the Afghanistan War." *Foreign Policy Analysis* 10, no. 3: 265–288.

McChrystal, General Stanley. 2013. *My Share of the Task: A Memoir.* New York: Penguin. Kindle edition.

McIntyre, Jamie, and Laurie Ure. 2008. "Surge or Splurge in Iraq." CNN, Cable News Network, March 19.

Merica, Dan. 2014. "Obama Subtly Pushes Back against Clinton, Panetta on Syria." CNN. Cable News Network, September 29.

Miles, Rufus E. 1978. The Origin and Meaning of Miles' Law. *Public Administration Review* 38, no. 5: 399–403.

Miller, Aaron David. 2013. "Does John Kerry's Peace Process Have a Chance?" *Politico*, January 8.

Mintz, Alex. 1993. "The Decision to Attack Iraq: A Noncompensatory Theory of Decision Making." *Journal of Conflict Resolution* 37, no. 4: 595–618.

———. 2004. "How Do Leaders Make Decisions? A Poliheuristic Perspective." *Journal of Conflict Resolution* 48, no. 1: 3–13.

Mintz, Alex, and Karl DeRouen, Jr. 2010. *Understanding Foreign Policy Decision Making.* New York: Cambridge University Press.

Mintz, Alex, Nehemia Geva, Steven B. Redd, and Amy Carnes. 1997. "The Effect of Dynamic and Static Choice Sets on Political Decision Making: An Analysis Using the Decision Board Platform." *American Political Science Review* 91, no. 3: 553–566.

Mintz, Alex, Shaul Mishal, and Nadav Morag. 2005. "Evidence of Polythink? The Israeli Delegation at Camp David 2000." Discussion paper, Yale University, UN Studies.

Mintz, Alex and Carly Wayne. 2014. "Group Decision Making in Conflict: From Groupthink to Polythink in Iraq," in *The Handbook of Conflict Resolution: Theory and Practice*, eds. Peter Coleman and Morton Deutsch, 331–352. San Francisco: Jossey-Bass, Inc.

Mitchell, David. 2005. "Centralizing Advisory Systems: Presidential Influence and the U.S. Foreign Policy Decision-Making Process." *Foreign Policy Analysis* 1, no. 2: 181–206.

Moreh, Dror. 2013. "Diskin: Netanyahu Too Weak." *Yedioth Aharonoth*, January 3.

Murray, Donette. 2010. "The Carcass of Dead Policies: Lessons for Obama in Dealing with Iran." *Contemporary Politics* 16, no. 2: 209–223.

Nasr, Vali. 2013. "The Inside Story of How the White House Let Diplomacy Fail in Afghanistan." ForeignPolicy.com, March 4.

National Intelligence Estimate. 2007. "Iran: Nuclear Intentions and Capabilities."

New York Times Editorial Board. 2013. "Britain's Syria Vote in Perspective." *New York Times*, September 3.

———. 2014. "The Slippery Slope Begins: Is U.S. Policy on Fighting ISIS Already Changing?" *New York Times*, September 16.

News Research Center. 2009. "Iraq War Casualties Database."

Obama, Barack. 2007. "Renewing American Leadership." *Foreign Affairs* 86, no. 4: 2–16.

Office of the Press Secretary. 2013. "Remarks by the President at the National Defense University." Whitehouse.gov, May 23.

Oren, Amir. 2011. "On Sale: Just 499 Casualties in a War with Iran." *Haaretz*, November 13.

Panetta, Leon. 2014a. "Leon Panetta Criticizes Obama for Iraq Withdrawal." CBSNews. CBS Interactive, October 2.

Panetta, Leon. 2014b. *Worthy Fights: A Memoir of Leadership in War and Peace.* New York: Penguin Group.

Parmar, Inderjeet. 2010. "Plus Ca Change: American Foreign Policy under Obama." *Political Insight* 1, no. 1: 14–16.

Parsi, Trita. 2012. *A Single Roll of the Dice: Obama's Diplomacy with Iran.* New Haven, CT: Yale University Press.

Parsons, Christi, and Kathleen Hennessey. 2012. "Obama's Search for 'Balance' Defines His Decision-making." *Los Angeles Times*, November 2.

Pelosi, Nancy. 2006. "Bringing the War to an End Is My Highest Priority as Speaker." *Huffington Post*, November 17.

Pew Research Center. 2014. "Bipartisan Support for Obama's Military Campaign against ISIS." Pew Research Center for the People and the Press RSS, September 15.

Pfiffner, James P. 2005. "Presidential Decision Making: Rationality, Advisory Systems, and Personality." *Presidential Studies Quarterly* 35, no. 2: 217–228.

———. 2009. "The Contemporary Presidency: Decision Making in the Bush White House." *Presidential Studies Quarterly* 39: 363–384.

———. 2011. "Decision Making in the Obama White House." *Presidential Studies Quarterly* 41, no. 2: 244–262.

Pinter, Eitam. 2013. "Fat Man and Little Boy: Group Decision Making or Polythink?" Poster presented at the 2013 conference of the International Society for Political Psychology.

Pollack, Kenneth M. 2011. "American Policy toward Iraq after 2011." Testimony before the U.S. Senate Committee on Armed Services. Brookings Research, November 15.

"President Bush Addresses Nation on Iraq War." 2007. *Washington Post*, January 10.

Putnam, Robert D. 1988. "Diplomacy and Domestic Politics: The Logic of Two-Level Games." *International Organization* 42, no. 3: 427–460.

Ratnesar, Romesh, and Michael Weisskopf. 2002. "How the FBI Blew the Case." *Time*, June 3.

Rice, Condoleezza. 2011. *No Higher Honor: A Memoir of My Years in Washington.* New York: Crown.

Ricks, Thomas E. 2009. "Understanding the Surge in Iraq and What's Ahead." Foreign Policy Research Institute, May 1.

Risen, James, and Mark Mazzetti. 2012. "U.S. Agencies See No Move by Iran to Build a Bomb." *New York Times*, February 24.

Roberts, Dan. 2014. "Obama on U.S. Foreign Policy: Principled Realist or Failed Isolationist?" *The Guardian*, August 29.

Rogin, Josh. 2014. "Obama's Ex-CIA Chief Slams White House for 'Hesitation and Half Steps.'" *Daily Beast.* Newsweek/Daily Beast, October 2.

Rogin, Josh, and Eli Lake. 2014. "Why Obama Backed Off More ISIS Strikes: His Own Team Couldn't Agree on a Syria Strategy." *Daily Beast.* Newsweek/Daily Beast, August 28.

Rohde, David, and Warren Strobel. 2014. "Special Report: How Syria Policy Stalled under the 'Analyst in Chief.'" Reuters, October 9.

Rosenau, James N. 1969. *Linkage Politics: Essays on the Convergence of National and International Systems.* New York: Free Press.

Rothkopf, David. 2014a. "Obama's 'Don't Do Stupid Shit' Foreign Policy." *Foreign Policy,* June 4.

———. 2014b. "National Insecurity: Can Obama's Foreign Policy Be Saved?" *Foreign Policy,* October 4.

———. 2014c. "The Pendulum and the President." *Foreign Policy,* October 28.

Rubin, Jeffrey Z., and Bert R. Brown. 1975. *The Social Psychology of Bargaining and Negotiation.* New York: Academic Press.

Rudoren, Jodi. 2013. "Former Israeli Security Chief Calls Netanyahu a Poor Leader." *New York Times,* January 4.

Rudoren, Jodi, and David Sanger. 2013. "US and Israel Share a Goal in Iran Talks, but Not a Strategy." *New York Times,* October 3.

Russett, Bruce, Harvey Starr, and David Kinsella. 2006. *World Politics: The Menu for Choice.* Boston: Wadsworth.

Rynhold, Jonathan. 2008. "President Obama and the Middle East Challenge." Bar Ilan University, Begin-Sadat Center for Strategic Studies Perspective Papers, no. 50.

Sadjadpour, Karim, and Diane de Gramont. "Reading Kennan in Tehran." *Foreign Affairs* 90, no. 2.

Sagan, Scott D. 2006. "How to Keep the Bomb from Iran." *Foreign Affairs* 85, no. 5: 45–59.

Sage, Andrew P. 1991. *Decision Support Systems Engineering.* Hoboken, NJ: Wiley.

Sanger, David E. 2012. "Obama Order Sped Up Wave of Cyber Attacks against Iran." *New York Times,* June 1.

———. 2013. "In Step on 'Light Footprint,' Nominees Reflect a Shift." *New York Times,* January 8.

Sanger, David E., and Thom Shanker. 2010. "Gates Says U.S. Lacks a Policy to Thwart Iran." *New York Times,* April 17.

Schafer, Mark, and Scott Crichlow. 2010. *Groupthink Versus High-Quality Decision Making in International Relations.* New York: Columbia University Press.

Schneeweiss, Christoph. 2003. *Distributed Decision Making.* New York: Springer.

Schultz, Kenneth. 2003. "The Politics of Peace." Paper presented at the Gilman Conference on New Directions in International Relations, Yale University, New Haven, CT.

Sciolino, Elaine. 2000. "Compulsion to Achieve." *New York Times,* December 18.

Sengupta, Somini. 2014. "In Dealings on Syria, Security Council Exposes Its Failings." *New York Times,* May 8.

Shelton, General Hugh, Ronald Levinson, and Malcolm McConnell. 2010. *Without Hesitation: The Odyssey of an American Warrior.* New York: St. Martin's Press.

Shenon, Philip, and Mark Mazzetti. 2006. "Records Show Tenet Briefed Rice on Al Qaeda Threat." *New York Times,* October 2.

Shleifer, Andrei, and Daniel Treisman. 2011. "Why Moscow Says No." *Foreign Affairs* 90, no. 1: 122–138.

Shultz, Richard H., Jr. 2004. "Showstoppers: Nine Reasons Why We Never Sent Our Special Operations Forces after al Qaeda before 9–11." *Weekly Standard* 9, no. 19 (January 26).

Sink, Justin. 2014. "Dems Want Whitehouse Shakeup." *The Hill,* October 12.

Snyder, Richard C., H. W. Bruck, and Burton Sapin. 1962. *Foreign Policy Decision-Making: An Approach to the Study of International Politics.* New York: Free Press.

Spiegel, Peter, Jonathan Weisman, and Yochi J. Dreazen. 2009. "Obama Bets Big on Troop Surge." *Wall Street Journal,* December 2.

Starr, Barbara. 2014a. "Hagel Wrote Memo to White House Criticizing Syria Strategy." CNN.com, October 31.

Starr, Barbara. 2014b. "White House Struggles to Find Hagel Successor." CNN. Cable News Network, November 26.

Suedfeld, Peter, and Dana C. Leighton. 2002. "Early Communications in the War against Terrorism: An Integrative Complexity Analysis." *Political Psychology* 23, no. 3: 585–599.

Suedfeld, Peter, Philip E. Tetlock, and Carmenza Ramirez. 1977. "War, Peace, and Integrative Complexity in Speeches on the Middle East Problem, 1947–1976." *Journal of Conflict Resolution* 21, no. 3: 427–442.

Sullivan, John F. 2007. *Gatekeeper: Memoirs of a CIA Polygraph Examiner.* Dulles, VA: Potomac Books.?

't Hart, Paul, Eric K. Stern, and Bengt Sundelius, eds. 1997. *Beyond Groupthink: Political Group Dynamics and Foreign Policy-making.* Ann Arbor: University of Michigan Press.

Taber, Charles S. 1992. "POLI: An Expert System Model of U.S. Foreign Policy Belief Systems." *American Political Science Review* 86: 888–904.

Tenet, George. 2007. *At the Center of the Storm: My Years at the CIA.* New York: HarperCollins.

Walker, Lauren. 2014. "Panetta's Memoir Blasts Obama on His Leadership, Blames Him for State of Iraq and Syria." *Newsweek,* October 10.

Walker, Stephen G., Mark Schafer, and Michael D. Young. 1999. "Presidential Operational Codes and Foreign Policy Conflicts in the Post-Cold War World." *Journal of Conflict Resolution* 43: 610–625.

Waltz, Kenneth N. 2012. "Why Iran Should Get the Bomb." *Foreign Affairs* 91, no. 4: 2–5.

Washington Post Editorial Board. 2014. "Mr. Obama's Half-hearted Fight against the Islamic State." *Washington Post,* October 25.

Wayne, Stephen J. 2011. "Presidential Character and Judgment: Obama's Afghanistan and Health Care Decisions." *Presidential Studies* Quarterly 41, no. 2: 291–306.

Weisman, Jonathan. 2014. "The House, in Rare Unity with Obama, Will Leave the Trail for an ISIS Vote." *New York Times*, September 11.

Whitlock, Craig. 2014a. "Dempsey Raises Possibility of Involving U.S. Combat Troops in Fight Against Islamic State." *Washington Post*, September 16.

———. 2014b. "Rift Widens between Obama, U.S. Military over Strategy to Fight Islamic State." *Washington Post*, September 18.

Woodward, Bob. 2010. *Obama's Wars*. New York: Simon and Schuster.

World War II History Info. 2010. "Pearl Harbor." *Worldwar2history.info*, April 5.

Yetiv, Steve A. 2003. "Groupthink and the Gulf Crisis." *British Journal of Political Science* 33, no. 03: 419–442.

———, ed. 2004. *Crude Awakenings: Global Oil Security and American Foreign Policy*. Ithaca, NY: Cornell University Press.

Index

Lightning Source UK Ltd.
Milton Keynes UK
UKOW04f1808041117
312145UK00001B/76/P